DESK REVOLUTIONARIES

DESK REVOLUTIONARIES

THE MEN of the FRENCH DIRECTORY, 1795–9

BIANCAMARIA FONTANA

REAKTION BOOKS

To the memory of Bernard Manin, who liked this unheroic revolution

Published by
REAKTION BOOKS LTD
2–4 Sebastian Street
London EC1V 0HE, UK

www.reaktionbooks.co.uk

First published 2026

EU GPSR Authorised Representative
Logos Europe, 9 rue Nicolas Poussin, 17000, La Rochelle, France
email: contact@logoseurope.eu

Printed and bound in Great Britain by Bell & Bain, Glasgow

A catalogue record for this book is available from the British Library

ISBN 978 1 83639 249 1

CONTENTS

Jean-Joseph-François Tassaert, after Fulchran-Jean Harriet, *The Arrest of Robespierre and His Supporters at the Hôtel de Ville on 27 July 1794*, *c.* 1794, etching.

Prologue: Surviving Terror

> Our revolution has made me feel that history is like a novel.
>
> MAXIMILIEN ROBESPIERRE, 21 December 1792

In the modern imagination, the French Revolution of 1789 continues to represent a major landmark in European history, the archetype of all revolutions to come. We are all familiar with the stories of the taking of the Bastille, of the victims led to the guillotine, and, later, of Napoleon Bonaparte's military exploits. But when was the Revolution finally over, and what happened between then and the time Napoleon came to power? Were the sweeping changes made by the revolutionaries preserved or set aside?

For most historians, the Revolution ended with the *coup d'état* of Thermidor, on 27–28 July 1794, when the Convention (the National Assembly) turned against the Jacobin leaders and Maximilien Robespierre with his close allies went to the scaffold, where in the past they had sent so many of both their enemies and their friends. Another *coup d'état*, that of Brumaire, on 9–10 November 1799, made the young General Bonaparte head of the French Republic, the first step towards becoming emperor. Those five years, between 1794 and 1799, have left no memorable image to posterity, no charismatic figure to embody them, yet they played a crucial role in shaping France as we know it today, and, by reflex, most of continental Europe. This book is about those forgotten years and their legacy, more precisely about a group of men who, having survived revolutionary Terror, struggled, not always successfully, to establish in its place a normal constitutional government, the first modern liberal republic.

At the beginning, in 1789, when Louis XVI summoned the Estates General – an old institution with purely consultative powers – to address the kingdom's financial crisis, nobody was planning or expecting a revolution, and only very few intellectuals imagined that France could ever become a republic. The initial project had been to 'regenerate' the monarchy, giving the country a constitution with a charter of rights and representative assemblies, following the example of the English monarchy. It would then be possible to adopt the fiscal and administrative measures necessary to rescue the State's finances – measures that the king had been unable to enforce. Until then, despite the advice of such progressive ministers as Anne-Robert-Jacques Turgot and Jacques Necker, any attempt at reform had been sternly opposed by the privileged social groups who benefited from the status quo, especially those (such as the wealthier landed nobility) who were exempt from paying the most substantial share of taxes.

The first promoters of the move towards constitutional rule were themselves grand aristocrats from the younger generation (some, such as the Marquis de Lafayette, had fought for America's independence); they were followed by the *noblesse de robe* (the lesser nobility who held posts in the magistracy), by the professional and commercial bourgeoisie, and by part of the clergy. All were inspired by the Enlightenment ideals of freedom and equality, and also by their own direct experience of the malfunctioning of the French administrative and judicial system. Some of the most flamboyant future leaders belonged to a familiar stereotype: the sons (and daughters) of relatively prosperous families, who rebelled against their parents' authority and against traditional values; a few had even been arrested and imprisoned for 'immorality' at the instigation of their own relatives. But the majority of the men elected to the revolutionary assemblies were not essentially rebellious types; they were conventional provincial notables or ambitious young professionals who adjusted to the new circumstances of the Revolution as in the past they might have settled into the routine of traditional offices.

Initially things seemed to follow the plans of reformers. The Estates General – formed by representatives of the three orders: clergy, nobility and the Third Estate – were replaced by a single Constituent Assembly entrusted with drafting a declaration of rights and a constitution (until then France, like England, had had no written constitution, only a customary one). The principles of popular sovereignty, equality of rights and religious freedom were established, while the most archaic measures of the old regime – such as the *lettres de cachet*, a legal device that permitted arbitrary arrests – were abolished. Soon afterwards, however, the course of events took a far more radical turn, fuelled by violent urban and peasants' riots that put pressure on the deputies. Historians have been debating ever since the causes of this *dérapage*, the vertiginous sliding from a moderate policy of reform into revolutionary dictatorship.

All things considered, a variety of converging factors contributed to this outcome. To begin with, the deputies failed to introduce in the new constitution adequate guarantees of an effective separation of powers; fearful of reproducing any form of aristocratic council (similar to the English House of Lords) or personal power, they opted for a single legislative assembly and gradually undermined the authority of all executive figures, from the ministers to the king. In this way the Legislative Assembly elected in October 1791 – and its successor from September 1792, the Convention – became the only legitimate power, without any kind of counterweight. Lacking any experience of parliamentary politics and divided in rival affinities, the partisans of constitutional monarchy, who had been the majority in the Constituent Assembly, rapidly lost control of the subsequent assemblies, succumbing to such better-organized radical groups as the Girondins and the Jacobins.

For his part King Louis XVI, who in October 1789 had been forced by an angry crowd to leave Versailles for Paris, proved unable to sustain his new role of constitutional monarch. At the same time, he was reluctant to resort to using the regiments of his guard – formed by foreign mercenary troops – to put down popular unrest, as his entourage urged him to do. In June 1791, eluding surveillance at the palace of the Tuileries, he tried unsuccessfully to flee the country with his family. Arrested near the frontier at Varennes, he was imprisoned, tried and finally executed in January 1793; Queen Marie-Antoinette was tried and guillotined in October the same year. In the absence of alternative candidates for the crown (Louis' only son was still a child), the disappearance of the king as head of state led, in September 1792, to the proclamation of the Republic. France thus became republican more by default than by design.

Another destabilizing element was the aggravation of economic circumstances. The financial crisis at the origin of the Revolution had two main causes: the vast debt accumulated by the monarchy over a long period; and an inefficient – as well as grossly unfair – fiscal system that exempted from the bulk of taxation the wealthiest privileged elites, on account of their aristocratic status. Moreover, taxes were collected not directly by the State but by financial intermediaries, the *Fermiers généraux*, who loaned the Crown the expected tax returns and retrieved their loans by exacting payment from the people. It was a method clearly open to all manner of miscalculation and abuse. The reform of this fiscal system was generally accepted as a necessity, although it was unclear how it might be effected. On the other hand, the option of simply cancelling the national debt – why should the Republic pay the debts of the monarchy? – was rejected. The main reason for this choice, apart from the fear of causing public panic, was that many deputies, being themselves holders of State bonds, were reluctant to face a bankruptcy that would directly affect their own private fortunes.

In a move reminiscent of the suppression of the English monasteries by Henry VIII, on 2 November 1789 the Constituent Assembly had voted for the confiscation of the vast properties of the Catholic Church in France, and these were now placed 'at the disposal of the nation'. These Church lands should serve as guarantee for a new type of paper money, the *assignats*. However, in a climate of growing insecurity, the new currency was rapidly devalued, while a sequence of bad harvests led to a rise in bread prices and consequently to riots. Such protest had been a recurrent feature in the past, but now it acquired a new, more alarming political significance. The appropriation of the patrimony of the Church, meanwhile, was perceived as an attack against religion as such, leading to the rebellion of some deeply Catholic regions, among them the Vendée, while 'refractory' priests, who refused to profess their allegiance to the French State, became the targets of persecution. While the revolutionary assemblies were prepared to confiscate the properties of the Church and, later, of those aristocrats who had fled the country, the lands were then auctioned off to wealthy investors; the possibility of distributing them to the peasantry was never considered. The revolutionary political class remained firm throughout in its defence of individual property, despite the demands of proto-socialist militant groups.

But the most crucial factor in the radicalization of the Revolution was the outbreak of war. In April 1792 the French king was pressed into signing the declaration of war on Austria, on the thin pretext of some long-disputed territorial enclaves. For some revolutionary groups, such as the Girondins, this was an opportunity to defuse civil conflict within the country, turning it instead against foreign enemies. At the same time those royalists who wished to see the Revolution fail hoped for a rapid defeat of France – which was by all accounts unprepared for war – and for the restoration of the monarchy to its former status through the intervention of foreign armies. At the beginning of the Revolution the other European monarchs had not been sorry to see Louis XVI struggling with domestic difficulties, keeping France away from the international power game. However, after the declaration of war on Austria and the proclamation of the Republic, they became aware of the dangers of a 'revolutionary' and 'democratic' contagion in their own countries. Following the example of Prussia, they joined forces against France, encouraged by aristocratic émigrés – such as Louis XVI's two brothers – who had found refuge at their courts.

The war had a double impact. On the one hand it strengthened the new regime, reinforcing popular patriotic sentiments; on the other it created a climate of fear that justified the violation of the rights and liberties so recently acquired. The war led to the mobilization of all the country's resources. After the recruitment of a few battalions of volunteers, an unprecedented number of men (about 300,000) were called up to serve in the army; all had to be equipped and fed as well as trained, and even the country's most prominent scientists were mobilized to produce gunpowder. Since food became scarce for the population in the towns, the prices of necessities were fixed by law, and anyone suspected of hoarding or speculating became the target of public fury.

Thousands of high-ranking officers had fled the country to join the anti-French coalition, and their desertion led to the promotion from the ranks of a new generation of talented young officers, many of them destined, like Napoleon, for spectacular careers. Their efforts, combined with the improvements to the artillery effected during the previous decade, made it possible to stop the Prussian invasion in the battles of Valmy and Fleurus, turning the fortunes of war unexpectedly in favour of France. The untrained and somewhat disorganized citizens' army played an essential role in saving the Revolution. However, for fear of further defection or some military coup, the conduct of the war was always kept under the strict control of the civil authority; commanding officers were frequent targets of accusations of treason, and many later became victims of the Terror.

Once the war had begun, the Republic also faced the rebellion of some towns – among them Toulon, France's main port at the time – that were ready to go over to the enemy at the first sign of defeat.

This threat, combined with the rumours of real and imagined anti-revolutionary conspiracies, led to the adoption of a series of emergency measures. Following a wave of spontaneous violence carried out across the country by groups of militant sans-culottes – such as the massacre of hundreds of prisoners in Parisian gaols in September 1792 – the Assembly finally resolved to take control of the domestic struggle against counter-revolutionaries. The new republican constitution, voted for in June 1793 (Year I), was suspended in August of the same year, together with judicial guarantees. A new law, the Law of Suspects, passed in September 1793, condemned not just subversive activities but any suspected anti-revolutionary sentiments; a month later a special Revolutionary Tribunal was created to pursue such crimes. In this way the politics of Terror – the words 'Terror' and 'Terrorist' were used in that context for the first time – was legitimated and given legal form.

In a climate of growing paranoia, anyone could be accused of crimes so broadly defined. No proper prison system existed at the time, and the available places of detention soon proved insufficient to house those awaiting trial, so that all manner of buildings – from former convents to royal palaces – were adapted to the purpose. Luckily the relatively slow judicial process meant that many victims managed to survive until the collapse of the regime. Initially directed against broad categories of potential suspects, such as aristocrats and refractory priests, as well as against presumed spies and enemy agents, the Terror soon became an instrument through which the rival revolutionary factions fought one another. In a scenario familiar from twentieth-century revolutions, the revolutionary leadership proceeded to self-destruct through mutual trumped-up accusations of corruption and treason. The Girondins, a faction that had been especially active in the earlier phase of the Revolution before being defeated by the Jacobins, were the largest contingent of deputies to be tried and executed, while several of them, who had escaped arrest, committed suicide. The groups of Jacques-René Hébert and Georges

Danton were soon to follow the Girondins to the scaffold. The fear, spreading through the Convention, of seeing one's name on the next list of suspects was a decisive factor in bringing about the coup of Thermidor.

But who was responsible for these policies? How was the republican government run between 1792 and 1794? When the monarchy was set aside, there were no precedents for a republic in a large country; until then republics had been city states, like Venice and Geneva, or federations of small territories, while France's population of about 28 million was the largest in Europe. The only comparable recent example – for the extension of territory, not for the population, which was much smaller – was the United States of America; but America was a federation, while the French Republic had maintained the united and centralized structure of the old kingdom, repressing any attempts at administrative autonomy. To prevent any form of personal rule reminiscent of the monarchy, the only legitimate authority was the Legislative Assembly of about 750 members. Executive power was exercised on behalf of the assembly by a growing number of legislative subcommittees that replaced ministerial departments.

The most important of these was the Committee of Public Safety, formed by twelve members, who acted in practice as a kind of shadow cabinet. Yet the composition of the Committee itself was dependent on the floating majorities within the assembly; contrary to popular historical representations, its most famous members – such as Danton and Robespierre – had far less personal power than any English prime minister. All things considered, the Revolution had produced no strong leadership, even though some charismatic speakers gave the impression of being in command and were occasionally accused of aspiring to tyranny. Moreover, France had no experience of party politics; political factions were loosely organized, with unstable central and local structures. When at Thermidor the Convention turned against Robespierre, his supporters were unable to offer any resistance, while their attempts to mobilize the Parisian Jacobins failed.

What had looked like a strong dictatorship dissolved so easily that observers abroad could not at first believe that the regime of Terror was truly over.

What happened afterwards? For more than a year the existing ruling institutions – the Convention and the Committee of Public Safety – remained in place, although naturally they were now run by those who had taken part in the conspiracy. Prisoners were freed and prosecutions initiated against former 'Terrorists', a highly questionable exercise, since many Thermidorians had themselves been responsible for arrests and even mass executions in the rebel towns. It is impossible in retrospect to generalize the motives that had led many deputies belonging to the moderate centre of the assembly to endorse repressive arbitrary measures; sincere belief that it was the only way to save the Republic, sheer opportunism and just fear for their lives all played a role. As one of them, Emmanuel Sieyès, memorably replied when asked about it, they had just survived. While some of those accused of Terrorism spoke out to defend their own conduct, the policy of Terror was now universally rejected. In the circumstances the repression was rather limited. Some symbolic figures, such as the former prosecutor of the Revolutionary Tribunal, Antoine Fouquier-Tinville, went to the guillotine, but the image of the scaffold, now haunted in the popular imagination by bloodied ghosts, had become so repellent that from then on political enemies were generally sentenced to the 'dry guillotine' – deportation to some remote colony.

Meanwhile a low-profile Commission of the Eleven was entrusted with drafting a new constitution. Initially the idea had been to bring back the suspended Constitution of 1793; however, in a far less radical climate, there was little enthusiasm for reviving a too 'democratic' text, one that introduced universal male suffrage and recognized the citizens' right to public assistance in case of need. The authors of the Constitution of 1795 (Year III) were especially preoccupied with guaranteeing the separation of powers that the Constituent Assembly had failed to establish in the past. Legislative power was now exercised by two assemblies: the Council of the Elders (*Anciens*) and below it that of the Five Hundred (*Cinq-Cent*).

To prevent any emerging individual authority, executive power was entrusted to a council of five members elected by the two Councils. There was no head of government and decisions were collegial. The model of collegial government was inspired by the examples of classical antiquity, and by the institutions of the republics still present across Europe in Italy, Switzerland and the Low Countries. Its name was borrowed from the juridical jargon generally associated with the running of commercial companies: Directory (*Directoire exécutif*). The first Directory was elected at the end of October 1795, and the story that follows begins a few days later.

Introduction:
At the Luxembourg

Five men . . . chosen in anger, came to power
in the most unfavourable circumstances.

GERMAINE DE STAËL,

Considerations on the French Revolution (1820–21)

The beginnings were not very promising. On 2 November 1795 four members of the newly elected French government, the Directory – Paul Barras, Louis-Marie de La Révellière-Lépeaux, Étienne-François Le Tourneur and Jean-François Reubell – made a low-key entrance at the vacant, icy-cold palace of the Luxembourg. There should have been five of them, but the most distinguished nominee, Emmanuel Sieyès, had refused the position, and his replacement, Lazare Carnot, had not yet been appointed. They arrived in two hackney cabs, with a motley escort of ragged foot soldiers and dragoons. The last owner of the palace, the Count of Provence (the future Louis XVIII), had fled the country in 1791.[1] During the Terror the deserted building, stripped of all its elegant furnishings, had been used as an improvised prison.[2] The new arrivals had to rely on the caretaker to find an old table, some chairs, and wood for the fireplaces. They had prudently brought with them, from the premises of the old Committee of Public Safety at the Louvre, paper and writing materials.

Things improved in due course; files and maps were brought over from across the river, the original furniture came out of storage, and rooms were refurbished and decorated with paintings by old masters, Gobelins tapestries and Aubusson carpets. However, the palace – built by Queen Marie de Medici in the 1610s as a copy of the Florentine Palazzo Pitti – had needed substantial repairs long before the Revolution. The Count of Provence had failed to raise the money to complete its restoration, and the rooms remained for the most part dilapidated and uninhabitable. Its new occupants ended up crammed in some discomfort, in some cases with their families, into the small annex known as Petit Luxembourg.[3]

The reason the Directors found themselves in such an unwelcoming setting was that they represented a kind of constitutional experiment. With the Constitution of 1795 (Year III), France had officially acquired a republican executive for the first time. At the beginning of the Revolution, while the monarchy was still in place, executive power was exercised by the king and his ministers, although their authority was being increasingly undermined. Since the proclamation of the Republic in September 1792, all power had been concentrated in the legislative assembly, the Convention. To avoid the emergence of some over-popular minister, executive functions were exercised by a growing number of legislative subcommittees that took the place of ministerial departments.[4] Even the most important of these, the powerful Committee of Public Safety, had ruled under the appearance of being a mere emanation of the legislative. As for the 'executive council' imagined by the Marquis de Condorcet for the Constitution of 1793 (Year I) – a nine-member body elected directly by the people – it had been set aside with the Constitution itself on account of the war, before it could come into being.

Because the Directory was the first official government of the Republic, it seemed necessary to confer on it a certain exterior dignity. The obligation to live, not just work, in the semi-royal palace of the Luxembourg was part of this strategy; no other French constitution, before or after, has dictated where the members of government should live, although over time the Republic has acquired various official residences, such as the Élysée Palace. In a similar spirit the painter Jacques-Louis David was commissioned to design the extravagant attire the Directors were expected to wear whenever they appeared in public: white silk trousers and tunic, long red coat with gilded trimmings, black hat topped by tricoloured feathers. A set of these outfits was hastily made up at great cost by a maker of theatrical costumes, justifying Director Barras' contemptuous qualification of the result as 'a masquerade'.[5] In addition, the Constitution imposed on the single Directors a personal escort of two republican guards 'to accompany them outside', in a peculiar combination of pomp and surveillance.[6]

Of course, the constitutional experiment was not confined to exterior appearances. The Directory's mission was to ensure the transition from the extra-constitutional regime that had been in place since 10 October 1793, to face the war against the coalition of European monarchies, towards normal constitutional rule, now embodied in

Anonymous, *Luxembourg Palace*, 1794–1850, engraving.

the Constitution of 1795. In drafting this new constitutional text, French legislators were unable to follow the model of the American Constitution of 1787, with an elected president as head of the executive; in France, entrusting power – even temporarily – to a single individual was too evocative of the old monarchy. Instead, they opted for a five-man executive that was collegial, without a head of government; a rotating presidency, elected for three months, had a purely formal role.

With no experience of republican institutions, the French found this collegial formula, inspired by the ruling councils of traditional republican regimes – such as those of Venice or Geneva – somewhat disconcerting. Indeed, when the Constitution was discussed many, on both the right and the left of the Convention, raised the question of who precisely would be responsible for the government's actions; which of the five would rule? Decisions within the executive required a majority of at least three, and most of the time, to avoid conflict, the Directors divided the different departments and geographical areas among themselves. They were seconded by several ministers (six to eight), who did not form a council but were appointed by and depended on the single Directors. The move from the position of minister to that of Director and back was not uncommon, so that the perimeter of the executive was somewhat wider than the narrow circle at the top.

As for legislative power, this was now divided into two Councils, the Five Hundred and the Elders (with 250 members). Laws were first proposed and voted by the lower Council, then submitted to the Elders for approval. Fear of the excessive power exercised by the single legislative assembly in the recent past had finally convinced French legislators to adopt the bicameral system that the Constituent Assembly had rejected in 1789, judging it too close to the English 'aristocratic' constitution. The prerogatives of this dual legislative remained extensive, although, according to Article 144, the government oversaw 'the internal and external safety of the Republic'; in other words, the

Directors had a wide margin of action running foreign policy, conducting wars, appointing the army's commanders and, crucially, monitoring popular unrest and intervening to repress domestic disorders and foreign conspiracies. The assemblies were renewed by a third selected by lot every year, and these recurrent elections, designed to ensure the democratic character of representation, led to frequent shifts in parliamentary majorities, becoming a permanent source of political instability. Directors were elected by the Elders from lists submitted by the Five Hundred. One of the five was supposedly deselected by lot every year, but there was no control over the balloting, which did not take place in public, and some contemporary sources suggest that these yearly departures were negotiated rather than being left to chance.[7]

Casting the Directors

Between 1795 and 1799 the Councils elected thirteen Directors, some of whom served for a very short time, while others stayed long enough to make their mark on government. Only one of the thirteen, Barras, remained in charge for the whole four years. But what sort of men came to occupy the position? One relevant factor was generational. Under Article 134 of the Constitution, Directors must be at least forty years old: a mature age at the time, suggesting seniority and experience.[8] This meant that, unlike the younger generation of revolutionaries, the members of the new executive had imagined their lives and planned their future under the monarchy without any prospect of significant political change.[9] They had also had time to acquire solid experience in their respective professions, learning about the complexity and dysfunctional aspects of existing institutions.

By 1795 most of the grand aristocrats who had initiated the Revolution and led the Constituent Assembly were in exile, if not dead. The background of the Directors was firmly set within the middling ranks, which in France meant a combination of minor nobility and bourgeoisie, since the two classes frequently intermarried. They were sons of provincial notables and local magistrates, with no large family fortunes to rely on, but generally with the advantage of a good education.[10] Most had trained for the law and had seen their prospects of positions in the royal administration jeopardized by the reforms tentatively introduced by the monarchy in the 1770s and '80s; a few were military engineers, with a solid mathematical and scientific background; only one, Sieyès, had followed the ecclesiastical career to which his family had destined him, but without having any kind of religious vocation. As the Republic consolidated its unity, their geographical provenance was more diverse than in the past, and the presence in the government and its entourage of men from the newly acquired regions of Alsace and Lorraine had a significant impact on France's foreign policy.[11]

The mode of election of Directors was designed to ensure that they represented the different political currents present in the assemblies. Some had been close to the Jacobins or the Girondins and could still rely on the electoral support derived from their past associations; the majority had no clear partisan affiliation and generally belonged to the *plaine*, the moderate centre of the Convention, a fact that had contributed to ensure their survival during the Terror. By 1795 even those with a radical past had converged on a political line of compromise, placing order and stability at the top of their priorities. As a rule, they were not famous; the Republic was tired of inspiring pamphleteers and brilliant speakers, and was taking a break (a short one, as it happens) from charismatic leadership. The lists submitted by the Five Hundred were filled with names better known to the deputies than to the wider public. The two exceptions were Carnot – the 'organizer of victory' who had saved the Republic in 1793 by masterminding France's military defence – and Sieyès, the eloquent advocate of the Third Estate, but Carnot had no apparent political ambitions and Sieyès had published nothing of great popular appeal since his pamphlets of 1788–9.[12]

Despite their different backgrounds, the Directors did have a common political profile. Two discriminating choices defined their identity. The first was their shared moral, if not direct, complicity in the regicide. Most of them had initially been in favour of constitutional monarchy, but in time had come to regard the conduct of Louis XVI as inept and even treasonous. Not all had voted for the king's death at his trial in December 1792; some were not members of the Convention, or were away from Paris at the time, and two – La Révellière-Lépeaux and Le Tourneur – had sided with the unsuccessful 'Appeal to the People', the Girondins' proposal to decide the king's fate by referendum.[13] However, all subscribed to the view that the suppression of the monarchy was justified, and that the Republic represented a point of no return, a conquest to be defended at all costs. The second defining choice was their complicity in another symbolic execution, that of Maximilien Robespierre. Whatever their past relationships with the Jacobin leader, and whatever part they had played at Thermidor (none of them was among the leaders of the conspiracy), the Directors were united in their retrospective repudiation of Terrorist policies and factional violence.[14]

French revolutionary politics had never recognized the legitimate role of parties within representative institutions. The negative perception of partisan organizations originally came from the identification of parties with the corporations of the old regime: associations dedicated to promoting their own interests against the general interest of the nation. In the absence of a parliamentary tradition, the revolutionary assemblies expressed no proper parties, only fluctuating and disorganized affinities. Insofar as more structured formations, such as the Jacobins, emerged, they aimed at gaining hegemony over the assembly and eliminating all rival groups. Mistrust of parties as intrinsically corrupt and opposed to the common good had been present also in the English and the American political discourse. However, both David Hume in his analysis of English parties and James Madison in discussing their role within the American Constitution considered that parties could perform a useful function by controlling one another and giving visibility to particular interests.[15] No such hopes of the balancing role of parties seemed confirmed by the French experience; on the contrary, the unfolding of murderous factional infighting, watched from alarmingly close range, had reinforced in the mind of survivors the belief that the action of government must be preserved as far as possible from partisan divisions, the latter being a permanent source of danger and instability.

A murderous task

A relevant factor of a different order that united the Directors was their awareness of the magnitude of the task they were facing. A contemporary observer, the writer Germaine de Staël, compared the conditions of the disaffected Luxembourg in 1795 to those of the French State, which was, she wrote, 'in no better order than the palace'.[16] The Republic had forestalled the danger of a foreign invasion that might have crushed it, but the burden of the cost of the war was very heavy, draining resources that were needed badly elsewhere. Because of the war, manufacturing and commerce were suffering; even if the Revolution had never attacked private property, the climate of uncertainty discouraged investment, and most of the confiscated lands that had been auctioned remained unexploited by their new owners. Colonial trade had been seriously disrupted by the slaves' revolts that had unfolded in France's Caribbean colonies since 1791. Although slavery had officially been abolished by the Convention in 1794, the decision had little real impact on the position of former enslaved people, who were still bound to forced labour on the land; thus the overall situation, complicated by ongoing conflict with Spain, remained volatile. Most important of all, the questions of public debt and the continuing devaluation of the currency had not been confronted.[17]

Besides the war, domestic security continued to represent a major problem. Some of the 'plots' feared by the revolutionaries were probably the product of their paranoid imagination, but others were real enough. There were enemy agents and spies acting under cover in France, mainly in England's pay. This was the case, for example, with one of the clerks who took notes at the meetings of the Committee of Public Safety, the records of which were not public; he reported directly to London, providing future historians with a valuable source. The coalition had various plans to land troops on the northern coast of France with the support of local royalists, and militant radical groups in the suburbs of Paris were preparing insurrections. After becoming First Consul in 1799, Napoleon would be the target of several assassination attempts; although murdering any of the Directors would have little political impact, buying off one or other of them to organize a coup was a strategy seriously pursued by the agents of Louis XVIII.[18]

Another pending question was that of the relationship between central government and local administrations. During the Revolution, fear of the loss of parts of the national territory through local insurrection or foreign military occupation had led the government to reinforce its centralized policy. In 1793 a group of 31 Girondin deputies had been sentenced to death on the charge of being 'federalists' and therefore enemies of national unity. While the charge was unfounded, since none of the accused had seriously considered the possibility of turning France into a federation, the pressure to offer greater autonomy to the provinces persisted, and relations between central and local government continued to be characterized by mutual grievances and misunderstandings. (Indeed, this is still a cause of tension within the 5th Republic of the twenty-first century.)

The Directors had spent enough time sitting on one or other of the various legislative subcommittees to realize that much of the legislation voted since 1789 had proved inapplicable, and that local administrations as well as tribunals were simply unable to understand the new measures, let alone enforce them. While the offices of the royal administration had been suppressed, replacing them with new ones and recruiting the necessary personnel were proving difficult, and in any case the required resources were not available. Although all these problems had been apparent for some time, in the past the opaque and often litigious organization of power made it hard to tell who was responsible for what, and the Assembly and Committees kept claiming the fault was the other's. Now, as members of the new executive, the Directors were in charge – at least nominally. The paradox they were facing was that, on the one hand, peace seemed a necessary precondition for resolving these problems, but on the other, without the continuing pressure of the war, it was unclear that the revolutionary government would survive.

The new executive's initial response, at least for the first period, was to display an intense rhythm of activity. This was something the Directors were well used to, since they belonged to that minority of deputies who had carried on behind the scenes most of the painstaking bureaucratic work of the revolutionary governments: drafting reports, amending legislative texts, advising local administrations, and answering floods of correspondence and petitions from all over the country. One of them, the former Girondin La Révellière-Lépeaux, recalled their punishing daily routine:

> Meetings began at 8 a.m. precisely. They stopped only at 4 p.m. At 8 in the evening they started again, to end by 4 in the morning at best. This kind of life continued for six months. All issues were so pressing, the chaos that reigned was so bewildering, that we were unable to provide for everything. I cannot understand how such rhythm of work did not kill all five of us.[19]

Even when the first impact of their daunting task was over, the volume of work dispatched by the executive remained impressive. In time the financial situation was brought under control, as the government finally resolved to cancel two-thirds of the debt and run the risk of bankruptcy, an operation they managed to effect without any great shock to the system. The position of the buyers of confiscated lands, renamed national properties, was stabilized; ministerial departments as well as tribunals were restaffed and reorganized, and legislation rewritten. Reforms were implemented in different domains, from fiscality to education, from local administration to agriculture, commerce and industry; transport was improved and the country became generally more secure from marauding bandits. From facing the imminent prospect of a military disaster, the Republic went on to occupy neighbouring territories and was able to sign advantageous peace treaties with the powers of the coalition. Even those historians who tend to convey a negative image of the Directory are prepared to admit that the reforming achievements of the Consulate were built on the efforts made by the Directorial Republic between 1795 and 1799.[20]

Thermidorian vices

So why is the Directory generally perceived as a weak regime, or corrupt, or at best a transitional episode of little consequence? On the first point, the immediate answer is because it failed to attain stability and to ensure the long-term survival of the Republic. Consequently, it also lacked the time and opportunity to popularize its own achievements and build up its own positive reputation. The same incapacity to stabilize republican government can be imputed to the Jacobin leadership; however, the executions that preceded and accompanied Thermidor have conferred to the defeat of the Jacobins the mark of tragic heroism, while the bloodless liquidation of the Directors at Brumaire looks far from glorious. In the eyes of posterity, Danton, Robespierre and their friends go to the scaffold surrounded by an aura of martyrdom that masks to some extent their many faults and errors. By contrast, the Directors' safe retreat to their comfortable private residences (or to the lucrative seats of Napoleon's Senate) suggests only ineptitude or opportunism.

As will emerge from this narrative, different factors contributed to the fragility of the Directorial Republic: an ill-designed organization of powers that led the executive to act systematically outside the limits of the Constitution; the volatility of public opinion, unsettled by a sequence of traumatic upheavals; the continuing threat of military defeat and of rebellions and conspiracies. If the Constitution of 1795 established the separation of powers, it also created a somewhat opaque articulation of the prerogatives of the legislative and executive bodies. The authors of the text had tried to form a compromise between the traditional doctrine of the superiority of the legislative over the executive, and the intuition that the executive should be able to 'think for the government', making decisions and taking independent initiative beyond the mere application of the law.[21] In addition, they entrusted the Directory with the preservation of national security, a task difficult to accomplish without stretching their powers to face unexpected crisis. The inevitable result was constant tension, if not open conflict, between the Councils and the executive.

However, in a more stable context the defects of the Constitution might have been remedied by consolidating some working practices, without any major constitutional revision. The real difficulties for the Republic came from the executive's incapacity to master popular consensus. The Directory had been designed as an institution that stood above partisan struggles. Its members were no party leaders; indeed, in most cases, either by inclination or by choice, they were not even party men. Most of the time they focused their energy on rebuilding the machinery of the State, rather than on securing a majority in the Councils or winning elections. The same qualities that made them reliable administrators proved a handicap when it came to monitoring partisan dissent. The only way they could find to stay afloat was the recurrent resort to the annulment of elections or the purging of Councils, and this sequence of what were to all effects minor *coups d'état*, partial attempts against the Constitution, finally led them to that final coup of Brumaire that brought their republic to an end.

For a long tradition of pro-Jacobin historiography, the Directory's weakness was the inevitable outcome of their 'betrayal' of democracy. By abandoning the revolutionary commitment to government by the people (whatever that might mean), the Thermidorian political class and their republic of proprietors paved the way for the authoritarian regime of Napoleon. At the beginning of the Revolution, French territory had been divided into new administrative districts called *départements*, designed to provide comparable electoral constituencies. While their square shape was ridiculed at the time by the politician and philosopher Edmund Burke as an absurd invention contrary to natural geography, they still serve today as basic administrative units.[22] Given the large size of the population (with an unprecedented mass of several million potential electors), elections took place in two stages whereby primary assemblies elected the citizens who would then vote for the deputies. During the Revolution there was disagreement as to the conditions for voting in the primary assemblies; a varying fiscal contribution was required, while all men in a dependent economic position, such as domestic servants (which made up about 10 per cent of the population), were excluded. As to the vote for women, which Condorcet proposed to the Constituent Assembly, it was ruled out as being contrary to current popular opinion.[23]

The Constitution of 1795 established a limited electoral suffrage based on census. Voting rights had been nominally more extensive under the Constitution of 1791, and even wider in the never-applied text of 1793, which introduced universal male suffrage. In practice, however, popular participation in the vote had been declining steadily since 1792 under the impact of the war and the Terror, so that there was no significant restriction of the electorate in 1795. Even with somewhat reduced participation, the elections that took place under the Directory produced significant swings between left and right in the composition of the Councils, showing that democratic opinion had not been suppressed and that dissent was still very much alive.

The problem was that political opposition did not produce, with the changes of majority within the assemblies, a normal confrontation between competing agendas for government. Instead, both left and right worked on the prospect of overturning the Republic through some insurrection or coup, in view either of reviving the power of the Parisian sections or of paving the way for the return of the Bourbons. Paradoxically, the Directory did have the support of most citizens with voting rights, but this silent bourgeois electorate, frightened by the extremes, was ready in the end to support the establishment of a strong, authoritarian executive. Naturally after Brumaire, the new consular regime, faced initially with the same political instability, justified its own actions by magnifying the faults and inadequacies of the Directorial Republic it had replaced. The fact that some of the Directors were party to the coup, and that those who were not put up only feeble resistance, contributed to reinforcing this judgement, masking the continuity of agenda and personnel in the transition of 1799.

The grounds for the second allegation, that of corruption, are less apparent. All political regimes at moments of unpopularity are liable to be perceived as 'corrupt', a term that merely conveys the vague impression that rulers serve their own private interests rather than the common good. In the case of the Directorial Republic, however, the accusation is more specific, as if the actions of the executive in those years had been characterized by systematic disorder and the plundering of public resources. The description of the Directory as a 'corrupt regime' has been echoed insistently by commentators from all political sides and has become, by the simple effect of repetition, a standard assumption in historiographical reconstructions of the period. In fact, if we look at the individual circumstances of the Directors, there is no evidence that they took bribes, sold their influence or misappropriated public funds. While some of them were, or became, quite wealthy, that was through their professional activities, their official salaries and the investment opportunities that emerged at the time.[24] The only one who was clearly guilty of corruption in the proper sense of the term, Barras, had committed his misdeeds long before the advent of the Directory, when he served on different missions on behalf of the Convention.[25]

The notion that the Directory was generally corrupt has one important source in the division of competences between the Councils and the executive. The Constitution gave the Directory no independent access to finance; under Article 162, the executive's accounts had to be submitted regularly to the Councils for approval, a requirement that was frequently neglected, especially when it came to promoting and conducting military operations. Over time the Councils made repeated attempts to deprive the executive of whatever financial autonomy it possessed.[26] This rather peculiar arrangement provided the Councils with a convenient weapon to which they resorted whenever they wished to get rid of a particular Director. The members of the executive were accused on various occasions of misappropriating public funds; the accusations, once investigated, proved unfounded, but the rumours of embezzlement duly voiced by the press were sufficient to force the accused to resign. The scenario has often been reproduced in the history of modern democracies.

Besides its use as a weapon in the conflict of powers, the charge of corruption reflected the radical change in the attitude towards money and wealth brought about by Thermidor. The end of the Terror encouraged a return to the 'normal' enjoyment and display of wealth, which revolutionary ideology had reproved and denounced as suspicious, leading well-off citizens to conceal their fortunes. The sudden display of ostentatious luxury, the lavish, sometimes orgiastic parties that followed the liberation of political prisoners, the reappearance in public of surviving aristocrats who were no longer forced to hide – all were perceived by many as the betrayal of patriotic austerity and republican virtue.[27] In the concluding passage of Jules Michelet's influential *History of the French Revolution* (1847–53) a young boy is surprised, in the days following Robespierre's execution, when he hears a coachman address some potential customers – a crowd of elegant theatregoers – as 'master'; the word, the historian claims, was unknown to him. The implication of the narrative is that capitalism and social domination had suddenly reappeared in France after the death of the Jacobin leader.[28]

As we have seen, during the Revolution, if the shortages caused by the war had produced episodic witch-hunts against supposed hoarders and profiteers, the rights of property as such had never been questioned. For all their professions of republican equality, revolutionary governments had never passed legislation against private wealth, only against aristocratic privilege.[29] In a changed ideological climate, the Directorial Republic was even more explicit in indicating property as the founding element of political association; citizens were metaphorically the shareholders of the nation. In practice, the Revolution and the war had opened up new prospects for social advancement and economic gain. The lands confiscated from the Church and of the émigrés, often inadequately exploited, had passed to new investors; the devaluation of paper currency and suppression of the debt inherited from the monarchy favoured all manner of speculation; and the market in military supplies and the occupation of foreign territory offered promising business opportunities.

This process of economic transformation was not confined to the years 1795–9 but rather unfolded from the time of the Constituent Assembly throughout the Consulate and the Empire. The patriotic propaganda of the revolutionary regime had only masked the reality of this shift of resources within the wealthier social groups. The only episode that fell immediately under the Directory's control was the abolition of the *assignats*, the paper money that had been created in 1789, and on that occasion the government put in place severe measures to contain speculation, including closing the Paris Stock Exchange for a time.[30]

By contrast with the excesses of some prominent Thermidorians (and with the sole exception of Barras), the Directors' lifestyle was far from ostentatious. They remained at heart respectable provincial notables with no time or taste for extravagant or licentious habits.

Some of them did, however, apply themselves seriously to the objective of improving their private fortunes. In common with many other exponents of the political class, they profited from the economic opportunities created by the Revolution, acquiring national properties, making some advantageous investments and developing contacts with the bankers and businessmen who financed the war. Clearly the frontier between the legitimate pursuit of wealth and the corrupt exploitation of one's public position is very thin and depends on political perspective. Even so, there is no evidence that the Directors and their ministers were generally more rapacious or dishonest than their equivalents in the revolutionary, consular or imperial governments. However, those nostalgic for Jacobinism and the partisans of Napoleon have found it convenient to confine all suspicion of corruption to the short-lived Directorial Republic, an ideological orphan that left no immediate political legacy.

Desk revolutionaries?

All things considered, in the eyes of posterity the main fault of the Directors is not so much their dubious morality or inadequate performance as their dismally unheroic profile. Squeezed chronologically between the fierce tribunes at the rostrum and a victorious general back from the pyramids, the men of the bourgeois liberal Republic have little to offer the modern imagination. Even the flamboyant disguise created by David could not transform a set of ordinary middle-aged politicians into popular heroes. At the one occasion on which the Directory indulged in a Roman-style triumph with the spoils of the first Italian campaign, in September 1798, the celebrations focused on the prosaic inventions of French industry, such as coloured pencils and mechanical clocks.[31] While they lacked the heroic glamour of Robespierre or Napoleon, the Directors also failed to achieve the reputation for Machiavellian duplicity that has turned two of the Directory's ministers, Joseph Fouché and Charles-Maurice de Talleyrand, into legendary masters of intrigue, ever present in all narratives about the period; instead, they have been written off as commonplace opportunists.

Their unexciting outlook and lack of visibility have conveyed the impression that the men of the Directory were merely 'desk revolutionaries', who spent the years after 1789 in the safety of some cabinet, to emerge in 1795 unscathed by the dramas that had unfolded around them. The most recent version of this representation consists in describing them as 'technocrats', an expression suggestive of competence in the service of the power in place, to the exclusion of any political or ideological commitment. This reading by contemporary historiography is somewhat paradoxical. Long before the Revolution, the kings of France, especially Louis XIV, had often chosen their ministers on grounds of competence rather than birth, with a view to limiting the power of the grand aristocracy and ensuring the efficiency of the royal administration. In addition to the crowd of lawyers decried by Burke (some of them excellent jurists), the revolutionary political class included from the start many distinguished mathematicians, philosophers and scientists.[32]

The creation of a system of State education accessible to all ranked high on the agenda of 1789. The aim was, in the first instance, the basic instruction of the citizenry at large, but the creation of specialists in all areas through a network of *grandes écoles*, to replace the royal academies, was also a priority.[33] The Directory contributed to these educational projects by reorganizing schools and introducing scholarships and competitions for the recruitment of public servants. Since then, the ambition to create a meritocratic elite of experts has been a constant feature of all post-revolutionary French regimes, yet somehow the opposition of partisan militancy on the one hand and expertise on the other has never disappeared, as if competence – although in principle accessible to all – represented a form of unjust privilege and undemocratic discrimination and was necessarily incompatible with true political commitment.

The Directors' survival during the Terror possibly depended not just on prudence or sheer luck, but on their usefulness in carrying out those indispensable tasks of government that required specific skills. Yet it is unfair, as well as false, to describe them as strangers to political engagement. If one puts together their individual experiences, the older ones had defied their social superiors by contributing to the drafting of the *cahiers de doléances* – the documents by which the various regions presented their grievances to the Estates General – and had taken the famous Oath of the Tennis Court that established the Constituent Assembly in 1789. All had stood in various elections, facing their constituencies in the provinces; all, although no brilliant speakers, had addressed the difficult audience of the assembly on various occasions. They had presided over tribunals, run murderously litigious local administrations or dealt with intractable military commanders on the front line. Just like many of their fellow revolutionaries, they had been threatened with death by their own colleagues and had anxiously followed the rumours of conspiracies and lists of proscription; some had even known exile, deportation and imprisonment. Such experiences may have contributed to making them disillusioned and even cynical, and, in common with all survivors of a collective tragedy, they carried the guilt of being still alive; but on balance their revolutionary record, with its load of risk and harsh confrontations, cannot be faulted.

The modern Republic and its enemies

Unpopular in its own time, the Directory has no apparent heirs in French political history. In the four republics that followed it the model of collegial government has never again been taken into consideration; all have been parliamentary or presidential. By an odd set of circumstances, today the only surviving example of government modelled on the French Directory is the Federal Council of the Swiss Confederation: a body of seven members elected by two legislative assemblies, who rule collegially without a premier; one of the seven serves in turn as president for a year, but the office is merely ceremonial. The executive directory was imported into Switzerland by the French occupation of 1798, with the Constitution of the Helvetic Republic.[34] It was revived in 1848, when the Confederation finally adopted a central federal government. The lasting success of the Directory's Helvetic incarnation brings out the elements that were missing in the original French context: a secular republican tradition of councils of peers; a stable structure of political consensus that makes it possible for all major parties to sit together in government, sharing ministerial departments according to what is ironically (but also proudly) called 'the magic formula'; and a federal organization of the territory into small political and administrative units.[35]

While in France the Directory was quickly dismissed as a failed constitutional experiment, its ideological heritage continues to prove controversial. For a long time in the tradition of pro-Jacobin, socialist and Marxist historiography, the Republic of 1795 was associated with the transformation of the supposedly democratic society created by the Revolution into a bourgeois rule of proprietors. Consequently, it marked the end of the Revolution itself and the return to despotism. More recently, the indictment of the Directory has focused on a different aspect of its political profile, namely the recurrent ambition to govern France from the centre, overruling partisan divisions and bridging the traditional opposition between left and right.

The substance of the accusation is the same: that the Directory has become a 'non-place of memory' because, by promoting inequality and limiting popular participation, it has led the revolutionary Republic towards the 'precipice' of anti-democratic powers, from Napoleon's Empire to the 5th Republic of General Charles de Gaulle. In addition, it is argued that, by creating the illusion of a dynamic republic 'marching' towards modernity (a transparent allusion to the centrist movement En Marche of 2016), the Directory has consigned the French State to the immobile rule of technocratic *fonctionnaires*.[36] Quite apart from the entrenched hostility of the French left towards the institutions of the presidential 5th Republic, these renewed attacks against the Directory reflect contemporary concerns about the decline of ideology, the demobilization of political militancy, and the breaking down of both left and right political parties.

Setting aside the partisan nature of these arguments, the detractors of the Directory are right in identifying a continuity between the choices made by the men of 1795 and the predicament of contemporary democracies. Their tentative, shaky regime was the first *modern* republic to be established in Europe, in the sense in which the term was used by the liberal writer Benjamin Constant in his famous 'Speech on the Liberty of the Ancients and the Moderns' of 1819: a large commercial nation ruled by non-hereditary representative institutions.[37] Until then, republics had existed only in small territorial units, such as city states, or within leagues and confederations. The only other contemporary example of a republic in a large country, the United States of America, was a federation, while France, for reasons that were both traditional and circumstantial, maintained the centralized state of the old monarchy.

Because the modern Republic ruled over a large population too numerous to assemble in public meetings, it was also by necessity a 'representative (rather than direct or pure) democracy': a new term that appeared in the writings of political theorists in the 1790s.[38] The same theorists pointed out the analogy between representative government and the division of labour described by Adam Smith in *An Inquiry into the Nature and Causes of the Wealth of Nations* (1776); the citizens of modern republics, unable to rely on the work of slaves and occupied full-time by their own private business, were bound to delegate the running of public affairs to a professional class of representatives. The positive side of this solution was that citizens were free from constant civic obligations, while their collective interests were cared for by competent procurers; the negative was that representatives must be constantly controlled to prevent them from abusing their power.[39]

The delegation of civic responsibilities inevitably created a distance between the people and their elected deputies, a distance that, in the case of the French Republic of 1795, partial yearly elections were insufficient to bridge. The perception of the political class as a kind of elected aristocracy, a caste alienated from the people and their concerns, has become a constant feature of modern democracies – a phenomenon recurrently denounced as a crisis or deficit of representation, and now ever present in populist rhetoric. In 1795 the survivors of the Revolution were the first to be confronted with the problem, which was added to the other complex practical difficulties associated with the new republican model. Their choice at least was clear. In one of his many unpublished manuscripts dating from 1792, the future Director Sieyès outlined the opposition between *ré-publique* and *ré-totale*: the *ré-totale* was the totalitarian democratic republic of the Jacobins, which in the future must be avoided at all costs to make way for the true Republic.[40]

Hidden in plain sight

While it does offer a sympathetic reading of the Directory and its protagonists, this book is not meant as a retrospective apology for the lost bourgeois liberal Republic, an appendix to the never-ending trial to which it has been subjected since 1799.[41] Instead, it looks at the Directory as the reflex of two largely neglected aspects of the French revolutionary experience that deserve to be better known and understood. The first of these is the hidden side of the Revolution that the Directory embodied: its tenacious, if unheroic, bureaucratic vocation. Between the symbolic abolition of feudal privileges by the Constituent Assembly on 4 August 1789 and the equally symbolic adoption of the new civil code by the Consulate on 21 March 1804, fifteen years of patient labour were necessary to turn abstract principles into viable legislation, and imagined institutions into functioning administrative structures.

This largely invisible backroom activity constitutes the most durable and solid conquest of 1789, one that could not be easily suppressed or reversed in the alternation of regimes that followed. Mostly attributed by traditional historiography to Napoleon's empire-building ambitions, in recent decades this painstaking consolidation of the revolutionary achievements has been reconstructed and analysed by the historians of law and institutions. Yet it remains hidden, as it were, in plain sight in a series of unconnected specialized studies; as to the men responsible for it, they are forgotten names buried in the pages of decrees and parliamentary records.[42]

The second aspect is the emergence of the difficult relationship between democracy and government. In his study of the Constitution of 1795, Michel Troper suggests that the experience of the Directory represented for France the 'invention' of government: in other words, the realization that governing meant something more than the mere application of the law.[43] But then, how could this 'excess' of initiative on the part of the government be performed without violating the mandate of electors? How can a political regime be truly democratic, yet function efficiently without paralysing impediments? Is it possible to reconcile popular participation and good governance? The French revolutionaries were sincerely committed to the ideal of the sovereignty of the people, even when they differed in estimating the desirable extension of voting rights. However, they imagined that once just laws were made, the execution of those laws should be a simple mechanical exercise, while the people would naturally be prepared to endorse their lawmakers' choices. Instead, the revolutionaries were taken aback by the density of the obstacles they encountered once in government, both from the rigidity of practices and institutions, and from the entrenched hostility of the public. Soon the temptation to seek shortcuts, acting on their own judgement alone, became irresistible.

This early discovery of the intractable nature of democratic governance is relevant to the understanding of contemporary democracies.

While popular participation is potentially far wider than it was two centuries ago, everywhere the technical implications of political decisions have moved further from the grasp of most ordinary citizens and their representatives. In the 1790s the revolutionary governments could at least rely on their own elected experts; today crucial choices – in subjects as diverse as public health, environmental issues, and policies relating to energy or finance – are delegated by necessity to the competence of unelected bodies, largely independent from democratic control. Recent populist attacks against political decisions made on the grounds of scientific advice (during the COVID-19 pandemic which began in 2020, for example) highlight this difficulty. In facing this puzzling situation, the tentative and confused responses of the past, the Directors' search for a compromise between principles and reality, between popular expectations and governance, can still prove instructive.

In order to avoid, as far as possible, the never-ending ideological war over the true identity of the French Republic, this study is constructed around a gallery of biographical portraits, a formula borrowed from the great historian R. R. Palmer's unforgettable tableau of the members of the Committee of Public Safety.[44] Out of the small crowd of men who served on the Directory, I have selected six profiles, those of Paul Barras, Jean-François Reubell, Lazare Carnot, Merlin de Douai, Nicolas François de Neufchâteau and Emmanuel Sieyès; in addition to these, a chapter is dedicated to their minister Jean-Jacques-Régis Cambacérès, a character almost unknown to today's readers, who nevertheless exercised a major influence not just on the Directory's reforms, but on those of the Consulate and of the Empire.

The selection of this Directorial 'dream team' is somewhat arbitrary. I believe it includes the most representative and interesting figures, but no doubt I have been guided partly by my own preference and curiosity. Following these, and in the attempt to circumscribe the scope of my research, some deserving characters have been left out. That is the case, for example, of the Girondin Louis-Marie de

La Révellière-Lépeaux, a lawyer who offered his steady support to Reubell's policies; as deeply anticlerical as most of his colleagues, he distinguished himself by attempting unsuccessfully to promote in France the religious doctrine of theophilanthropy, originally set forth by the Welsh philosopher David Williams. Another unjustly neglected figure is Balthazar François de Barthélemy, who served only briefly on the Directory, but had a long and influential diplomatic career that ran from the reign of Louis XVI to the Empire and the Restoration.

In ordinary times the faults and merits of the Directors might have been those of any random set of politicians or civil servants, whatever their ideological orientation. Instead, their lives unfolded on a unique historical stage, marked by extraordinary dramas and spectacular turns of events, giving their actions a depth and resonance that most of them had neither anticipated nor wished for. Looking at their individual trajectories carries the risk of incoherence, since even within a shared experience, personal interpretations and attitudes are bound to diverge. Moreover, most of the (abundant) evidence provided by the protagonists themselves in their memoirs and correspondence is obviously distorted by their desire to present their own actions in the most favourable light, at the expense of those of others. Even so, I think the risk is worth taking, to break down their stereotyped collective image and gain a more illuminating understanding of their experience.

Avy (Swiss, 1776–1814), *Paul François Jean Nicolas, Viscount of Barras*, 1804–5, miniature on ivory.

I

The Viscount on Horseback: Paul Barras (1755–1829)

On 9 November 1799, the day of the coup of Brumaire, a frequent traveller, Germaine de Staël, on her way back to Paris from Switzerland, stopped for a change of horses a few miles outside the city. While she was waiting, she heard from the postilions that Director Paul Barras had just gone by, speeding in the opposite direction towards his château of Grosbois, accompanied by a military escort. While it was obvious that something out of the ordinary was taking place – troops were stationed around the capital and the Councils had been summoned, allegedly for security reasons, away from the city, at Saint-Cloud – it seemed odd that Barras should be not at the heart of events, but running away from them. Barras was the only one of the Directors with whom de Staël, an influential presence in liberal circles, was on friendly terms; while he was in power, she had pestered him with requests and complaints about the government's actions, and she must have felt she knew him well enough; yon this occasion she was genuinely puzzled.[1]

Barras' place in the history of the Directory is as central as it is difficult to define. On the one hand he remains for posterity the face (or possibly the mask) of the regime, the only name that is still immediately associated with it in people's minds. On the other hand, he cannot be described as its most typical or representative figure, since he did not have much in common with the men who shared his main political adventure; he was, to all effects, the odd one out.

During the four years of his mandate – he was the only one to last the whole course, from November 1795 to November 1799 – he presented himself, and was widely perceived, as the dominus of the Directory, the 'king' of the post-revolutionary Republic, an attribute that is recurrent in later historical accounts. His unexpected rise from near obscurity to the limelight of the Thermidorian political stage, and his swift disappearance from it at Brumaire, has been rightly described as 'meteoric'. Barras was 40 when he was elected to the Directory: the minimum age required by law, but a late start at the time for a national political career; he was 44 when he was forced into bitter retirement for the three decades that remained of his life.[2]

A major difficulty in assessing Barras' position is the scarcity of reliable evidence. His posthumous image is the combined product of the poisonous allegations of his enemies from all political sides, and his own glorious and heroic self-representation. Both are obviously unreliable, but it is impossible to tell to what extent. A somewhat biased account of events is of course to be expected in the memoirs of a period marked by such quick reversals of fortune; many former revolutionaries attempted to justify their own actions in retrospect, while denouncing the faults and responsibilities of others. However, in most cases these discrepancies concern single events or specific issues, while the general narrative corresponds broadly to what is known from other sources. In Barras' case his extensive *Memoirs* – supposedly just edited but in fact largely composed after his death by his former secretary Alexandre Rousselin de Saint-Albin – read like a work of fiction, full of picaresque adventures, malicious anecdotes and extravagant claims. Unfortunately, for significant segments of his life there are simply no alternative sources to set them against.[3]

The adventurous viscount

The first significant difference between Barras and the other Directors was his background. While they came from bourgeois families or the lesser administrative nobility, he was descended from an ancient aristocratic lineage dating back to the Crusades. The Barras belonged – like the Mirabeau, the Pontevès and the Castellane – to the old nobility of Provence, but their strained financial circumstances made it necessary for their son to pursue a career or seek some sort of position along with his less illustrious counterparts. To ensure their social advancement, his future colleagues received a suitable education preparing them to become men of law, provincial administrators or army officers. The young viscount, however, barely had time for superficial schooling before enrolling, at the age of sixteen, as a *cadet* in a colonial regiment, following in the footsteps of his uncle Vice Admiral Jacques-Melchior de Barras.

The commander of the Regiment of Pondichéry, Antoine de Labrillane, was a relative of the family; a knight of Malta, he occupied the position of governor of the Isle de France (now Mauritius). Barras approached his military career in the old way, relying on personal connections and experience rather than facing the selective examinations and training required by the technical corps: navy, engineers and artillery. For all the accusations subsequently levelled against him of being a traitor to his class, he remained at heart a true aristocrat from the old regime: trusting patronage and his superior personal qualities, his natural dash and style, rather than relying on any acquired skill.

By his own account, Barras' military engagement resulted in a series of exotic adventures. During the American War he took part in the siege of Pondichéry (now Puducherry, India) and was taken prisoner by the English; he was shipwrecked on a small island of the Maldives, met Captain Cook and seduced the wives of various colonial dignitaries. These colourful vicissitudes did not lead, however, to any advancement or any serious prospects, and by 1782, disappointed, he had resigned his post of under-lieutenant on the pretext of ill health and returned to civilian life. His suggestive allusions in the *Memoirs* to a personal clash with the minister of the navy, the Duke of Castries, have found no independent confirmation.

In different circumstances, Barras might have been one of those adventurous young aristocrats who used their participation in the American War of Independence to build up their reputation in revolutionary politics. Unfortunately, unlike the Marquis de Lafayette or the brothers Alexandre and Théodore de Lameth, he was not the heir to a large fortune, which would have enabled him to pay for his own regiment, or to a high-ranking military position, the necessary conditions to join that campaign. Even so, the years of his military service in the colonies proved an unexpected asset several years later, when he was finally elected to the Convention. Thanks to them he was seen as a man with military experience but who was no longer attached to the army; in the eyes of a watchful civil government, suspicious of any interference from the military, this was a desirable combination and led to his early appointments as deputy 'on mission' by the Assembly.

Another aspect of Barras' career that differs from those of his colleagues is the puzzling obscurity of his life between 1782 and 1790. Other future Directors spent years in relative anonymity before the Revolution raised them on the political stage, but we do know roughly what they were doing: working in a private legal practice, holding some administrative post, serving in the army or publishing pamphlets. But the account of those years given in Barras' *Memoirs* reads like a picaresque novel. The narrative mentions his association with such characters as the famed libertine the Duke of Richelieu, the writer Nicolas Chamfort and the future political leader Honoré-Gabriel de Mirabeau; it features such equivocal if colourful personalities as the protagonists in the scandal of the queen's necklace: the fraudster Jeanne de La Motte, her hapless victim the Cardinal of Rohan and the magician Cagliostro; it does not, however, provide any information about Barras himself.[4] His enemies claimed that he made a living working as a croupier in the gambling houses of the Palais Royal, or even from prostitutes' gains; needless to say, there is no evidence of any such activity.

It seems reasonable to assume that, while in Paris, Barras frequented a mixed and sometimes equivocal society until, discouraged by a lack of prospects, he finally decided to go back to Provence. What is notably absent from the picture is the indication of any interest on his part in ideas of reform, or in those political questions that were the object of heated debate at the time. In the *Memoirs*, the events of 1789 are related with the obligatory display of revolutionary sentiment, but the narrative reads like a second-hand account full of conventional rhetoric. At best it is the testimonial of a puzzled and detached observer.

It was only after he returned to Provence that Barras began to see in the new political setting the opportunity to make a career. In 1790 he joined the Jacobins of Marseille, a good entry point into local politics, but also the focus of inextricable parochial conflict. The most divisive of these concerned the status of Avignon. An enclave belonging to the Papal States since the thirteenth century, Avignon (along with the surrounding region, Comtat Venaissin) was annexed to France by the Constituent Assembly in 1791. Although this initiative was endorsed by a local vote, it provoked the stern opposition of the rural population of the commune of Carpentras, which remained deeply attached to Catholicism and papal authority. There were violent attacks on both sides (the most famous being the massacre of the Glacière) that Barras and other political envoys, hastily dispatched to the region to mediate, were unable to settle.[5] Despite this lack of success, in September 1792 Barras was elected 'substitute deputy' to one of the eight seats for the *département* of the Var in the new assembly, the Convention; a month later he became deputy in his own right when one of the eight elected, Edmond Louis Alexis Dubois-Crancé, opted for another constituency.

Meanwhile Barras' mother had arranged his marriage to the daughter of a local bourgeois family, with a view to providing him with a stable revenue and possibly an incentive to remain in the region. In practice, however, the new Madame Barras lived with her mother-in-law in the village of Fox-Amphoux, while her husband pursued his activities elsewhere. The couple had no children and shared a house only during the last years of Barras' life, when he became an invalid in need of care; indeed, most of his Parisian friends ignored the fact that he was married. A handsome and dashing man, Barras liked to boast of his success with fashionable society ladies, and it has sometimes been suggested that he was Joséphine de Beauharnais' lover before she married Napoleon. Although there may be some truth in such stories, those contemporaries who knew Barras well believed that he preferred men.[6] Whatever the truth, he led a consistently celibate life.

Controversial missionary

Barras' performance in the Convention was rather low-key since he was, by all accounts, a poor speaker and unsteady in his political allegiances. For a while he was close to the Girondin minister Jean-Marie Roland; the *Memoirs* report his surprise when, summoned to the minister's house, he found that they had to discuss politics in front of Roland's wife, Manon, one of the leading women active in the Revolution. It was an arrangement that Barras found frankly shocking, although it was customary to the couple.[7] Whatever the relevance of his relationship with Roland, in the end Barras distanced himself from the Girondins to side with the Montagnards, the radical group present within the Convention. It was a prudent choice, since Manon Roland was executed during the Terror and both her husband and her lover François Buzot, who had escaped arrest, committed suicide. At the king's trial, Barras voted for his death, along with all the other deputies for the Var – a choice for which in later years he produced convoluted, garbled justifications.

In March 1793, on the strength of his military experience, Barras was sent on a mission to the Hautes and Basses Alpes, and a few months later he was appointed commissioner to the Armée du Midi (the future Armée d'Italie).[8] He was paired with another deputy, the journalist Louis-Marie Stanislas Fréron, whom Barras later described as his 'adjutant', but who at the time – being from a wealthy family, with high-placed connections – was far better known than he was.[9] The situation the missionaries found in Nice, Toulon and Marseille was extremely chaotic and virtually out of control. The Convention had on the one hand to face the counter-revolutionary rebellion of the towns; the port of Toulon – the most important in France at the time – had just been handed over by the rebels to the English fleet, and that of Marseille was about to follow. On the other hand, the envoys struggled to discipline the local Jacobins, whose radical initiatives were partly responsible for the disaffection of the population. Ensuring the recruitment of troops all along the coast in response to the decree for mass mobilization issued by the Convention – the official purpose of their presence in the region – seemed practically impossible.

In the circumstances Barras proved himself to possess both energy and initiative, justifying the harsh means employed by the desperate situation. Less guarded, Fréron boasted of several thousand executions (no figures have ever been confirmed) and admitted to occasional theft ('we pillaged a little').[10] Following the recapture of the port of Toulon by the French – the first noted military exploit by Napoleon, for which Barras later tried to take credit – the town suffered a ferocious repression.[11] As for Marseille, a decree issued on 6 January 1794 stated that the commune, having proved itself 'criminal', would be 'de-baptized', remaining provisionally 'nameless'. Both deputies were accused not just of occasional misappropriation, but of the systematic extorting of the population, and of selling pardons to those accused of counter-revolutionary activities. Yet, whatever excesses the two may have committed – the summary executions, the looting and corruption – these were not the reason for their recall to Paris, contrary to what has been suggested in many later reconstructions. The main concern, from the viewpoint of the Committee of Public Safety, was the two men's inability to collaborate with the local Jacobins, rather than causing harsh personal confrontation.

The circumstances that ended Barras' mandate as missionary are relevant here, since they help to clarify his role in the events of

Thermidor. The most common version of events claimed that Robespierre himself, shocked by the allegations of abuses and corruption, was at the origin of Barras' recall. Faced with the stern condemnation and hostility of the Jacobin leader, and fearing for his life, Barras then naturally contributed to the conspiracy against him.

Barras' *Memoirs* endorse this narrative to some extent, except of course that in his account the allegations of corruption were false. Indeed, he provides a colourful touch to the story by describing the meeting he and Fréron had with Robespierre on their return to Paris. In his narrative, they visited him at his 'humble residence' – the phrase conveys contempt rather than appreciation for the modest set-up – where the Incorruptible lodged with the family Duplay. Robespierre, wrapped in a sort of robe, had just emerged from the hands of his barber, and was brushing away the remnants of white hair powder from his clothing. As the two visitors illustrated the dramatic situation in the South, he pursued his grooming routine, cleaning his teeth, spitting, washing his face, without uttering a single word. His thin lips became even thinner, and the frustrated visitors left without getting any response out of him. Whatever the truth about the episode, Barras had not expressed at the time any marked hostility towards Robespierre, and there is no evidence of a personal clash between the two. Indeed, he seems to have considered Robespierre more moderate and reasonable than other members of the revolutionary government.

The letter of recall of the 'missionaries' was signed by two other members of the Committee of Public Safety, Jacques-Nicolas Billaud-Varenne and Jean-Marie Collot d'Herbois, who were irritated and alarmed by the escalation of the conflict with the local authorities. Quite apart from the idea of de-baptizing the town, the last straw from their point of view was the order to arrest the president of the Revolutionary Tribunal of Marseille, Augustin Maillet, and the public prosecutor, Joseph Giraud.

Recent research on Thermidor questions the notion of one major conspiracy, presenting Robespierre's fall as the outcome of a series of different initiatives, rather than the result of a single orchestrated operation.[12] Barras' position has also been reconsidered, and his role somewhat reduced in importance. Whatever reading is given of the events, Barras must have been aware of the tensions within the Committee of Public Safety and in the Convention; yet, like many others, he simply waited to see how things would turn out, adopting the cautious attitude he had manifested all along. He did not speak at the tribune of the Convention on 9 Thermidor – but then probably no one expected him to intervene.

After the arrest of Robespierre and his associates, however, Barras benefited once again from his military reputation, being entrusted with the defence of Paris in the eventuality of an insurrection to free the Jacobin leaders who were kept in custody at the Hôtel de Ville. He retained that position for a few days, until the crisis was over. The only noticeable incident during these convulsed hours was his visit to the *enfants Capet*, the king's son and daughter in captivity at the Temple, since the rumour had spread that they had been allowed to escape. The episode predictably became the source of fantastical speculation in later years, including Barras' alleged complicity in a plot to replace the dauphin (who died in prison in June 1795) with another boy.[13]

Riding to power

Throughout his life, the image of himself that Barras liked to promote (and probably believed in) was that of a man of action, resolute and decisive in his interventions at moments of crisis. To some extent this was true. He could indeed prove energetic and effective once he had decided on a line of action, but he was extremely cautious, and reluctant when it came to choosing sides. Contrary to his claims of an early commitment to Jacobinism, he had hesitated between the moderate group of the Feuillants and that of the Jacobins before joining the latter; later, as a member of the Convention, he had manifested the same indecision when it came to siding with the Girondins or the Montagnards. A similar caution marked his attitude to the events of Thermidor. A retrospective comment by Benjamin Constant, although sarcastic, captures something of Barras' personality: 'Every time a crisis was announced, it was said that Barras was ready to mount his horse; unfortunately, one never knew on behalf of which side he was going to ride.'[14]

This elastic disposition is another significant difference between Barras and his colleagues. As had most survivors of the Terror, all Directors had shown a degree of political opportunism; their prudence was dictated partly by fear for their lives, and partly, no doubt, by calculation and ambition. However, their opportunism was framed by the resolution to achieve some basic objectives, whatever it took. Even those who had contributed to Terrorist measures were ready, in retrospect, to defend their actions as necessary steps towards the establishment of a stable constitutional government. Besides, some of them had invested considerable energy in promoting reform in their favourite domains, be it education, the law, agriculture or administration; for them, these were lifelong engagements not to be sacrificed to any power. Somehow, their experience limited their political choices but also shaped and guided them.

The same description does not apply to Barras' attitude. The rebellious sentiments that animated the 'Jacobin' or 'Red' viscount were somewhat unfocused, closer to the aristocratic spirit of the Fronde than to any revolutionary ideology. As such they could take on any colours, leaving as the only criterion for allegiance the chance of success. He had no clear vision of a future republic, no past achievements to consolidate, and no specific agenda of reform to promote. The fact that he had never held prominent posts in government favoured his conversion to anti-Jacobinism, since he was not a prime target for personal attack. In common with the other missionaries accused of misdeeds in the provinces, he was the object of investigation by the Convention for his conduct in the South, but the situation there was confused and individual responsibilities difficult to establish. All things considered, he was not important enough for his case to be examined seriously.

Unsurprisingly, given the general chaos, Barras found it quite easy to make people forget his radical past. After Thermidor he served briefly as secretary of the Convention, then he joined the Committee of General Security, now led by a Girondin majority. Both were rather safe positions, and neither offered much in the way of power or responsibility. Finally, in February 1795 he was elected president of the Convention. At the same time, he continued to promote the image of himself as one of the main authors of the 'liberation' of France from the Reign of Terror. With his old friend Fréron and his new one, the journalist Jean-Lambert Tallien, he became the embodiment of the new Thermidorian political class: opportunistic and corrupt in the eyes of many, but in their own view daring, ambitious and open to opportunities.

Countless narratives have described the widespread sense of relief that followed the end of the Terror, but also the moral and political confusion that characterized Thermidorian society: the mixing of former enemies who now met in the salons; the emergence of new fortunes founded on profiteering and speculation; the return of the émigrés; and the licentious parties of the survivors. The reaction against former Terrorists – in the form of both legal prosecution and summary revenge – gave scope to the royalists, now represented in Paris by the fashionable crowd of the dandified *Muscadins*. In this precarious setting Barras was quite at ease. For the first time since the beginning of his public career his personal qualities were well suited to the circumstances; his aristocratic manners were appreciated and he was received in the new fashionable circles, making himself known and forming useful connections.[15] Above all, his natural inclination to sit on the fence, keeping the balance between Jacobin and royalist influence, had become the common strategy of most of the surviving political class.

During his presidency of the Convention, Barras was twice called to mount his horse and save Paris from the threat of insurrection, although by then he had resigned his official position of commander of the Armée de l'Intérieur (domestic defence force). The first occasion was on 1 April 1795 (12 Germinal), when the people from the faubourgs, exasperated by the scarcity of food supplies and the rise in prices, took to the streets to demand the return to the Jacobin Constitution of 1793.[16] They also attempted to free four Jacobin leaders who had been put on trial on account of their Terrorist past: Billaud-Varenne, Collot d'Herbois, Bertrand Barère and Marc-Guillaume Alexis Vadier.[17] Before the extent of the protest was clear, Barras firmly declined to intervene; he was apparently unwilling to attack a starving crowd, especially since he had himself criticized the government's failure to ensure supplies reached the city. Instead, he pressed the unwelcome honour on the reluctant General Charles Pichegru.

On the second occasion, on 5 October 1795 (13 Vendémiaire), Barras was entrusted with the defence of the Convention against the threat of a royalist coup. As in Toulon, he enlisted the services of Napoleon, who was then in Paris between employments, and who dispersed the insurgents without great difficulty.[18] This second episode allowed Barras to shine once again as saviour of the Republic. However, the exploit lost him the support of some moderate and royalist voters, and gave him a poor result in the elections of the Year IV that took place in October–November 1795, shortly after the adoption of the new Constitution. Even so, his balancing act during the previous year ensured his election as one of the five members of the new executive.

The choice of the Directors by the Councils reflected a preference for a middle course, combining a republican past in one or other of the factions, with the rejection of Terrorism. On this point Barras' conversion, like that of many others, was suspicious to say the least. However, on balance his profile conformed to the common pattern, with the additional advantage of moderate visibility. The question is how he progressed from low-profile nominee – one who obtained the fewest votes of the five – to apparent leader of the executive.

The Republic's accountant

Unlike his colleagues, Barras, however effective and energetic he might be, did not possess any professional skills. He was not a lawyer, magistrate or engineer; he had never run a local administration, presided over a tribunal or drafted legislation, nor was he willing to learn to do any of these things. In the words of a contemporary, 'he had no aptitude for administration and government.'[19] The judgement was shared by Napoleon, who claimed Barras had 'no opinion whatever on any subject of public administration'; moreover, although he might have been able to mount a horse, he had, according to the emperor, no real military experience.[20]

So why, despite his limitations, did Barras end up playing such a prominent role in the Directory? To start with, he was the only one willing to keep the executive together, ensuring its functioning – and the only one capable of that. The Constitution of 1795 had since the beginning been the constant object of varied criticism, but one point that has not been sufficiently appreciated is the difficulty of running a collegial executive consisting of members chosen randomly from among hundreds of deputies. In traditional republican regimes, the members of ruling councils came from the same closely knit local elite, with a long practice of mediation and interaction: an endogamous model that clearly did not apply to the French political class. In modern parliamentary systems, the head of the executive co-opts the ministers, commanding a degree of loyalty from them and limiting the risk of personal conflict. In addition, when the members of government belong to some party, the parties themselves act as a moderating element against the inevitable personal clashes.

Instead, the mode of selection of the Directors, without a head of government in charge and without structured parties, offered no guarantee that they would get on with their colleagues or indeed be prepared to work with them at all. If we look at the first set of five, with the single exception of the friendship between Lazare Carnot and

Étienne-François Le Tourneur (both military engineers), they all disliked, even detested, one another. Emmanuel Sieyès' decision to refuse the post when he was first elected in 1795 was generally attributed to his strong aversion to his prospective colleague Jean-François Reubell, a lawyer from Colmar. Reubell was indeed notoriously difficult; abrasive, abrupt and ungracious, he easily became loudly abusive. Although less intractable, Carnot and Louis-Marie de La Révellière-Lépeaux were equally lacking in social graces and diplomatic skills; hard-working and focused on their own projects, they made no allowances for collegial interaction. The replacements that occurred year after year, sometimes following fabricated allegations of conspiracy or corruption, did not improve things on the relational front.

Naturally the Committee of Public Safety – the legislative committee of twelve that served as executive cabinet during the Revolution – had also been an arena for violent personal confrontation. Even in more ordinary settings, nobody expects the members of any government to like and appreciate one another. However, in a small group of five, without any leadership or mediation, personal hostility could prove paralysing. Most of the work of the executive was carried out individually, each Director being responsible for a specific domain (Barras supervised the interior) with the assistance of the ministers who depended on them; there was also an implicit sharing among the five of broad geographical areas, based on their provenance and electoral constituencies. Even so, some collegial initiatives and decisions were necessary.

Barras took on the task of coordinating, if not directing, the action of the executive. Most of the time he did so by forming a sort of 'triumvirate', the composition of which varied over time, that dictated the government's line; a majority of three in agreement on some measure was sufficient to pass it. Early on he adopted the practice of keeping track of things by writing after each meeting a short summary of what had been decided, since there were no formal minutes. In his *Memoirs*, Barras explained that he regarded himself as a sort of 'accountant' responsible for the moral and material balance of his administration towards his 'natural controllers', the citizens, so he wished to see the accounts updated every day. This notion of accountancy is sufficiently unusual to sound authentic, rather than being a posthumous invention of the editor.

All things considered, Barras seems to have developed the capacity to ensure a degree of coherence in the government's action, influencing and subduing his colleagues and avoiding major conflict as far as possible, although, as time went by, his relationships with the two Directors who were not part of his 'triumvirate' became increasingly strained. His presence in office for the entire duration of the Directorial Republic contributed to placing him in a central position. Was the fact that he was never deselected by lot accidental or contrived? The odd coincidence that his name never came up for deselection is one of the factors that raised suspicions of a rigged ballot, but no conclusive evidence has survived. It may have been chance, or he may have been the only one who was always willing to stay on.

The mask of the regime

Barras' ability to extract a degree of cooperation from his reluctant colleagues went together with another distinctive function he acquired within the Directory: the public representation and staging of the new republican power. Until then, for all the ideological mistrust of individual ambition, public attention had been focused on the leaders of the National Assembly. These popular personalities were charismatic speakers who had become the incarnation of the Revolution, the subject of legend and fantasy – even when they orchestrated their own mutual destruction. By contrast the Directors, despite their long and active political careers, were almost unknown to the wider public. This relative anonymity was not appreciated by a popular audience that had always been used to more visible and recognizable incarnations of authority.

The authors of the Constitution of 1795 had tried to enhance the status of the new government by conferring on the Directors some exterior signs of prestige, but this did not elicit much response on their part. While he firmly refused to wear the fancy costume of his function, Barras was the only one who undertook with enthusiasm the mission of surrounding himself with the visible marks of power. Proud of his aristocratic origins and uninhibited by any republican modesty, he was determined to make the most of his high position. One question was the Directors' forced 'communal' residence. Barras had no intention of sharing the makeshift apartments at the Petit Luxembourg with his colleagues. Instead, he took over and hastily refurbished a set of rooms in the larger palace next door, including the gallery, overlooking rue de Vaugirard, that housed the paintings by Peter Paul Rubens illustrating the lives of Henri IV and Marie de Medici.[21] Two years later, in 1797, Barras crowned his ambitions by acquiring the Renaissance château of Grosbois in Val-de-Marne, yet another of the Count of Provence's confiscated properties that were auctioned off at an advantageous price.

The Directors were obliged to be available regularly to those citizens who wished to submit petitions or complaints. For most of them, these audiences were the whole extent of their public appearances, unless they were called on to preside over some public event or celebration. Barras was not satisfied with such formal occasions, however, and took advantage of his palatial accommodation to hold receptions and parties in suitable style. His easy generosity and natural love of ostentatious display placed him at the heart of a small court that included useful political contacts, fashionable socialites (he had no taste for the arts and sciences) and the inevitable crowd of hangers-on.

To all effects, Barras turned himself into the public face of the Directory, its recognizable identity, and this convinced many observers, in France as abroad, of his primacy within the government, exaggerating to some extent his personal power and influence. As in the case of other leading figures of the Revolution (Robespierre being the most striking example), popular imagination attributed to Barras near-royal prerogatives that he did not in fact possess. In retrospect, this also made him the ideal scapegoat for the Directory's real and supposed vices. As Napoleon shrewdly observed, while Barras' display of luxury was not achieved at public expense, it was still suggestive of hidden corruption, with a demoralizing impact on public opinion.[22] The atmosphere of licence and intrigue that floated around his entourage was naturally extended by detractors of the Republic from all political sides to his dull, respectable colleagues, creating the overall illusion of widespread dissipation.

Inside the besieged fortress

If he was engaged in making the executive work, Barras did not seem to have any vision of what their mission should be, beyond ensuring their own immediate political survival. The close of the Terrorist phase of the Revolution, and the return to a normal constitutional regime, had put an end to the spiral of self-destruction, but it had also created new problems for the government. With the prospect of free elections, the Directory had to keep an uneasy balance between the resurrected royalists and the diehard Jacobins, both of whom were competing for control of the Councils. In addition, the rumours of conspiracy and insurrection from both political sides persisted, rather than dying out. One dangerous legacy of the years of emergency rule was the problem of differentiating between the change in parliamentary majorities resulting from free elections, and the use of extra-constitutional means to get rid of political opponents; somehow the frontier between democratic competition and *coup d'état* had become too easy to cross.

While his colleagues struggled with the conduct of the war, or focused on improving the economy, Barras concentrated on keeping the regime afloat between opposing forces: the right working towards the restoration of the monarchy, the left fighting to reassert the power of the Parisian sections. Caught between the two, he behaved like the defender of a besieged fortress, constantly watching the political horizon for the moves of potential assailants. Every day he would get reports from his agents on his own and on the government's popularity, in a prefiguration of the modern obsession with opinion polls.

On one point at least, Barras' political line was quite clear, without his usual balancing between left and right: the pursuit of the war. In 1795 the Treaty of Basel (which France signed with Prussia, Spain and Hesse-Kassel) marked a point of arrest in the military conflict. Should the Directory continue to negotiate peace with the forces of the coalition, bringing the war to an end and focusing instead on domestic issues? Or should France continue to fight, intervening in those neighbouring countries where revolutionary patriots called for its help? Foreign policy was the domain in which the executive had a freer hand and was less subject to the control of the legislative, but it was also the source of open disagreement among the Directors.

On the one hand, Carnot, backed by Le Tourneur, defended the Jacobin principle that France should have no territorial ambitions beyond the consolidation of its natural frontiers. Carnot's military experience made him fully aware of the huge resources, both human and economic, necessary to pursue the conflict, resources that could be more usefully employed at home. Anxious for a return to normality, he saw the war as a major obstacle to the stabilization of the Republic. On the other hand, Reubell, preoccupied with the safety of his own region, Alsace, was keen on pursuing a policy of territorial expansion. Barras sided with the latter, securing the support of La Révellière-Lépeaux and tipping the majority in favour of the pursuit of the conflict.

Barras' objective was not so much the patriotic defence of the frontier of the Rhine that preoccupied Reubell, nor the spreading of revolutionary institutions abroad, but rather the financial gains that military conquest could bring, as shown by the spoils of Napoleon's first Italian campaign. Barras also saw military success as a means of strengthening the position of the Directory and boosting their prestige against the attacks of their opponents. In 1797 he managed to get rid of Carnot, falsely implicating him (as he openly admitted) in the royalist conspiracy of Fructidor; this left the Directory free to support the occupation of Switzerland and to promote Napoleon's new campaigns in Italy and Egypt. Barras' calculation of the potential political and economic advantages of military conquest was correct, but his assumption that he would be the main beneficiary of such policy was, to say the least, ill-judged.

A conspiracy too far

When did Barras decide that the Directory was no longer a viable political option? More importantly, how did he fail to take control of its liquidation, given his central position in the government? It is difficult to obtain an accurate picture of his role in the sequence of events, once again not because the evidence is lacking, but rather because most of it is contradictory or unreliable. Barras' own retrospective accounts of the coup of Brumaire consist of a flood of accusations against everyone involved, mainly Napoleon, but also Sieyès, Joseph Fouché and Charles-Maurice de Talleyrand (whom he had appointed minister of foreign affairs on Germaine de Staël's insistence), all of whom were charged with wicked duplicity and betrayal. As to the testimonials of others – protagonists as well as observers – they provide an excess of conjecture, opinion and allegation, generally without proof.

It is reasonable to assume that by 1799 Barras had been thinking for some time of a possible exit from the 'government of balance' to which the Directory was constrained both by its limited constitutional powers and by fluctuations in popular consensus. After all, the best guarantee against the risk of a *coup d'état* is to organize one yourself.[23] His decision to replace the intractable Reubell (officially deselected by lot) with Sieyès, whom he considered easier to control, went in the direction of some initiative to bring the Directorial Republic to an end. But if the Directory had reached its terminal stage, what could take its place?

One possible solution was the restoration of the Bourbon monarchy. Barras' aristocratic birth meant that he was regarded as a natural interlocutor by Louis XVIII's agents. Perhaps optimistically, those agents saw in the weakness of the Directorial Republic the ideal opportunity for the king's return; they also believed, with some reason, that Barras' attachment to republicanism did not run very deep.[24] There is, however, no evidence of serious negotiations between him and the royalists. It was rumoured that he had asked for a large sum of money (20 million *livres*) and a ducal title, yet the intermediaries in the transaction may have been acting without authority, or simply making it up. A written report addressed to Louis XVIII by his informers after Brumaire denounced the cowardice of Barras – that *sardanapale populaire* – in running away from Napoleon with a severity that suggests there had been hopes of different conduct on his part.[25]

More significantly, at the Restoration Louis XVIII's attitude towards Barras was consistently gracious. The fact that he was pardoned for having voted for the king's death (and allowed to remain in France) was not in itself the sign of special treatment; during the Hundred Days a panicked Louis XVIII had promised amnesty to those former regicides who did not rally to Napoleon, and Barras obviously had no intention of doing so. However, even after the emperor's final defeat, there were courteous exchanges between the king and the former Director, possibly favoured by the minister of the royal household, the Count of Blacas, who was related to Barras' family.

While the project of restoring the monarchy seemed hazardous, the alternative was to change the republican constitution so as to give greater powers to the executive. Apparently, no one had a precise notion of what form this change might take. Even the constitutional oracle Sieyès arrived on the day of the coup with 'some ideas' but no definite project. On the other hand, it seemed the support of the military would be indispensable, since the Councils were unlikely to surrender their powers willingly. Barras' encouragement of Napoleon's career was clearly instrumental to the project of radical change in government. Just like Sieyès, he made a double miscalculation. First, he assumed that the army's intervention was necessary, when in fact the coup was brought about without any arrests or a single shot; second, he regarded the military partner in the operation as an indifferent tool (any general might do), rather than as a political actor with designs of his own. As Fouché (who knew Barras well) cruelly observed, 'he was not very good at politics.'[26]

In any case, Barras behaved in the circumstances as he had at other turning points in his career: hesitating and taking the time to see how things would turn out. Since he had convinced the public of his own dominant role in the government, he had also convinced himself that nothing could be done without him. The realization that it was not so must have come as a considerable shock. His friends (just like his biographers) were surprised by his passive, unresponsive attitude to a political exclusion that was to prove final. On the morning of 18 Brumaire (9 November) two of the Directors, Sieyès and Roger Ducos, who were party to the conspiracy, signed their letters of resignation from the executive. Two others, Louis-Jérôme Gohier and Jean-François Moulin, who were not, opposed furiously any suggestion that they should do the same; indeed, Moulin (another general) threatened to have Napoleon shot, although it is unclear how he proposed to do this. Barras might have tipped the balance by joining them, holding on to his post in the executive, but when they tried to confer with him, they were unable to do so; the Director, they were told, was taking what turned out to be a very long bath. When he finally emerged from his ablutions, it was to sign his own letter of resignation, without showing any kind of reaction, and shortly afterwards he left the Luxembourg for the very last time.[27]

'Citizen General'

Was Barras already resigned to the idea that this was the end of the road for him, or did he have other hopes? After the coup the First Consul offered him various posts, all outside France, that he refused. Napoleon was quite happy to recruit some of the former Directors, making use of their professional competence and experience for his new institutions, the Senate and the Council of State. However, Barras had little to offer in the way of administrative skill, and his reputation was too compromised. He had turned himself into the incarnation of the past regime, with all the faults and vices that were now denounced to justify its liquidation. Moreover, the new master of France did not trust him.

For a few years, Barras chose to exile himself in Brussels, avoiding the constant surveillance of the police, to which he was subjected by his former fellow Jacobin Fouché, who suspected him of conspiring with both the royalists and the left. In 1805, once the new power was consolidated, he returned to France, first to a country property near Marseille, then to a house at Chaillot, then to the outskirts of Paris. For thirty years (he died in 1829) he brooded over the duplicity and ingratitude of his former associates and, as he saw them, protégés and subordinates.

The last glimpse we have of Barras comes from the pen of the young Alexandre Dumas, who was an occasional dinner guest at Chaillot.[28] The former Director, now confined to a wheelchair, liked to describe himself as a 'hermit'; however, he kept an open table for the usual mixed and diverse company, including some other survivors from the golden circle of Thermidor who had fallen on hard times, such as Tallien. Curiously (was he losing his memory?) Barras insisted on being addressed not as 'Viscount' but as 'Citizen General', as if he expected to be called at any moment to mount his horse and save the Republic.

2

The Difficult Lawyer from Alsace: Jean-François Reubell (1747–1807)

In Jacques-Louis David's famous drawing from 1791 celebrating the Oath of the Tennis Court of 20 June 1789 at Versailles, when the delegates promised to give France a constitution, Jean-François Reubell occupies the centre left of the scene. As the deputies raise their arms towards President Jean-Sylvain Bailly, who is reading the oath standing on a table, Reubell is shown in profile and in full light, about to embrace the black-robed silhouette of the delegate of the clergy for Nemours, Anne Alexandre Marie Thibault. The gesture was probably introduced by the painter to create some variety of movement in the composition, while showing the fraternal unity of the three estates. David's choice was unwittingly ironical, as it happens, since Reubell was not generally given to such fraternal embraces of the representatives of any religion. In any case, the identity of the tall deputy in lacy jabot and silky redingote was destined to fade rapidly from collective memory.[1]

The name of Jean-François Reubell appears frequently in histories of the French Revolution, but he is generally mentioned in relation to specific topics: the controversy over the status of the Jews from Alsace; some contested financial measure; the diplomatic negotiations over the Batavian and Helvetic republics. He is largely forgotten – except perhaps locally, being the only major figure in national government produced by Alsace at the time. Yet, after a long and industrious political career that stretched from the Estates General to the Five

Hundred, Reubell was possibly the most influential member of the Directory. He was also, after Barras, the longest-serving one; he was elected in 1795 and replaced by Emmanuel Sieyès only at the very end, a few months before the liquidation of the Republic at Brumaire. His responsibilities within the executive – foreign affairs, finance and (briefly) justice – meant that he orientated the government's action in some crucial domains, and insofar as the Directory had any coherent policies, he was responsible for them. Barras admitted that Reubell was the soul of the Directory, but perhaps it is more appropriate to say that he was its backbone.[2]

Reubell's colleagues found him impossible to deal with, since he was authoritarian, obstinate and ill-tempered (Barras dismissed his behaviour haughtily as 'vulgar'). At the same time, they were ready to acknowledge his many qualities: a very good knowledge of all branches of the administration down to the finest legal details; a phenomenal memory; an impressive capacity for hard work; and the ability to make considered decisions when faced with the most intricate questions. In personal relations, however ungracious, he was reliable and very loyal. Napoleon – who was also confronted with Reubell's difficult personality – claimed that he was the only one of the Directors to possess the stature of a statesman.[3] When he died in retirement in 1807, the emperor intervened to assist his family, who were left in difficult financial circumstances; the accusations directed against Reubell of having squirrelled away millions accumulated through corruption turned out to be unfounded.

The deputy from Colmar

In some ways, Reubell's background was like that of other Directors, consisting of years of solid professional experience leading to his election to the Estates General in 1789. The son of a royal notary, he chose instead a career at the bar and, appointed *batonnier* (chairman of the bar) in 1782, became a successful lawyer with a lucrative practice. His

Henri Félix Philippoteaux, *Jean-François Reubell at the Siege of Mainz, 1793*, 1862–84, oil on canvas.

abrasive character was perhaps not apparent in his ordinary relations with clients. In November 1796 the English writer Henry Swinburne, who happened to be present at one of Reubell's weekly audiences at the Luxembourg – a routine Reubell followed scrupulously – was struck by the Director's attentiveness to and patience with the dissatisfied members of the public who came to consult him.[4] His professional reputation was established in the mid-1770s, when he defended the Alsatian county of Riquewihr-Harbourg in a tangled legal dispute against the Duke of Württemberg over the payment of feudal dues. Reubell was apparently not driven by any ideological opposition to feudalism; he simply thought the duke's claims to a share of the county's revenue, based on some intricate and questionable line of succession, were legally unfounded. The episode enhanced his popularity and contributed to his being chosen later as an Alsatian delegate for the Third Estate.

What did make Reubell's position somewhat different from those of his future colleagues was his deep attachment to his place of origin. While others, once in central government, lost touch with the concerns of the regions they represented, Alsace's complex situation continued to be the focus of Reubell's political commitment throughout his life. Annexed to France by the Treaty of Münster in 1648, in the late eighteenth century Alsace was still far from resembling a French province. Administratively it was a patchwork of independent cities and residual German feudal domains, with a Sovereign Council in place of the customary French parliament.[5] Colmar itself – the second most important centre after Strasbourg – was part of a *décapole*, a set of ten allied towns; at the time of the elections to the Estates General, the constituency that Reubell represented, Colmar-Schlestadt, had been created by dividing the territory somewhat arbitrarily into three zones and assimilating for electoral purposes the local *Bürgers* (bourgeois) to the members of the Third Estate.

Alsace's religious circumstances were also unusual. A deeply Catholic region, where the Church owned two-thirds of the land, it had a significant Protestant presence guaranteed by the terms of the Treaty of Münster, as well as an important and largely self-contained Jewish community.[6] Despite various royal decrees imposing linguistic conformity, German, rather than French, was still the prevailing language, and Reubell's own studies at the University of Strasbourg had been carried out in German. While other French provinces retained some distinctive local practices and institutions, Alsace's administrative differences from the rest of the kingdom were more important and, because of the region's considerable demographic and economic weight, could not be ignored. Unlike the other small German enclaves within France, this was a vast and prosperous territory, with a population of about 600,000 and a rich agriculture centred on the production of wine and tobacco; it also enjoyed fiscal privileges and custom-duties exemptions dating back to the time of the annexation.[7]

In 1789, along with most deputies, Reubell went to Versailles to convey the demands of his electors. He hoped the royal administration would prove more responsive to local concerns than it had been in the past, given that Alsace had more substantial prerogatives to defend than other French provinces. The experience of the Constituent Assembly led him, in common with many others, to switch from a local to a broader national perspective; striving to transform the Alsatian patchwork into a viable administrative unit, he supported the suppression of the Sovereign Council and, as a result, his house in Colmar was besieged by an angry mob, who threatened to burn it down. Later, he opposed the Girondins' proposal to create a network of departmental assemblies, since he considered the project a danger to national unity. However, he never lost the sense of Alsace's distinctive position. Even before the war against the European coalition began, the circumstances of the region made it especially vulnerable. Its geographical situation, its long tradition of administrative independence, its proximity to German culture and the influence of the dispossessed Catholic Church all were elements that exposed the territory to the risks of foreign occupation or even annexation. These concerns fed Reubell's obstinate patriotism and his determination to keep Alsace French at all costs. His actions during the Revolution and the Directory were largely shaped and orientated by these sentiments.

Among the fairly conservative Alsatian delegation, Reubell stood out as a committed revolutionary, yet he was at heart a moderate with an ingrained dislike of radical excess and a genuine horror of mob rule. As a representative of the Third Estate, he fully deserved his place in David's commemorative tableau. Not only did he vote with Sieyès to form the Constituent Assembly, but he was part of the Alsatian delegation who met the minister Jacques Necker and demanded the replacement of the collective vote by order with the vote by head, a decision that gave the Third Estate a large majority.[8] Being in favour of reducing the power of the executive, Reubell was against the royal veto, and against the king's prerogative to declare war. When the Constituent Assembly debated the conditions for *active* citizenship, in other words for the right to vote, he sided with the more democratic proposal of fixing the requirement to the equivalent of three days' wages.

While he disliked such aristocratic leaders as Honoré-Gabriel de Mirabeau and the Marquis de Lafayette, Reubell was, like them, in favour of constitutional monarchy. He was reluctant to accept the hasty proclamation of the Republic in 1792, exposing himself to (unfounded) accusations of supporting the dynastic ambitions of the Duke of Orléans. Although no impressive speaker, he made regular interventions at the Constituent Assembly, especially on juridical and economic questions (he joined the Finance Committee in August 1790). Indeed, it was on a juridical issue that the endless complications in Alsace caught up with him. In December 1789 the assembly debated the status of French Jews. The general view was that Jews, just like Protestants, should be given full civil rights, but there were reservations about the Jewish communities of Alsace and Lorraine. Of different origins from the rest of the French Jews (Ashkenazi rather than Sephardi), these communities were unwilling to be assimilated into French society, preferring to maintain their own language, customs and administration.

In Alsace the Catholic clergy demanded harsh laws against the Jews. For his part, Reubell was opposed to any discriminating measures but believed that full civil rights should be accorded gradually, conditional on the willingness to be integrated. Differences of cult, he explained in a private letter on 28 January 1790, were irrelevant, but 'by keeping their own practices and separate administration', Alsatian Jews effectively 'excluded themselves from citizenship'.[9] Reubell's viewpoint was shared by most of the members of the Constituent Assembly, and in 1790 the Assembly voted in favour of civil rights for French Jews to the exclusion of those from Alsace and Lorraine. Meanwhile Reubell himself had become the target of virulent attacks by Jean-Paul Marat and by Camille Desmoulins, who claimed his opinions were 'unworthy of a professed patriot'.[10]

Following these denunciations, Reubell has acquired an undeserved reputation for antisemitism. There is in fact no evidence that he held any racial prejudices, since he was in favour of the attribution of civil rights to freed slaves in the colonies. As to religion, he placed State authority above confessions and was sternly opposed to any church or cult that failed to conform to secular rule. Despite his Catholic background, he had voted in favour of the Civil Constitution of the clergy; faced with the counter-revolutionary influence of the Church in Alsace, he acted with extreme severity against those refractory priests who refused to profess their allegiance to the Republic, jeopardizing the support of his own Catholic electors as a result.

However, as Reubell knew very well, the difficulty over Alsatian Jews was not merely religious or cultural. The community was the most important source of credit for local landowners and held the largest share of the local debt, a fact that accounted to some extent for the reluctance to recognize their status. Peasants, believing that Jews would be the main buyers once Church lands were sold off, were afraid of being evicted from their farms. In the end the question of assimilation was inextricably connected both with ancient prejudice against 'Jewish usurers' and with contemporary anxiety over money and the redistribution of property. This second, more tractable aspect became the focus of much of Reubell's subsequent political activity.[11]

The left bank of the Rhine

On 17 October 1791, a month after the dissolution of the Constituent Assembly, Reubell – who had opposed in vain the decision to make the former members of that assembly ineligible for membership of the new Legislative Assembly – went back to Colmar to take up the position of Procureur-Général Syndic (a kind of governor) for the *département* of Haut-Rhin. The post was the main executive office in the region, and Reubell had been elected to it a year before with a large majority by the departmental assembly of Belfort. Shortly afterwards he was received as a member by the Jacobin club of Colmar, although in Paris he had left the Jacobins for the moderate Feuillants.

Whatever his original plans for his mandate back home, Reubell's year in office was dominated by the question of national security.[12] Before the declaration of war against Austria on 20 April 1792, the main threats were the presence of émigrés (some of them former members of the Constituent Assembly) and refractory priests, and the counter-revolutionary activities of the Bishops of Basel and Strasbourg (the latter, Cardinal Rohan, being famous as the gullible protagonist of the scandal of the queen's necklace). When asked by a correspondent what caused the greatest difficulties, Reubell replied: '1) the priests; 2) the priests; 3) the priests'. His efforts to have the rebel clergy deported caused him to be described as a revived Nero or, alternatively, a 'savage Huron'.[13]

Once the war began, the Legislative Assembly sent three deputies, one of them the future Director Lazare Carnot, on a mission to verify the loyalty of the regiments stationed in the area. As it happens, four of their commanding officers – Generals Nicolas Luckner,

Armand-Louis de Gontaut Biron, Adam-Philippe de Custine and Alexandre de Beauharnais (Joséphine Bonaparte's first husband) – would be sent to the scaffold in 1793 and 1794. For the revolutionary government, the distinction between failure to hold the front and treason was becoming very thin indeed.[14] The prevailing atmosphere of panic and defeat is well captured by an episode that Reubell himself reported. While on a mission to Basle in June 1792, he encountered at the Hôtel des Trois Rois – the inevitable meeting point for all those crossing the border on the Rhine – various characters (an elderly émigré marquise, two eccentric Swiss travellers), all of whom were ready to assure him, to his great dismay, that France was going to be dismembered and that its northeastern territories were about to be taken over by Austria.[15]

Reubell held the office of Procureur until 2 September 1792, when he was elected to the Convention with the largest number of votes of the eight Alsatian deputies. However, his election did not take him back to Paris and to national politics, and he was to spend most of his mandate on various missions. A fluent German speaker with a working knowledge of English and Italian, he was appointed on 11 October 1792 to the Diplomatic Committee, where he joined Carnot and another future Director, the Girondin Louis-Marie de La Révellière-Lépeaux. In his new role Reubell was involved in two unsuccessful military operations: the occupation of Mainz (Mayence) and a failed attempt, the first of many, to end the revolt in the Vendée. Mainz had been occupied by the French army at the beginning of the war, with the support of local revolutionaries; it was surrendered to Austria by General Custine after a three-month siege, although this was a controversial decision, since some thought resistance was still possible. (The town returned to France in 1797, when Napoleon signed the Treaty of Campo-Formio.) After the siege, the army of the Rhine was employed, unsuccessfully, to 'pacify' the rebellion in the Vendée.

These frustrating experiences with the running of the war show the difficult role of civilian commissioners, who were supposed to assist army commanders – interacting with the local population, mobilizing revolutionary sympathizers, indoctrinating the troops – while at the same time keeping tabs on the officers' performance and loyalty.[16] The revolutionary government's determination to keep strict control over the conduct of the war, leaving nothing to military initiative, created endless complications and fed misunderstandings on both sides. In addition, at the beginning of the war all high-ranking officers were aristocrats, since under the old regime, patents of nobility (often bought or made up for the purpose) were a necessary condition for occupying such posts. Inevitably, despite their loyalty to the Republic, their social status exposed them to recurrent suspicion of desertion and betrayal. As for civilian officials on missions from Paris, they were often blamed for military failures for which they were in no way responsible.

Reubell emerged from the Mainz episode with a mixed reputation. His supporters, especially those in Alsace, saw him as a hero of the siege, an image consolidated by his posthumous portrait by Philippoteaux; his enemies however claimed that Custine's surrender, which cost the general his head, was partly Reubell's fault. The fact that several trunks filled with precious objects originally belonging to the Elector of Mainz were found in Reubell's house (allegedly stored in preparation for delivery to the Jacobins of Colmar) brought accusations of looting and misappropriation. Being away from Parisian factional struggles had contributed to Reubell's survival, but the controversy over the siege exposed him to further attacks that he could overcome only by keeping a carefully low profile. One significant effect his military missions had on the Alsatian lawyer was to convince him of the duplicitous role played by Louis XVI in the war by encouraging desertion and plotting with France's enemies. While he did not vote for the king's death (he was away from Paris at the time), his correspondence shows that he fully approved of it; his favourable opinion of constitutional monarchy as a suitable political system for France had been destroyed by a profound sense of disillusionment and betrayal.

Even with the Elector's silver stored in his house, Reubell was not a prime target for accusations by the Committee of Public Safety and had no personal contention with any of its members. If anything, he thought Maximilien Robespierre 'too soft' in conducting the war. Reubell was not involved directly in the events of Thermidor, although, like many others, he behaved afterwards as if he had made a significant contribution to them. However, he was ready to take advantage of the political space that had suddenly opened, making steady progress within the Thermidorian institutions. Not having been directly involved in any Terrorist policies, he was naturally ready to join in the general disavowal of the past regime. Some weeks after the liquidation of Robespierre, Reubell spoke up against the lack of turnover in the Committees of Public Safety and General Security, proposing some rules against the re-eligibility of their members that were adopted by the Convention on 29 August 1794. He also criticized the current practice of multiplying special commissions as a source of confusion and opacity in the conduct of government. On 6 October 1794 he joined the Committee of General Security; he was then elected president of the Convention, and he finally joined the Committee of Public Safety on 5 March 1795.

Meanwhile the question of national security took Reubell away from Paris once again, back to France's iron frontier on the Rhine.[17] In April 1795 he was in Basle to negotiate the peace treaty with Prussia. Deeply hostile to Austria, Reubell had always favoured the project of a Franco-Prussian alliance to stabilize the northeastern border. He was then sent to The Hague; the French armies had occupied a large portion of the United Provinces, and in May 1795 the Treaty of The Hague established the Batavian Republic, the first of the satellite (or, as they were called, 'sister') republics created by French revolutionary expansion. These diplomatic settlements made evident the basic disagreement that had marked the conduct of France's foreign policy by revolutionary governments since the beginning of the war.

Some negotiators – such as Merlin de Douai and Merlin de Thionville – were against the annexation of territories with German populations. More generally, they were opposed to a politics of conquest, or 'liberation', that would stretch France's borders beyond its supposedly natural frontiers, in this case the left bank of the Rhine. Indeed, Carnot – a stern opponent of expansion – suggested that the Moselle, rather than the Rhine, should be regarded as France's natural frontier, leaving the German enclaves on the other side. On the contrary, Reubell regarded the occupation of the Rhineland as essential for the protection and stability of Alsace. On 18 September 1795, after the capitulation of the Duke of Württemberg (Reubell's old opponent in the dispute over feudal duties), he wrote to the Committee of Public Safety:

> It is essential that we should not prove too accommodating on the question of the left bank of the Rhine. The happiness of mankind will be the result of this position [*systhème*]; it is only with the help of occupied countries that we can re-establish our finances and fix the assignats at their right value. It is necessary to keep the Rhine by securing the left bank and by watching closely the right bank to avoid any threat to the integrity of the Republic's territory.[18]

While the reference to the happiness of mankind sounds far-fetched, to say the least, the impact of the occupation of new territories on the value of the *assignats* and, more generally, on the Republic's credit was clearly established in Reubell's mind. A compromise was finally set forth by Merlin de Douai: the permanent annexation of Belgium and the temporary occupation (until the end of the war) of German territories. However, the profound strategic and ideological differences over the status of occupied regions continued to poison relations between the two Directors once they found themselves together in government.

Chasing vampires

Following his successful progress through the Committees, in October 1795 Reubell was elected by several *départements* to the new assembly of the Five Hundred, and shortly afterwards he was designated one of the five Directors, coming third in terms of the number of votes received. The downside of his promotion to the executive was the prospect of forced collaboration with men whom he disliked. While Sieyès had allegedly declined the post to avoid working with him, Sieyès' replacement, Carnot, was someone with whom Reubell had already clashed over France's territorial expansion. As for Barras, Reubell despised his ostentatious lifestyle and uninhibited opportunism, and was suspicious of his relationship with the royalists, although in time he managed to form a kind of strategic alliance with him. Luckily, Reubell was at least able to develop a fruitful collaboration with the finance minister, Dominique-Vincent Ramel-Nogaret, and, later, with the minister of the interior, Nicolas François de Neufchâteau. Ramel-Nogaret, a lawyer from Carcassonne, had, like Reubell, been a member of the Constituent Assembly, the Convention and the Thermidorian Committee of Public Safety.[19] Their good understanding was crucial, since finding a way out of the Republic's financial crisis was the first object of Reubell's acts as a Director.

Reubell had been interested in financial matters since the beginning of his political career. Now that he was, to some extent at least, in charge, he saw the restoration of French finances as an essential condition for the survival of the Republic.[20] Predictably, in pursuing this objective he met with considerable practical difficulties, and he was also confronted with the paradoxical position in which the new government found itself. On the one hand, returning to normal constitutional rule meant abandoning the special measures introduced by the revolutionary regime to control the economy: regulation of prices, requisition of stock and, above all, the use of paper money (the *assignats*) as official currency. On the other hand, getting out of this artificial economic framework back into a normal market economy was a perilous exercise that required illiberal authoritarian interventions. One additional difficulty was presented by the fact that the Constitution of 1795 entrusted the control of finances to the legislative Councils rather than to the executive, leaving the Directors with a narrow margin of action and causing endless conflict between the two powers.[21]

The repeal of the *maximum* – the imposed limit on the price of necessities – was the occasion for protest and even attempted revolt that was unhesitatingly repressed. Always the magistrate at heart, Reubell had no sympathy for any form of popular unrest and dreaded the revival of Jacobin militancy. On 21 January 1796, celebrating the anniversary of the king's execution, he described the Jacobin experience in retrospect as 'a time of anarchy and terror'. Yet besides popular discontent, the abandonment of the *assignats* was a risky operation that might bring about the economic collapse of the Republic. Reubell had been faced with the same problem in 1790, when, convinced that the Church's confiscated lands were insufficient to guarantee the value of the *assignats*, he had proposed to the Constituent Assembly the forced borrowing of 1,700 million *livres* at a rate of 5 per cent, as well as the obligation to declare any private stocks of gold and silver. While this project had been rejected by the assembly as illiberal and in violation of property rights, Reubell's assessment of the inadequacy of the available resources had been more than confirmed by subsequent events.

By 1795, following the steady devaluation of paper currency – 18 billion *assignats* had been printed since their adoption in April 1790 – the *livre-assignat* was worth one-hundredth of its nominal value, or 2,400 *livres-assignats* to one gold *louis* (one gold *louis* was originally equivalent to 24 *livres*). After some initial hesitation, the Directory finally decided to abandon the *assignats*, and on 19 February 1796 the moulds for the printing presses were destroyed in a solemn public ceremony. However, on the initiative of the Five Hundred, the *assignats* were replaced on 18 March by a new form of paper money, the territorial bonds (*mandats territoriaux*), which were supposedly guaranteed by the profits generated by the sale of State-owned land, especially forest, the value of which could be realized easily by cutting down trees.[22] Unsurprisingly, these new bonds went the same way as their predecessors, depreciating very rapidly, and not even State employees accepted them in payment of their wages. The solution adopted by Ramel-Nogaret (with Reubell's support) on 30 September 1797 was the bankruptcy the revolutionary assemblies had always refused to consider. Two-thirds of the debt were cancelled, reducing it from 250 to 83 million *livres*; in practice, only a third of the amount was consolidated, while the rest was lost for investors, who found themselves in possession of worthless bonds.[23]

One inevitable side effect of the attempted return to a market economy was the revival of popular unrest, and even of plans to restore the Jacobin regime and the Constitution of 1793. The most famous of these, immortalized in the tradition of revolutionary communism, was the Conspiracy of the Equals promoted by François-Noël (Gracchus) Babeuf. A journalist, friend of Jean-Paul Marat and editor of the *Tribun du peuple*, Babeuf had already been arrested and prosecuted on various occasions before Thermidor, on account of his radical views; he was especially vocal in his denunciation of the evils of private property. In May 1796 he was at the heart of an attempt to overturn the Directory with the support of former Jacobins and of some insurrectional committees within the army; however, the members of the secret 'Committee of Public Safety' created to mobilize the insurgents were denounced by an informer and arrested. Most of those implicated in the conspiracy were acquitted, but a few were sentenced to deportation, while Babeuf was guillotined in 1797.[24]

Another important consequence of the suppression of paper money was the flourishing of speculation. On 6 January 1796, shortly after taking office, Reubell closed the Paris Stock Exchange, that 'den of brigands and speculators', that had been reopened only a few months earlier. On 30 March 1796, after the introduction of territorial bonds, the Director raged in his correspondence against the 'vampires' who took advantage of the situation to enrich themselves. Such bloodsucking activities culminated in the scandal of the Compagnie de Dijon, a consortium created specifically to speculate on the currency.[25]

There was, however, one category of vampires that the Directors could not do without, namely military subcontractors. Subcontracting army supplies had been standard practice under the old regime. The Convention had tried to limit the corruption associated with such operations by multiplying bureaucratic controls, without any notable success. Now these *compagnies de fournisseurs*, halfway between traders and bankers – men like Jacques-Rose Récamier, Jean-Frédéric Perregaux and Gabriel-Julien Ouvrard – became essential not just to supply the armies, but to levy taxes in occupied territories and to provide the government with credit abroad.[26] Until then, all attempts to convince the assemblies of the necessity to create a single national bank for the financing of such operations had failed; the project was finally realized by the Consulate with the creation of the Bank of France in 1800. One of the reasons the Directors acquired a reputation for corruption was their inevitable proximity to this opaque speculative galaxy. As to Reubell, his use of words (bandits, vampires and so on) shows that he shared the traditional mistrust of revolutionaries towards money and financial activities, and there is no evidence that he profited personally from such transactions.

Another obvious means of improving the Republic's financial resources that the revolutionary governments had failed to pursue was the reform of the fiscal system. This had been a major objective at the beginning of the Revolution, but, although all agreed in principle on its necessity, in practice they were reluctant to undertake it. Their hesitation came from the belief that, even in a regime of fiscal equality, such reform would inevitably lead to the introduction of new taxes, reviving popular feelings of oppression associated with the monarchy.

Reubell and Ramel-Nogaret were now determined to confront the problem. They redesigned the categories of direct taxation, adding to the *impôt foncier* (land tax) the taxation of other forms of property insufficiently covered by the revolutionary *impôt mobilier*. They reintroduced different forms of indirect taxation, such as customs and stamp duties and the tax on windows (the broad lines of their system remained in place until 1914, when the finance minister Joseph Caillaux finally introduced the income tax). To assess and reallocate the contributions of the *départements*, they created the Agence Départementale des Contributions Directes, an indispensable institution that was maintained under the Consulate. Finally, in 1797 the principle of a budget presented and made public every year by the government was adopted, a measure that had not been attempted since the controversial publication by Jacques Necker of the monarchy's budget in 1781.[27] As minister of the interior and, later, Director, Neufchâteau contributed to Reubell's and Ramel-Nogaret's efforts to improve local fiscality and relaunch French industry and trade, which had been crippled by the double impact of the Revolution and the war.[28]

The pitfalls of conquest

Despite these long-lasting economic achievements, the economic viability of the Republic at the time remained heavily dependent on the success of military operations and the contributions of occupied territories. Inevitably, Reubell's energy was focused once again on the question of France's frontiers. The fear of counter-revolutionary activities orchestrated by France's enemies abroad continued to weigh on his mind. As ever, Alsace's position was at stake, and the elections of March 1797 (Year V) resulted in the affirmation of royalist candidates in the Haut-Rhin after their success in the Bas-Rhin the previous year. Reubell's eagerness to consolidate the safety of the region by pursuing the occupation of neighbouring countries led him to form an alliance with Barras and with the amenable La Révellière-Lépeaux. Together the 'triumvirs' exploited the failed royalist conspiracy of Fructidor (September 1797) to get rid of Carnot, the main opponent in the

Directory of this strategy of territorial expansion. Falsely accused of plotting with the royalists, Carnot was sentenced to deportation but fled the country before he could be arrested (see Chapter Three).

After the annexation of Belgium and the creation of the Batavian Republic in the Low Countries, an agreement had been reached with Prussia for a swap of territories that gave France control of two-thirds of the Rhineland. Reubell had been especially keen on this arrangement; the region was rich in raw materials, manufacturing and reserves of coinage, but above all it was in his eyes the rampart that protected Alsace from the possibility of Austrian invasion supported by domestic counter-revolutionaries. With the eviction of Carnot from the executive, the next step was, in March 1798, the military occupation of the Swiss Confederation and the establishment at the frontier of the Alps of another regime under France's control, the Helvetic Republic. The independent Republic of Geneva, traditionally placed under French protection, was annexed to France as the *département* of Léman, as was Mulhouse, an allied town of the Swiss Confederation within Alsatian territory. Reubell saw these initiatives as a means of acquiring more economic resources while preventing the occupation of some of the border regions by Austrian and Russian troops.[29]

This apparently successful sequence of territorial acquisitions resulted – just as Carnot had predicted – in new difficulties for the Directorial government. One major problem was the unstable situation in the new sister republics. Military occupation, accompanied by pillaging and requisitions, created resistance and unrest that the governments of the pro-French revolutionaries were unable to control. In Paris Reubell was in contact with various expatriates from the Rhineland, who were sympathetic to the annexation to France; similarly, he was acquainted with one of the promoters of the Helvetic Republic and member of its Directory, Peter Ochs, whom he had met at the time of his diplomatic missions in Basle. The problem was that many such pro-French patriots, some of them living in exile, had a limited or too idealistic vision of the circumstances of their own countries, and were poor judges of the impact of the French occupation on them.

Reubell's correspondence with Ochs and with another member of the Swiss Directory, Frédéric-César de La Harpe, reveals their growing difficulties and the inability, as well as the unwillingness, of the French government to offer them steady support beyond vague professions of fraternal sympathy. As in the case of the Batavian Republic, the imposition of a united, centralized state on a country with a secular tradition of federalism made the acceptance of the new institutions difficult, leading to political instability and several attempts to force a change in the constitution. Moreover, in Switzerland Reubell's reputation was seriously damaged by the conduct of his brother-in-law Jean-Jacques Rapinat, who was also a lawyer from Colmar. In his capacity as French commissioner to the Helvetic Republic, Rapinat soon stood accused of misappropriation and corruption, and although the allegations were never proved, they discredited Reubell by association in the eyes of the public and were later exploited by his political enemies in France.[30]

Another alarming consequence of the policy of conquest was the increasing power of some army commanders. Reubell remained faithful to the position of the revolutionary political class, who had always tried to keep the army under the control of civil authority; indeed, according to Napoleon he had all the traditional lawyer's prejudices against the military.[31] However, by promoting the occupation of new territories, the Directory had made it possible for ambitious generals to take the initiative, emancipating them from their own authority. The fact that generals were often forced to find the resources necessary to supply and pay their troops through requisition and the use of private contractors meant that their dependence on the government was considerably diminished, as was the power of the once-feared army commissioners.[32]

While Reubell continued to focus his attention on the northeastern frontier, Napoleon's victories in Italy shifted the balance of the war south of the Alps. The terms of the armistices the general signed at Leoben on 18 April 1797 and Campo-Formio (17 October 1797), without waiting for the government's approval, were a clear indication of the extent to which the Directors were no longer in control of a domain – foreign policy – that until then they had managed to keep, as it were, for themselves, protecting it from the Councils' interference. After Italy, the Egyptian expedition (financed by the confiscated treasure of Bern) opened yet another dimension of the conflict, centred on England, the colonies and the control of the Mediterranean, away from the original question of France's borders.

Reubell could only watch these developments with growing anxiety. The financial benefits of the Italian campaigns were obvious, as were those of an armistice with Austria, much as he might disapprove of some specific agreements. Yet he remained suspicious of military initiative. Barras' decision, in July 1797, to replace Charles-François Delacroix with Charles-Maurice de Talleyrand as minister of foreign affairs could only add to Reubell's feeling of being sidelined. The patriotic defence of the Republic – the cause to which he had been so passionately dedicated – was now replaced by a series of ambitious adventures with uncertain contours and unclear objectives.

The last defence

In the summer of 1798 Reubell became seriously ill and spent a few weeks recovering at the spa town of Plombières, where he found himself in the unexpected company of another *curiste*, Joséphine Bonaparte, who entertained him with the latest gossip about her husband's exploits in Egypt. However, while the Director was enjoying the benefits of the thermal waters, France's position in the face of the second coalition was deteriorating rapidly. Napoleon's engagement overseas had reduced French military potential on the continent, reviving the rivalries among the commanders who remained behind. Unable to control them, the Directors were held responsible for all ensuing military reverses in Italy and Switzerland. Despite the armistice signed by Napoleon at Campo-Formio in October 1797, the prospect of durable peace with Austria was also at risk. The meetings at the Congress of Rastatt to discuss terms were tragically disrupted when two of the French delegates – Antoine Bonnier d'Alco and Claude Roberjot, both members of the Diplomatic Committee and friends of Reubell – were ambushed and killed by a squad of Hungarian hussars (Hungarian regiments being at the time part of the Austrian Empire's army). Sent as ambassador to Vienna, General Jean Bernadotte had to defend the embassy from an angry mob after displaying the French flag outside the building. The precarious balance that had been achieved in the international arena seemed suddenly in jeopardy.

In France, meanwhile, the elections of April 1798 (Year VI) had given a majority in the Councils to the Jacobins. Although the results had been partly invalidated, Barras, sensitive to the drift in public opinion, now sided with the left, abandoning his former allies Reubell and La Révellière-Lépeaux to the retaliation of their enemies. In May 1799, at the annual ballot, Reubell was deselected from the Directory and his place taken by Sieyès, recalled from his diplomatic mission in Berlin. On the strength of his reputation as an early prophet of the Revolution, Sieyès did in fact enjoy the support of the Jacobins, although his political position was by then very far from the radical republicanism they attributed to him.

Unwilling to serve under Sieyès, Reubell refused the offer of the ministry of foreign affairs. As soon as he left the executive to take up his seat in the Elders, to which he had been elected a month before his deselection from the Directory, he became the target of a vicious campaign of libel. With his colleagues La Révellière-Lépeaux and Merlin de Douai, he found himself accused of crimes including corruption, mismanagement of public funds, violation of the Constitution and treason. Things went so far that even his enemies within the Directory took fright, since the accusations – which dragged up a long list of past incidents and episodes dating back to 1795 – inevitably implicated the whole executive.[33] In the end all charges were abandoned, but the long public career of the Alsatian lawyer – who made his last public appearance on 31 August 1799 – had clearly come to an end.

In his *History of the French Revolution* (1824), the liberal journalist François Mignet wrote that with Reubell's deselection, the Republic had lost its last defender.[34] In a similar vein, it has been suggested that had the ballot of 1799 indicated someone else, the coup of Brumaire might have met with a more vigorous opposition or even have had a different outcome.[35] Such comments imply that Reubell's exclusion from the Directory was a matter of chance, but in fact it is quite possible that it was the product of an agreement brought about by his own recognition that he could no longer remain on the political stage. These comments also imply that Brumaire marked the end of the Republic, an assumption, based on later developments, that was not apparent to many observers at the time. Whatever the nature of the ballot – genuine or contrived – Reubell accepted his eviction without resistance and took the agreed financial compensation. He might have felt some satisfaction a few months later, when the men who had contributed to his downfall were in turn excluded from power. However, unlike most of his colleagues, Reubell did not commit his personal thoughts and recollections to paper; rumours that drafts of his planned memoirs were destroyed by his family have never been confirmed.

How could someone who had carried the heavy responsibility of government for years simply give up on account of a strip of paper bearing his name? Bitterness, pride, disillusionment, but also exhaustion and ill health may have been the origin of his lack of reaction. Did he perhaps hope to make a comeback? Reubell was not one of those who were excluded on principle from the consular institutions on account of their past. If he did not sit on one of the legislative committees created immediately after the coup to draft the new constitution, his political record was still perfectly acceptable. The full implications of Brumaire were probably unclear to him, as they were to many of his contemporaries, including those who had contributed to bring it about. Yet he did understand enough to realize that he was out of his depth in the new setting. While Barras had spent the last year of his mandate exploring possible alternatives to the vacillating Directory, there is no evidence that Reubell ever looked beyond the horizon of the bourgeois Republic, that besieged trench against the past that he had fought so hard to defend.

In any case, the 'hard and vain' Alsatian – in Joseph Fouché's words – had no friends in the new regime, which was largely represented by men whom he despised, disliked or had quarrelled with.[36] He could rely only on the First Consul's esteem and goodwill, and he mainly used his residual influence to promote the career of his elder son, Jean-Jacques, an army officer who later became adjutant to Napoleon's brother Jérôme Bonaparte in Westphalia. Vague prospects arose of a lucrative post for himself, perhaps a position as senator or prefect, but that never materialized. Sadly, Reubell had failed to accumulate the millions he had been repeatedly accused of having stolen; he was forced to sell what property he had inherited or bought during his career to pay the debts of his dissipated younger son, François-Xavier. He finally retired to Colmar, where he died in 1807 at the age of sixty.

Drafted by the bureaucracy of the Empire, Reubell's death certificate described him soberly as a 'former representative of the people'. The Alsatian's patriotism had been an odd mixture of pride, obstinacy and lack of imagination as to other people's motives. During the long decade of the Revolution, he had fought pugnaciously with a lawyer's weapons: sitting on countless committee meetings, drafting regulations and reports, exploring loopholes, redesigning frameworks, rustling up resources – arguing, shouting, bullying, threatening, pleading. He made many compromises but never retreated from the ground he had undertaken to occupy and defend; to the oath sworn in 1789 at Versailles he was faithful to the very end.

Louis-Léopold Boilly, *Lazare Nicolas Marguerite Carnot*, 1813, oil on canvas.

3

Master of the Maps
Lazare Carnot (1753–1823)

Lazare Carnot was not there on the first day; on 2 November 1795 only four newly elected Directors – Paul Barras, Jean-François Reubell, Louis-Marie de La Révellière-Lépeaux and Étienne-François Le Tourneur – made their entrance into the empty rooms of the Luxembourg Palace. Emmanuel Sieyès should have been with them as the fifth elected member of the executive, but he refused the position, claiming he did not regard himself as 'apt' to occupy it. It is unclear whether this deliberately cryptic statement concealed his disapproval of the new Constitution or his dislike of his future colleagues (see Chapter Six). Carnot was elected as Sieyès' replacement on 4 November and accepted, despite his reservations, in order to preserve a significant republican presence in the executive. He was not there on the first day, but he soon made up for his late arrival. While the Luxembourg was hastily refurbished, he carted over from the premises of the defunct Committee of Public Safety in the Louvre the maps, charts and archives that had enabled the monitoring of troops and supplies in France's desperate defence during the terrible summer of 1793. In his *History of the French Revolution*, Jules Michelet confers a symbolic significance on Carnot's maps, describing Maximilien Robespierre's frustration in the face of a display of technical skill that he found deeply alien: 'He was seen occasionally staring at Carnot's maps, sad, with tears in his eyes, lamenting his own nature and his military incompetence.'[1]

Although Michelet's picture of the weeping Robespierre is probably a clever literary invention, it does capture the ambiguity of Carnot's presence on the stage of the Revolution. Was he one of those algid technicians who survive all political storms by virtue of their indispensable competence, the representative of a new breed of skilled military men who – as General Charles de Gaulle observed appreciatively – understood that order and discipline were the necessary preconditions of strength?[2] Or was he the patriot ready to break many rules of his military craft and to risk his head several times over in order to save the Republic from annihilation? Having gained a place in the pantheon of France's national heroes in the darkest hour of the Revolution (he was received into the real Panthéon in 1889), what was he doing in 1795 in a government of survivors like the Directory?[3]

A different kind of war

While Robespierre's misgivings about the military may have been justified, Carnot himself was not, by all accounts, a very martial figure. Only a couple of posthumous portraits show him wearing the epaulettes of military uniform; in contemporary ones he is in civilian clothing, a quiet bourgeois in a redingote (Michelet writes that he looked 'like a priest') among the plumed, beribboned, glittering marshals of the Empire. Napoleon claimed, somewhat ironically, that Carnot had no experience of war, but this was a malicious exaggeration.[4] In October 1793 Carnot had been in command on the field of Wattignies, the first victory for France after a long sequence of defeats, although after the battle he had gone back to his office in Paris, leaving his colleague Jean-Baptiste Jourdan to take the credit. The emperor admitted that Carnot possessed real moral courage; indeed, in those days even the battlefield was a safer place than the Convention.

Under the old regime, the young Carnot's duties as one of two hundred Royal Engineers had been those of a surveyor. Since his appointment in 1773 he had toured the north of France, inspecting fortifications and assessing their state of repair, or sitting in some office to check measurements and calculations. Only after 1793 were the competences of military engineers extended to other fields of activity, Carnot being a promoter of this change. Building on his early experience, he first acquired a national reputation in 1784, when his essay 'Éloge de Vauban' won a competition organized by the Academy of the Arts and Sciences of Dijon to celebrate Louis XIV's famous military architect, Sébastien Le Prestre de Vauban.[5] The essay established Carnot as an authority on the role of fortifications in modern warfare, a controversial subject at the time, and the object of fierce dispute within the army itself. More than twenty years later, in 1810, Napoleon commissioned from Carnot the definitive study on the subject, a handbook for the use of future military engineers entitled *De la défense des places fortes* (On the Defence of Fortresses).[6]

When Carnot was called to serve on the Committee of Public Safety in 1793, he soon found himself back on his old round of inspection of the northern front line. This time his task was to verify the location of the armies (not always known in Paris), the loyalty of troops to the new republican government, and the condition of their equipment and supplies. His was another kind of war from that fought on the battlefield. While he retained the rank of captain in the engineers (it never occurred to him to promote himself, even with fourteen armies under him), Carnot acted on behalf of the civilian authority, not as a military commander. It was a novel and perilous exercise dictated by the determination of the revolutionary government to retain full control over the conduct of the war, especially after General Charles-François Dumouriez's attempted defection to Austria in 1793.[7]

Raising and training troops on a large scale, mixing professional soldiers with volunteers and new recruits, keeping them all fed and armed, replacing the officers who had defected to join the émigrés, and deciding the overall strategy – all of this while reporting constantly to the Convention – represented the near-impossible mission Carnot had to face every day. In practice, it required a painstaking balancing act between the expectations of nervous, litigious politicians and the demands of the armies' commanders, vividly documented by the four huge volumes of his correspondence with the front line.[8] It was a minefield in which every decision, every move, each signature placed on a piece of paper might lead to the scaffold. Historians disagree over whether the initiative of concentrating French troops on the northern front, leaving the Rhine and Moselle fronts exposed – a choice that enabled a crucial breakthrough and reversed the fortunes of the war – was Carnot's own, or whether it was suggested by his staff officers; either way, he made the decision and took upon himself the risk of what might have been a debacle.

While Carnot was not a typical career officer, Robespierre was right in associating him with his maps. On his initiative, topography became an essential part of army archives and intelligence, and charts and tables were the constant support of his own activities. One of his earliest surviving writings is a large synoptic table he drew in 1770, at the age of seventeen, entitled 'Idea for the Systematic Classification of the Sciences and the Arts'.[9] It was based on the 'Preliminary Discourse' in the *Encyclopédie* (1751–72) of Denis Diderot and Jean Le Rond d'Alembert. D'Alembert himself had been a regular visitor to the Pension Longpré in Paris, the prep school where Carnot studied for his entrance examination to the École Royale du Génie (Royal School of Engineering) at Mézières (now Charleville-Mézières). The two met and exchanged views on several occasions, and d'Alembert was said to have been impressed by the boy's intelligence and mathematical talent.

It is because he was a gifted mathematician that Carnot decided to apply to Mézières, since engineering seemed a more congenial option than the other careers open to the sons of impecunious notables: the law (his father's profession) and the Church. Somehow his mathematical capacity and scientific vocation caused him to lead what amounted to a double life, a curious position for a man who was by nature incapable of duplicity. One life followed the path common to many of his contemporaries, socially ambitious professionals who wished to see their abilities recognized. Under the old regime they animated public debate, advocating the reform of French institutions; after 1789 they were ready to engage in politics. Carnot made his leap into politics in 1791, when the dissolution of the Constituent Assembly brought about the complete renewal of the legislative body. He was elected to the legislative as a representative for the Pas-de-Calais and served initially on the Committee of Public Instruction, which was in charge of designing a national system of education.[10]

Carnot's other (no doubt his first) life was that of the man of science. Even at the most difficult times of his public career, he never entirely abandoned his studies in mathematics and physics. His early scientific work on the dispersion of kinetic energy – *Essai sur les machines en général* – appeared in 1783, during relatively quiet times. While he did not publish during the Revolution, the dates of his subsequent works show the steadiness of his research: *Réflexions sur la méthaphysique du calcul infinitésimal* (1797); *De la correlation des figures de géometrie* (1801); *Géometrie de position* (1803); and *Essai sur la théorie des transversales* (1806). In 1794 he contributed to the establishment of the École Centrale des Travaux Publics in Paris (subsequently the École Polytechnique), and in April 1796 he was elected to the Institut de France – founded in 1795 to replace the old Royal Academies – in the Class of the Arts Méchaniques.

Carnot possessed the distinctive strengths of the scientist: method, endurance, rigour and imagination. At the same time, however, he displayed some typical weaknesses: single-mindedness, honesty and unworldliness. In Napoleon's cynical summing-up, he was easy to deceive.[11] His scientific persona shaped and sustained his political activities and provides the main key to understanding the nature of his commitment. Politics was a career for which, in his own words, he had not been destined, and to which he was unsuited. On two occasions he tried to disentangle himself from it, hoping to return to his scientific work: first when his name was proposed for election to the

Directory in 1795 and later when Napoleon offered him the ministry of war in 1800. It is impossible to say to what extent his reluctant acceptance of these new responsibilities was dictated by personal ambition or by a sense of patriotic duty; it was probably a combination of the two. But he could not have done either, as he could not have survived the Revolution, without the lifeline offered by his scientific self.[12]

Carnot's experience of politics in 1792–4 and his activity within the revolutionary government took place in exceptional circumstances that often led to the violation of constitutional principles and rules. In common with other future Directors, he accepted the arbitrary use of power on the part of the Convention as a necessity dictated by the war and the dangers of counter-revolution. He was ready to assume responsibility for the abuses he and his colleagues might have committed in that context, since he regarded them as inevitable. However, he also believed that the resort to arbitrary measures should be abandoned as soon as possible. His aspiration throughout was the establishment of a normal constitutional regime, in his own words 'reconciling the French with legal government'. Just as in his scientific research on the dispersion of energy, which focused on the difficulty of calculating friction, he was anxious to minimize the margin of hazard and uncertainty in the functioning of political institutions.

Carnot's love of order had nothing to do with the attachment to military discipline praised by de Gaulle. When in 1792 the Assembly discussed the enforcement of discipline in the army, Carnot supported the view that volunteers and citizen-soldiers could not be expected to offer the same passive obedience as the enlisted men of old, and that the readiness of revolutionary soldiers to follow orders must be subject to a reasonable understanding of what was asked of them – possibly sustained by an effort of instruction and indoctrination (a practice he promoted when in charge of recruitment). The order Carnot advocated and worked for was the capacity for the Republic to function without resorting to *coups d'état* or interfering with elections. It was the belief that the time had finally come for the normalization of political life, making the Republic secure in its foundations, that led him into the Luxembourg in November 1795, and out of it again, in unforeseen circumstances, in September 1797. Two months before his stormy eviction from the executive, during the celebrations of the anniversary of 14 July 1789, he declared: 'Yes, the Revolution is over . . . the time for exaggerations is also finished: it is no longer by the enthusiasm that makes revolutions, but by the prudence and firmness that consolidate them, that we can assure the grounds of our happiness.'[13]

The machine of government

An amateur poet in his spare time – it was at the literary circle of the Rosati in Arras that he first met Robespierre in 1786 – Carnot was generally reserved and disinclined to reveal his thoughts.[14] His correspondence was mostly factual and couched in conventional rhetoric; the memoirs published to defend his actions and celebrate his career were written by his brother Claude-Marie and his son Hippolyte. His talent as an orator was limited, and he used it sparingly. However, in two speeches he made at the Convention – the first before, the second after Thermidor – he broke his usual reserve, expressing clearly enough his views on the nature of the revolutionary government and its legacy.

The first speech, delivered on 25 March 1794, when Carnot was still a member of the Committee of Public Safety, illustrated his own proposal for the reorganization of the executive. On that day, the collective mind of the Convention was on entirely different matters. The radical leader Jacques-René Hébert had been executed the day before with about twenty of his partisans; Carnot had been busy trying to find replacements for those who had occupied posts in the ministry of war. Meanwhile another major revolutionary leader, Georges Danton, had been arrested with a group of his followers and was expected to stand trial. In this climate of ferocious factional confrontation

Carnot's proposed reform went almost unnoticed; it was voted in without opposition on 1 April.[15]

The decree Carnot submitted to the assembly abolished the Provisional Executive Council – formed by six ministers and dependent on the Convention – that had exercised executive power since the suspension of the king from his functions as head of government on 10 August 1792. Its place was to be taken by twelve Executive Commissions directly dependent on the Committee of Public Safety. The purpose of this change was twofold. On the one hand, it placed the executive formally under the authority of the Committee of Public Safety, which had controlled it in practice since its creation in April 1793. On the other hand, it broke down the competences of the departments so as to avoid the emergence of separate centres of power around a too popular minister or ambitious military leader. In this new setting, for example, the conduct of the war would require the cooperation of at least three different commissions dealing respectively with armament, supplies and military transport.

The philosophy behind this rearrangement conformed to the approach that had dominated the revolutionary regime from the start: that the legislative assembly was the only legitimate depository of popular sovereignty as the interpreter of the people's will.[16] The task of the executive was confined to the application of the legislative's decisions, and, although the Committee of Public Safety functioned in practice like an executive cabinet, its formal status remained that of a subcommittee of the legislative. From this perspective, the purpose of Carnot's reform was to make the enforcement of legislation as smooth and easy as possible, removing the obstacles that might surface in the transfer of laws and decrees from the Convention to the various agencies entrusted with their application.

To clarify his argument, Carnot evoked his own scientific work on the theory of machines, which focused on the difficulty of calculating 'frictions' (*frottements*) in certain physical conditions. The model he had analysed was the unloading of cargo in the port of Brest and the resistance exercised by the ropes used to shift heavy loads. The government was, he explained, a 'political machine' that, if it was to serve its purpose adequately, must be able to overcome the inevitable friction and resistance within its various parts. The accumulation of power in one single department or another had too often led to the paralysis of the entire machine, making legislation inapplicable and the action of the executive ineffective. The aim of the new distribution of competences was to avoid such blockages.

However, while apparently endorsing the vision of the executive as a docile mechanism in the service of legislative power, Carnot raised a crucial critical point. The government, he argued, existed in the first place to realize the people's will. Because decisions could not be made directly in a popular assembly on the scale of the whole nation, they were made by the legislative and enacted by the executive. However, the people were liable to be misled by demagogues serving their own purposes. What happened if the popular will was 'incoherent'? How could it be executed safely? His answer was that the Committee of Public Safety stood as a 'sentinel' against such mistakes, reserving for itself *la pensée du gouvernement* (the government's thinking), a formula that reappeared in the debate over the Constitution of 1795. The move from Jean-Jacques Rousseau's doctrine of the sovereignty of the general will to the suggestion that the government must think on behalf of the people may have escaped the attention of the panic-stricken deputies to whom the speech was addressed. But it is revealing of the evolution that Carnot's understanding of the role of government had undergone in the light of his experience on the Committee of Public Safety.

Carnot was familiar with Jacques Necker's work *Du pouvoir exécutif dans les grands États* (published in English as *On Executive Power in Large States* in 1792), which detailed the difficulties created by the revolutionary determination to leave as little scope as possible to the action of the executive. That project had its origins in the desire to suppress the monarchy, but once the Republic was established, it continued to hinder the functioning of its institutions. A stern republican and a believer in equality, Carnot did not think as Necker did that the expression of the general will through the vote should be restricted to a selected prosperous minority. However, he saw that the government must be allowed greater latitude to exercise its functions. The question, then, was to what extent this latitude – the task of thinking on behalf of the people – was compatible with normal constitutional rule. The Committee of Public Safety had been created to operate in exceptional circumstances. Clearly such an extraordinary set-up was not meant to last forever, but when would it end, and on what terms?[17]

Special means

The legitimate scope of the action of government was the implicit subject of Carnot's second speech. He made it on 23 March 1795 in defence of his former colleagues – Bertrand Barère, Jean-Marie Collot d'Herbois, Jacques-Nicolas Billaud-Varenne and Marc-Guillaume Alexis Vadier – all of whom were, like him, former opponents of Robespierre within the Committee of Public Safety, and who now stood accused of 'Terrorism'. Eight months earlier, in July 1794, Carnot had taken part in the Thermidorian coup against Robespierre. He had little choice in the matter, since his relationship with Robespierre himself and with his ally Louis-Antoine de Saint-Just had reached breaking point; indeed, during a stormy meeting the latter had threatened to kill him ('we shall have your skin!'). Carnot's main contribution to the conspiracy had been to make sure that Robespierre's supporters could not mobilize the national guard in his defence, by demoting their commanding officers in the days that preceded the coup. He did not address the Convention during the memorable sitting of 27 July, leaving the floor to more eloquent speakers, and spent the following day – the day of the executions – working as usual in his office. However, he felt that he must react against the proposal of putting on trial some former members of the Great Committee (he himself had resigned from it in October 1794) and thus making them the scapegoats for 'crimes' of which several prominent Thermidorians, not to mention the Convention at large, were equally guilty.[18]

Carnot argued his case by recalling the extraordinary, indeed unprecedented circumstances in which the revolutionary government had operated: the war and the threat of foreign invasion; the lack of trained soldiers, armaments and supplies; the betrayal of the army's high command; the penury suffered by the civil population. Such a desperate situation could be faced only by resorting to 'special means': requisitions, forced mobilization, arrests and even executions. The members of the Committee, he explained, signed three or four hundred orders every day, so they could not possibly follow what was done outside their own department. Yet he himself was ready to accept full responsibility for their collective actions, even those of which he had no knowledge at the time.

The question was: had they violated the law? They had done exactly what the people expected them to do, since popular opinion at the time was ultra-revolutionary and the legislators seconded it. The Convention could not place the will of seven hundred people – their own – above the general will without going against the very principle of democracy. Had they gone too far in their eagerness to be in tune with public opinion? Many deputies now claimed that they had voted for certain measures because they were threatened and feared for their lives. But this, Carnot pursued, was just cowardice on their part. If they thought popular opinion was mistaken, they should have tried to enlighten it, or resigned their position as representatives. By endorsing what they thought was wrong, they behaved like soldiers who desert their post when they have been charged with holding the line or standing guard.

As in the previous speech, there was an obvious shift from the view that the Convention and the revolutionary government were there to enact the people's will, and the notion that they had the duty to oppose it and correct that will if necessary. Carnot gave as an example the law of the *maximum*, the forced limitation of the price of necessities. The people had clamoured and petitioned to get it, until finally both the Convention and public opinion realized that the measure did not work and agreed that it should be changed. Clearly Carnot did not feel there was any contradiction in his own position; he had done what was asked of him with full conviction and did not think he should apologize for the means to which he had resorted. Voices demanding that he should be put on trial for the repression of the rebellion in the Vendée were quickly silenced. At the same time, he insisted on the unique nature of the events of the past, which, it was to be hoped, France would never have to face again. It is difficult to tell whether the speech had any real impact on the Convention. The pursuit of the accused was abandoned for a while, but a few months later they were tried and sentenced to deportation to French Guiana.[19] The experience left Carnot full of contempt for the hypocrisy of the Thermidorian leaders, some of whom would soon become his colleagues in the new government.

The government of balance

For all his misgivings about his associates, it cannot be said that by 1795 Carnot had abandoned all political ambitions. Although in principle he disapproved of what he called in one of his speeches 'professional politicians', by now he had effectively become one of them. Thanks to the controversial Decree of the Two-Thirds of 22 August 1795 (the measure designed to maintain in office the majority of deputies who held seats in the Convention), he moved directly from the old legislative assembly to the Elders, one of the two new bodies created by the Constitution of 1795.[20] At the same time, he was probably sincere when he claimed that, after years of relentless activity and nerve-racking conflict, he wished for a quieter, less prominent role. There is no indication that he aspired to be part of the new executive, particularly since he considered it an especially ill-designed institution, as did many at the time.

Carnot had not been a member of the Commission of the Eleven that drafted the Constitution of 1795, but he had offered his comments on some questions. These comments suggest that he had become reconciled to the idea of bicameralism, to contain the excessive power of a single assembly, but that he imagined the second chamber as a sort of organism of control occupied by men of special merit and distinction, elected for a longer period than ordinary legislators: something more similar to the Conservative Senate of the Consulate than to the Elders of 1795. He also formed the view that the executive should have greater independence and a wider scope of action than in past constitutional settings, but he mistrusted the idea of a collegial council that would make 'the destiny of the state dependent on the moods of five people'. On his own account, he finally agreed to stand for election to the Directory because of pressure from his republican friends. After Sieyès' defection, there was the risk that the post might go to the future Second Consul Jean-Jacques-Régis Cambacérès, a moderate who was widely believed at the time to have been involved in a royalist conspiracy (see Chapter Seven).[21]

It is difficult to give precise characterization to Carnot's contribution during the period of just under two years in which he served on the Directory. In the earlier months of their mandate the Directors worked day and night to face the most urgent questions, and even later much of the action of government consisted in responding to immediate crisis and difficulties rather than in developing a coherent programme. Since each Director was responsible for a particular department and geographical area, Carnot was predictably put in charge of the war and of the north of France. While this separation of competences allowed the executive to function without major interference or conflict, the five were soon divided into two rival groups: Carnot and his fellow military engineer Le Tourneur on the one hand, and the 'triumvirs' Barras, La Révellière-Lépeaux and Reubell on the other. Carnot tried in vain to build a working relationship with Reubell, who dealt with foreign affairs; when Le Tourneur was balloted out in

April 1797, Carnot found himself isolated, and he was evicted shortly afterwards.

Outside the Luxembourg, although the murderous factional struggle that had characterized the Terrorist phase of the Revolution was over, the shifts in public opinion between left and right, reflected in the varying majorities in the Councils, continued to threaten the government. To face these swings the Directory became, in Carnot's words, *un gouvernement de balance* a pendulum regime, ready to adjust to and counterbalance these fluctuations. In September 1797 Carnot's enemies, determined to exclude him from the executive, accused him of complicity in the attempted royalist coup of 18 Fructidor (4 September), which had just been uncovered. Although wholly unfounded, these accusations have left their mark on subsequent historiography, so that Carnot is often described as having moved significantly towards the right when he became a Director. In fact, he remained faithful throughout to his original revolutionary republicanism, and indeed, one of his earliest initiatives after joining the Directory was to appoint his Jacobin friends to all available administrative positions in the Pas-de-Calais.

The accusations of conservatism were prompted to some extent by the role Carnot played in May 1796 in the suppression of the so-called Conspiracy of the Equals organized by François-Noël (Gracchus) Babeuf. It was an operation Carnot conducted in collaboration with the ministry of police, a new department, before which the police had been under the responsibility of the ministry of justice. Carnot had first met Babeuf before the Revolution, when the latter canvassed for admission to the Academy of the Rosati at Arras. After Thermidor, Babeuf – who had often clashed with the Jacobin authorities – used his journal *Le Tribun du peuple* to attack the former Committee of Public Safety, denouncing Carnot himself for his supposed responsibility for the 'massacre' of the rebels of the Vendée. As a rule, Carnot did not take kindly to the retrospective (and opportunistic) accusations directed against the Great Committee; he also considered

Babeuf's attempts to associate the heritage of Robespierre with his own communist ideals simply ridiculous.[22]

Setting aside these considerations, Carnot felt towards the planned Conspiracy of the Equals just the way he felt towards the rebels of the northwest or the royalists' attempted insurrections. He was ready unhesitatingly to fight any attempt to destabilize the Republic, whichever side it came from. He was a 'conservative' only insofar as he wished to preserve the established constitutional regime. More than twenty years later he explained in a letter to a German friend:

> My opinion is not that the forms of government are indifferent, but that, once a given one is established, it is best to keep to it, or at least to modify it gradually to avoid new revolutions. This is why I have always worked to maintain a government that was in place: not because I thought it was the best, but because I believed it was less bad than a new revolution.[23]

Peace and war

The main grounds for conflict within the executive were not the preservation of public order and the repression of rebellion, a subject on which the Directors were generally in agreement. The question on which Carnot found himself increasingly at odds with some of his colleagues was the pursuit of the war. It is perhaps a paradox that the man who had contributed most to France's military success should be determined to see the conflict with the European powers end as soon as possible, yet sympathy for monarchical regimes as such did not come into it. In 1795 peace treaties had been signed with Prussia, Spain and Holland, but the war with Austria, England and Russia continued, and by the end of 1796, when Carnot found himself in charge again, things were not going well for the French armies, which were stuck at a standstill or in retreat on the various fronts. Carnot was prepared to fight on until the situation was reversed in France's favour, but his aim was to reach satisfactory peace conditions and to secure the frontiers, not to engage in the occupation of new territories. Unlike Reubell, he was not tempted by the advantages that military conquest seemed to offer.

The disagreement was in the first instance ideological, and had begun long before, during the first year of the war. On 14 February 1793 Carnot had presented to the Convention a document, *Report on Foreign Policy*, drafted at the request of the Committee of General Defence, the legislative committee in charge of the war and foreign relations before the Committee of Public Safety came into being. The report's object was the policy that France should adopt in relation to the territories occupied in the recent military campaigns. At the time these territories included such small 'enclaves' as Avignon and Nice, as well as larger areas, such as parts of Alsace and most of Belgium. Carnot began his report by stating two general principles: that peace was a supreme good; and that each nation had a right to independence and sovereignty. What these principles meant for him was that the Revolution did not commit France to annex other countries in the name of some crusade to free all nations from their rulers. 'By declaring ourselves protectors of the freedom of all peoples,' he maintained, 'we did not engage ourselves to become identified with them.' He added that the scope of France's sovereignty would be diminished rather than enhanced by stretching it ideally to the entire world: 'to say that sovereignty rests in the universality of mankind means that France has only a portion of sovereignty, therefore she has no right to establish at home the laws she desires.'[24]

Here Carnot took a stand against the line of the Girondins, in particular Jacques-Pierre Brissot, a member of the Diplomatic Committee who was strongly in favour of France's universal mission of liberation. Carnot also set forth some practical considerations. Those who pleaded for a policy of inclusion invoked the right of peoples to be in control of themselves, since in several of the towns and regions concerned the population had voted in favour of joining France. Without contesting the legitimacy of these consultations (which was generally questionable), Carnot stressed that the point was not what other people wanted, but whether it was in the interest of the Republic to extend its territory. Here he cited the authority of Vauban, who had argued that whenever France had tried to expand beyond its natural frontiers, the result had been disastrous. What exactly did constitute these 'natural frontiers' was debatable; Carnot took the traditional view that identified them with the Rhine, the Alps and the Pyrenees.

Three years later Carnot's position had not changed significantly, except possibly in identifying the Moselle rather than the Rhine as France's eastern frontier. He believed it was necessary to stop the war to end the Revolution and to stabilize the republican regime, yet the war could not be stopped until France was safely entrenched within its borders, an objective that he thought ill served by pursuing overambitious military campaigns.[25] A similar opinion had been expressed in the early months of 1795, during the negotiations for the Treaty of Basel, by the former artillery officer Pierre Choderlos de Laclos (better known as the author of *Les Liaisons dangereuses*) in a memoir entitled 'Of War and Peace' and addressed to the Committee of Public Safety. In his memoir Laclos warned the government against the risks of settling for a precarious peace; a short intermission in the war, he said, might give the coalition powers the opportunity to reorganize, while France would need more time to consolidate its political and economic position: 'We must consider France as an emplacement within enemy territory; in such circumstances our first concern must be to fortify it.'[26]

Laclos had clashed with Carnot before the Revolution over the question of the type of fortification required in modern warfare. However, they both agreed on the doctrine of natural frontiers, and both saw France as under siege and highly vulnerable to attack, so that the pursuit of durable peace remained the final objective.

When drafting the Constitution of 1795, the Commission of the Eleven had failed to reach agreement on a formula describing France's attitude to war and the rights of nations, similar to that of the

Constitution of 1791, where it was stated that France would never undertake war with the purpose of conquest, nor employ force against the freedom of another nation.[27] In the end, it had been decided to avoid the subject and concentrate instead on the definition of the respective competences of the Councils and the Directory in the conduct of foreign affairs – a domain in which the executive was given considerable scope of action.

By 1796 the difficulties Carnot faced in running the war were not ideological or constitutional, but essentially financial. During the great mobilization of 1792–3 the revolutionary government had been able to call on all national resources to supply the army. Now the Directory was struggling to restore the country's financial credit and could not resort to patriotic crusades to pay for the war, which had become merely an ordinary department of the administration, one with a limited budget. Carnot's state of mind at the time is vividly illustrated by a letter he wrote on 20 January 1796 to General Barthélemy-Louis-Joseph Schérer, commander of the Italian army. Schérer had been insistent in demanding additional funds from the Directory, while his army – dispatched to attack the Austrians in northern Italy – remained encamped near the frontier. Exasperated by Schérer's persistence and lack of initiative, Carnot replied in unusually blunt terms:

> How can we get out of the desperate inertia in which we are kept by the absence of means? . . . Money would get us out of our difficulties: but there is no money, there is none, none. Therefore, try to find a way to do without it or to get some where you can find it.[28]

Schérer was apparently unable to do without money, or to find any, and Carnot soon replaced him with his new protégé, Napoleon Bonaparte, who was prepared to supply his ragged soldiers through pillaging and speculative operations. Impatient to secure the command, he made (and kept) the promise to win the armistice with Austria in a few weeks.

It is understandable, especially in view of the rich profits brought by Napoleon's Italian campaign, that Carnot's colleagues should be tempted by the prospect of further territorial conquests. For Reubell the desire to see his native region stably united with France had a strong emotional appeal. The clash with Carnot occurred in 1797 over the plans to occupy Switzerland. The project had been set forth by some Swiss 'patriot' sympathizers of the Revolution – among them Frédéric-César de La Harpe and Peter Ochs – who solicited France's help to unseat the aristocratic regimes of the Swiss Confederation. According to their plan, the thirteen confederate states should be transformed into a united 'democratic' republic, the Helvetic Republic, modelled on France. As we have seen, Carnot was not squeamish about the means of military funding, but he did not consider Swiss territory a security risk for France. He thought the French Republic's resources were already stretched to the limit on the other fronts, without the creation of new ones, and was generally hostile to the idea of interfering with the free governments of other countries. Subsequent events confirmed his intuition; the Helvetic Republic survived for only a few chaotic years, until 1803, when Napoleon as First Consul decided to withdraw from Switzerland and the country returned to being an independent confederation.[29]

Meanwhile, in September 1797 the royalist conspiracy of Fructidor presented the 'triumvirs' Reubell, Barras and La Révellière-Lépeaux, now swinging towards the left, with the pretext to get rid of Carnot, together with many other political opponents. Wrongly accused of siding with the royalists and faced with a deportation order, Carnot walked calmly out of a back gate into the gardens of the Luxembourg while the soldiers sent to arrest him searched the palace.[30] After a few days in hiding, he fled to Geneva, where he benefited from the grateful support of local notables who knew of his opposition to the French occupation. Once again, the illusion of a normal constitutional regime had vanished into the thick fog of real and imaginary intrigue.

The last republican

Carnot's exile lasted for only a couple of years. In 1800, after the coup of Brumaire, the general amnesty issued by the First Consul allowed him to return to Paris. Shortly afterwards he was pressed into accepting the post of minister of war, but he occupied it for just a few months before resigning. Having failed to obtain a seat in the Senate, he was elected instead to the Tribunate. The Tribunate was, with the Legislative Body and the Conservative Senate, one of the three legislative assemblies created by the Constitution of 1799 (Year VIII), and its function was to discuss and vote on the laws proposed by the Legislative. To some extent what happened afterwards was simply the result of Carnot and Napoleon's incapacity to work together. Carnot had a great admiration for the First Consul, possibly more for his capacities as civil administrator than for his military talent; he was, however, unable to adjust to the servility, opportunism and intrigue of that 'normal' politics that he had so keenly advocated.

Napoleon, for all his somewhat malicious comments, appreciated Carnot's solid qualities and was an admirer of his scientific achievements; he was also dimly aware that the frosty engineer was the revenant of some terrifying adventure that he himself had not directly experienced. All the same, he found Carnot impossible to deal with, and in the end it seemed easier to offer him honorary positions and generous financial settlements than to have him around.

Beyond their personal differences, the two men were separated by a fundamental question of principle that Carnot finally spelled out in a memorable speech on 3 May 1804. Two years earlier, on 12 May 1802, he had been the only member of the Tribunate out of a hundred to vote against the transformation of the Consulate into a life appointment (the most vocal opponents, such as Benjamin Constant, had been evicted a few months beforehand). On that occasion he had reasserted his belief that in a republic all magistracies must be temporary. Now he rose to explain his vote (once again the only one) against the motion proposed by Jean-François Curée to declare Napoleon 'Emperor of the French'.

Carnot began his speech by professing his loyalty to the government and to Napoleon personally, stating his intention to abide by whatever decision the 'mass of the French citizens' should take. He then argued against the idea that republics were a more unstable form of regime than monarchies. Large republics, he explained, lacked stability not 'by the nature of their government', but because they had been established in troubled and stormy times. The proof of this was offered by the United States of North America, which had been conceived and organized after calm philosophical reflection; the New World had been able to teach the Old that 'it was possible to live peacefully under the regime of liberty and equality'. The main reason given by Curée to advocate the Empire was that a hereditary regime would be more secure than a republic. But how could a monarchy be secure, asked Carnot, when it was at risk from arbitrary and despotic rule? 'It is less difficult to form a republic without anarchy, than a monarchy without despotism.'

After Brumaire, and after the peace of Amiens – Carnot continued – Napoleon had been offered the unique opportunity to establish liberty upon solid foundations. He had been given the safe-keeping (*dépot*) of liberty and the choice between republican and monarchical rule. Why choose the latter? At times of crisis, it might be necessary to resort to short-term dictatorship, but in a context of peace there was no possible justification for 'a permanent and unmovable power'. Carnot then presented several other considerations on the possible reactions of foreign powers, the heritage of the Bourbons and so on. But these were only accessory considerations. The question he was asking was: should one be resigned to the idea that liberty was forever out of reach? His answer was a negative one:

> No, I cannot agree to look upon [liberty], this good so universally preferred to all others, without which all other

> goods are nothing, as a mere illusion. My heart tells me that liberty is possible; that the rule of liberty is easy, and more stable than any arbitrary government, than any oligarchy. I vote against the proposal.[31]

There is no record of the tribunes' reactions to Carnot's speech. For one last time he stood in front of the passive, docile assembly like the ghost of the Revolution, a reminder of what the ferocious, uncompromising patriotism of his generation had been about. Afterwards, although by now on frosty terms with the emperor, Carnot continued to serve on the Tribunate until its abolition in 1807, but the focus of his interests shifted away from politics to the activities of the Institute, and to scientific debate. Ever the man of patriotic emergencies, he returned to active service at a time of disaster, holding Antwerp for the emperor in 1814 and serving as minister of the interior during the fated Hundred Days. He finally retired into exile in Magdeburg, Prussia, during the Bourbon Restoration.

Double monuments

In 1889, on the centenary of the Revolution, Carnot's remains were moved from his Prussian grave to the Panthéon in Paris. The ceremony took place during the presidency of his grandson Sadi Carnot, who was head of the 3rd Republic from 1887 until he was assassinated by an Italian anarchist in 1894. Like his father, the president had been named 'Sadi' in honour of the thirteenth-century Persian writer Saadi Shirazi, his grandfather's favourite poet.

In addition to his promotion to the Panthéon, Lazare Carnot's double identity, and his double claim to glory, is officialized by his presence on two different Parisian monuments. His name is engraved on the north pillar of the Arc de Triomphe with those of some six hundred serving officers of the First Empire; he also features among the figures sculpted on the frieze. Not very far from there, across the

Pont de Jena and the Seine, his name is inscribed on the first floor of the Eiffel Tower (western side) in the more selective company of 71 other prominent French scientists. Several years after his death, his son Hippolyte was able to buy back a signet ring that had been stolen from the Luxembourg with other objects belonging to his father after his flight in 1797. The signet carried the Masonic image of the eye of justice (in common with many revolutionaries, Carnot had been a Mason) with the inscription *envers et contre tous* (against all opposition).

The motto on the ring did capture the fierce independence and lonely stand of its owner, and possibly it was on those terms of defiance that Carnot liked to see himself. But, unlike other claimants to the role of saviour of France, Carnot never considered himself a providential man or a man with a destiny.[32] For all his singular traits, he was the loyal servant of a collective cause, whatever that might be: France, the Revolution, the Republic, science; by no means a slave of the machine, but its watchful guardian.

Hilaire Ledru, *Merlin de Douai*, 1812, oil on canvas.

4

The Emperor's Beacon: Philippe-Antoine Merlin de Douai (1754–1838)

The emperor called him his *flambeau*, his beacon; in his recollections Napoleon explained how, during the meetings of the Council of State, Philippe-Antoine Merlin de Douai could always enlighten him whenever they struggled with some obscure legal question.[1] The law with all its ramifications was unquestionably not just Merlin's field of expertise, but his lifelong passion. Unlike other members of the revolutionary political class, who were the offspring of notaries, lawyers and local administrators, he did not come from a lineage of men of law. Instead, he was the son of prosperous tenant farmers (*censiers*), a social condition not requiring in principle any advanced education. He was encouraged to study because he was expected to undertake a career in the Church, but – to the disappointment of his pious relatives – he soon abandoned any pretence of religious vocation, choosing instead to train for the legal profession. In 1775, at the age of 21, he was admitted to the bar of the Flanders parliament at Douai. It was the beginning of a commitment, possibly an obsession, that lasted more than sixty years. In his eighties, under the July Monarchy, Merlin diligently attended the meetings of the restored Institute's legislative section (he had been a member since its foundation in 1795) until the day before his death in 1838.

Without the Revolution, Merlin's life would probably have followed the conventional path of a career at the bar and in the magistracy. As it turned out, the nature of his political engagement remains problematic. Was it an accidental detour, prompted by unforeseen circumstances? The choice of an easy opportunity for social advancement? Or did he view it as the means to pursue his ideal vision of justice?[2]

Seen from any of these perspectives, the ten years of Merlin's 'detour' into politics, from 1789 to 1799, cannot be explained away lightly. Between 1789 and 1794 he represented Douai in subsequent legislative assemblies; he also served as commissioner to the armies and sat on several parliamentary committees. After the fall of Maximilien Robespierre in July 1794, he became president of the Convention and entered the Committee of Public Safety during the last phase of its existence. He was appointed to the Commission of the Eleven that drafted the Constitution of 1795, and became minister of justice and police for the Directory, then a Director until the coup of 30 Prairial (18 June 1799), when a Jacobin majority took over the Councils and forced him to resign. Once Napoleon came to power in November that year, Merlin finally returned to the ranks of the magistracy, although he continued to serve in institutions close to the centre of power. He accepted a post in the Court of Review (*Tribunal de cassation*), was rapidly promoted to attorney general, and became a member of the Council of State, the new body of governmental advisors created by the Consulate.[3]

While he was politically active, Merlin was often accused by his enemies of being a shameless turncoat, ready to second any political regime. If so, it was a trait he shared with many of his accusers. This negative judgement has left its mark in most subsequent historiography, the most charitable version being that he was simply a competent professional, anxious to avoid conflict and largely indifferent to the colour of the power he served. It is true that during the years of his political career Merlin's position was often that of a legal expert, and that on occasion he put his competence in the service of policies he disapproved of. Yet, beyond the inevitable opportunistic adjustments, there was a guiding purpose to his engagement, a purpose that can be described as a tenacious legal utopia: the transformation of France into a country ruled by just, transparent and efficient laws. The reform of legal codes and of judicial institutions had been for centuries the holy grail of French magistrates and continued to be at the heart of the revolutionary project, although few of the legislators who espoused it were as fully aware as Merlin was of its complex practical implications.

Abolishing feudalism

By the time of his election to the Estates General in 1789 as one of the two representatives for the Third of the constituency (*bailliage*) of Douai and Orchies, Merlin had acquired considerable experience in his private legal practice. He was also a prolific contributor to Nicolas Guyot's *Répertoire universel et raisonné de jurisprudence*, an encyclopaedia of law published from 1786 onwards; more than five hundred out of four thousand entries were written by him.[4] Merlin's contributions reflected his two main fields of interest, the first of which was feudal rights. Through his professional practice he had become an expert in the many surviving ramifications of feudal law, since at the time landed property belonging to fiefs was still subject to an intricate system of constraints that dictated the conditions for its sale and inheritance. This situation was complicated even further by the peculiarities of the local common law. The region of Douai and Lille, known as French Flanders, had become definitively French only in 1713 with the Treaty of Utrecht, and the parliament of Douai had been established in the same year. It was to all effects a recent acquisition and, like other regional legal traditions, was poorly integrated into France's legal and administrative system.[5]

The second area of Merlin's interest was more theoretical and can be described as the creation of a comprehensive system of civil and penal legislation. This was an ambitious project that had begun to take form in the sixteenth century. As a system, it was intended to be built upon the universal principles of natural law and constructed as an orderly hierarchy of norms, from the most general down to the most specific and even transient prescriptions.[6] There was a direct connection between these two dimensions of Merlin's approach to jurisprudence, since both the peculiarities of regional common law and the arbitrary nature of feudal privilege were seen as signs of the disorder and unfairness of the entire system. In the circumstances, it was impossible for the French kings to fulfil their first obligation as sovereigns, that of dispensing equal justice to all their subjects.

Merlin subscribed to the influential narrative current in eighteenth-century historical works, which opposed the monarchy of the Middle Ages to modern absolute monarchy. By cutting its ties to the Estates and to the other legal councils that had surrounded it in the past, the latter had become detached from the body of the nation, losing any capacity to provide just rule. In common with many other members of the Constituent Assembly, Merlin moved without any great sense of discontinuity from his original ideal of the 'regeneration' of the monarchy through a return to its constitutional sources, to the principle of the sovereignty of the nation. The notion of social contract set forth in the writings of Jean-Jacques Rousseau (and also in those of Merlin's fellow Constituent Emmanuel Sieyès) provided him with the conceptual bridge between these two models of sovereignty. However, the transition from monarchy to republic, quite apart from its other disruptive consequences, did not solve the problem of the irregularity and incoherence of French law. The sovereign nation had the ambition to legislate on great matters of principle, for example abolishing feudal privilege and religious inequality, or condemning the practice of arrest by the infamous *lettres de cachet*, the documents that allowed the imprisonment of a person without providing evidence of their guilt to a tribunal. However, without the backbone of a new civil and penal code imposed on the whole of France, these enlightened reforms would remain mere ideological statements, rather than becoming effective measures of legislation.

Merlin's first encounter with this problem coincided with his emergence on to the national political stage. On the night of 4 August 1789 the Constituent Assembly had famously proclaimed the 'total destruction of feudal privilege'.[7] Some aspects of this destruction, such as the abolition of venal offices in the royal administration and the suppression of fiscal exemptions for the nobility, were quite straightforward. On the other hand, after several months of discussion, legislators were still unable to agree on the legal status of feudal domains. Because of his knowledge of the juridical background, Merlin was appointed to the Committee on Feudalism (*Comité de féodalité*), the legislative commission charged with studying the question, and on 8 February 1790 he reported on behalf of the Committee to the Assembly. His performance on that occasion established his reputation for knowledgeable and deft legal expertise, ensuring that his competence would be called upon repeatedly in subsequent years.[8]

The main difficulty came from the fact that the Constituent Assembly wished to remove the special status of feudal lands, transforming them into ordinary landed properties, without violating private property rights in any way. They considered that the benefits accruing to the owners of fiefs should be divided into two categories. Some derived simply from the ownership of lands, grounds and buildings, or had been established by contracts, whether between private individuals, or between the owners and the communes or local authorities. Such revenues constituted the legitimate returns of property and should not be abolished without some compensation. The second category, on the other hand, consisted of privileges that had been granted to feudal lords in the distant past in exchange for services they no longer performed, such as arming soldiers, administering justice or maintaining certain public venues. These often took the form of personal servitude, forced labour (*corvées*) being the most notorious but by no means the only example. Being no longer justified by the performance of some service to king or community, such privileges could be abolished without compensation.

Unfortunately, the distinction between these two types was far from clear-cut, since the different taxes, obligations, duties, prerogatives and exemptions had become hopelessly entangled over the centuries. In particular, some servitudes had been converted into monetary contributions through contracts between the parties concerned. The very distinction between 'lords' and 'vassals' made little sense, since in the feudal social pyramid everyone was both the lord and the vassal of someone else, and ultimately the vassal of the king. While feudal lords enjoyed benefits for which they provided no counterpart, they could not dispose freely of their property, which was subject to a variety of constraints, the rights of *ainesse* and *masculinité* (the entailment of a fief to the eldest son) being only the most obvious example. Merlin had struggled with such difficulties whenever he counselled his clients on the sale of a property or the drafting of a will. He could now advise the Constituents on how to establish a uniform regime common to all landed rents and charges.

The confiscation of property belonging to the Catholic Church in France, voted for by the Constituent Assembly on 10 October 1789, raised fewer legal difficulties. Such properties belonged not to private individuals but to corporate bodies: monastic orders, councils, confraternities and suchlike. Because corporations existed only insofar as the Crown acknowledged their legal status, they might be dissolved at any time, thus losing their right to ownership of property. Similarly, the later decision (made on 30 March 1792) to confiscate the fortunes of the émigrés aligned with the traditional prerogative of the Crown to appropriate the patrimony of those convicted of treason or crimes against the State.[9]

In the end, the decree embodying Merlin's elaborate legal distinctions between rights that could be suppressed and those that should receive compensation (*droits abolis* and *droits rachetables*) was never applied. The cost of buying back the legitimate share of feudal rights was huge, far greater than the already inadequate financial means of the revolutionary government, even after the confiscation and sale of Church lands. Moreover, peasants and tenant farmers were strongly opposed to the payment of any compensation for feudal benefits, and fought against the proposal. The question remained unresolved, the subject of recurrent discussion and reassessment well into the years of the Empire. In presenting his report to the Constituent Assembly, Merlin had stressed that general propositions, to be valid, must be directly applicable. 'It is not sufficient', he explained, 'to have established some principles; it is necessary, by an appropriate development of their consequences, to facilitate their being put into practice.' With these words the provincial barrister had pointed at the question that would dominate his political career.[10]

Uniting the nation

Throughout the years of the Revolution, all efforts to give a more orderly, structured form to the law had to contend not just with the density of practical questions, but with the vertiginous evolution of the political context. After the abolition of feudal rights, another major area Merlin was confronted with was that of local autonomy and the administrative uniformity of national territory. At the time of his election to the Estates General, Merlin, in common with many of his fellow deputies, had subscribed fully to the expectations of his electors, feeling directly responsible for the interests of the constituency he represented. As time went by, however, he looked increasingly at those interests from a national rather than a local perspective. Anxious to preserve his electoral base at Douai, he kept his official residence there and supported the town's promotion to capital of the new *département* of the Nord, against the claims of the rival town of Lille. Yet he no longer voiced those aspirations to local autonomy – strongly felt in a region of such recent acquisition – that had featured prominently on the agenda of the Estates.

With the beginning of the war in 1792, and the rebellions in various French towns against the revolutionary government, any reference to regional claims had become suspicious, even treasonous. In 1790 the Constituent Assembly had ordered the translation of public documents into the languages that were still spoken locally in some parts of France, such as Basque, Breton, German and Italian. But in January 1794 Bertrand Barère for the Committee of Public Safety argued for the suppression of all those local 'idioms', and Merlin proposed that Flemish should be added to the list of banished languages. On 20 July 1794 (a few days before the coup of Thermidor) it was at Merlin's proposal that the Convention voted for the exclusive use of French in all public acts, echoing the Ordinance of Villers-Cotterêts issued by King Francis I in 1539.[11]

Merlin's argument was that France as a nation was altogether different from the various populations – Bretons, Burgundians, Corsicans, Flemish and so on – that had come together to form it. Linguistic uniformity was, he maintained, the necessary premise to free French legal codes once and for all both from the surviving incrustations of Roman law, and from the common law of the various provinces. Like Francis I in the sixteenth century, the revolutionary assemblies were not altogether successful in their linguistic crusade; Flemish, for example, continued to be used for the drafting of private documents, such as wills or contracts, well into the second half of the nineteenth century.

All things considered, the sacrifice of local traditions to an allegedly national interest was relatively easy to justify, especially at times when the survival of the Republic was at stake. On the other hand, the annexation of foreign enclaves and the 'consolidation' of France's frontiers brought about by the war had far more questionable legal implications. In 1790 Merlin had subscribed, with Sieyès and Jean-François Reubell, to the doctrine set forth by the Constituent Assembly of the right of peoples to self-determination. On 20 May the deputies had voted for a resolution that engaged France to renounce any war of conquest and to abstain from using force against the freedom of other nations. This commitment was incorporated into the Constitution of 1791 and, again, into that of 1793, adopted when France was already at war with the European coalition. However, behind this apparent convergence on general principles, French legislators had rather different views on what those principles meant in practice.[12]

The differences were already apparent in 1790, when the Constituent Assembly decided to seize the papal enclave of Avignon, and they resurfaced in 1793 with the question of the annexation of the German enclaves in Alsace. They became more flagrant when France began extending its frontiers through war. Was it right to regard the inhabitants of the enclaves as 'peoples', according to Sieyès' definition (which Merlin endorsed) of 'nations united by a social contract'? And, if so, what counted exactly as the expression of their will? What happened when one of these 'peoples' could not agree on their own choices, as in the conflict between the citizens of Avignon, favourable to the annexation, and those of Carpentras, who were against it?

Looking further, how far should the Republic support those foreign patriots who wished to upturn their own governments? Should France take permanent responsibility for the survival of those revolutionary republics that had been created with its help, in the context of the war? Some deputies, especially those among the Jacobins, did not believe it was in France's interest to extend its dominion beyond its natural frontiers, taking permanent possession of those territories that had been occupied during military operations. By contrast with the doubts of some of his colleagues, such as Lazare Carnot, Merlin was, like Reubell, consistently in favour of policies of territorial consolidation and was ready to mobilize legal arguments to justify them. He argued that all agreements between monarchs passed under the old regime were illegitimate, since they had been made without the consent of the peoples concerned. Thus, Alsace was not French by virtue of the treaties signed after the end of the Thirty Years War in 1648; it was French because of the spontaneous participation of Alsatians in the revolutionary movement in 1790. In the same spirit, he was ready to accept as proof of the people's will the outcome of plebiscites that often reflected the position of militant minorities or had been carried out in the context of a military occupation. Somehow, he assumed that the will of the people must coincide with the decisions of those active groups of patriots who appealed for the help of the French Republic in view of 'revolutionizing' their own countries.

However, Merlin's main concern remained the position of his own province, French Flanders. In common with the Alsatian Reubell, he was anxious to see the territorial integrity of his region preserved, and, if possible, extended to include those districts that were part of the Austrian Empire. At the beginning of the war, in 1792, the coalition had briefly occupied French Flanders, but the territory had been recaptured by France the following year. When the revolutionary armies took over the Austrian Low Countries (Belgium) in 1794, Merlin was among those who advocated their permanent inclusion in the French Republic. The question was debated by the Thermidorian Convention the following year, and on 1 October 1795 Merlin obtained a vote in favour of the annexation of Belgium (the Belgian territories concerned had not been consulted on the matter).[13]

Following the decision to omit from the Constitution of 1795 all references to France's position in foreign politics, the Directory was no longer burdened with the universalistic aspirations of the Revolution. It has been suggested that the swift evolution from the ideal of the peaceful coexistence of nations to the endorsement of territorial expansion showed that Merlin (in common with others among his fellow jurists) had been converted by the revolutionary experience to the logic of reason of state, the defence of the interests of the Republic at all cost. In Merlin's case, however, there is no evidence that his views on the subject had changed significantly over time. The problem for him was, as usual, the relationship between ends and means. A just legal order could not be established unless the field of its application was viable and secure. This involved the creation of domestic administrative uniformity, but it also meant that the Republic must be protected from its enemies.

Ordinary and extraordinary justice

Another source of tension between legal principles and practice was the state of emergency established by the revolutionary government in 1793. The suspension of the new Constitution of 1793 was followed by the passing of 'extraordinary measures' to allow the pursuit of the enemies of the Republic operating within its borders, initiating what soon escalated into a generalized politics of Terror. Since Merlin did not at the time sit on the Committee of Public Safety, he was not directly responsible for the government's initiatives. The skeleton in his closet – a skeleton that continued to haunt him until the end of his life – was his expert contribution to the drafting of the decree introduced on 17 September 1793 and known as the Law of Suspects (*Loi des suspects*). The reputation he thus acquired of 'executioner in chamber' and 'atrocious jurist' pursued him well beyond the grave in later historiography.[14]

The decree was a response to the near-desperate circumstances in which the country found itself in the second year of the war. The French armies struggled to hold the front, while an invasion by coalition troops seemed imminent. There were rebellions in several major cities across France, and what amounted to a civil war in the Vendée. This led to a growing fear of the 'enemies from within' conspiring against the Republic: royalist spies and foreign agents, émigrés, refractory priests, traffickers and speculators, deserters and so on. Everywhere the government struggled to control the revolutionary militants who wished to deal with such suspects in their own way; the deputies sent to restore order in rebel towns were also inclined to take radical steps, ordering arbitrary arrests and executions, often on a large scale.

The Convention then instructed the Committee of Legislation, which was responsible for giving proper form to the laws voted for by the assembly, to produce a text defining precisely the notion of 'suspects' and the conditions for their arrest. Nominally the Committee had 48 members, but only a dozen of them were in Paris at the time, and even fewer attended the meetings. Competent and exceptionally hard-working, Merlin was – with his fellow lawyer Jean-Jacques-Régis Cambacérès (see Chapter Seven) – the obvious candidate for the task; once again, he was designated rapporteur to the Convention. The Committee's brief was a tricky one, since the decree must define not only criminal actions, but the intention or predisposition to commit them. All those who 'by their conduct, their relations, their words and writings' showed themselves to be 'partisans of tyranny and federalism' and 'enemies of liberty', meaning royalists, supporters of local revolts but also anyone supposedly harbouring anti-revolutionary views. Some specific categories of person were suspect because of their quality and position: former nobles (and their families); émigrés; public officials who had been dismissed or refused to serve in danger zones near the front; those who had been denied certificates of *civisme* because of their political past; and so on.

Understandably, the jurists involved were uneasy with this motley classification that punished actual criminal behaviour and presumed criminal intent in the same way, and their text was revised several times by the Convention to make it more flexible and inclusive. Significantly, however, the decree allowed for the detention of suspects (in 'adequate conditions', in practice under house arrest) only until their position was clarified or, eventually, until the end of the war. Possible suspects were identified by the local Committee of Surveillance, a kind of improvised police attached to the communes. This committee had to agree on the arrest by a majority of at least seven votes out of twelve; the arrest was then reported to the Committee of General Security (yet another subcommittee of the Convention that exercised police functions), and finally the suspect's dossier was transmitted to the Revolutionary Tribunal to be assessed by magistrates and by a jury.

It is only too easy to argue that the Law of Suspects, for all its complicated network of local and central committees, provided a thin legal veneer for the systematic elimination of political opponents. Unfortunately, the approximate number of those arrested, released or executed during the Terror remains controversial; in particular, because of the time lag, it is impossible to disentangle the impact of the decree of 17 September 1793 from the far harsher one of 22 Prairial (10 June 1794), introduced by Georges Couthon and Robespierre, and associated with what is known as the Great Terror. It is clear, however, that the Committee of Public Safety, dissatisfied by the sluggishness and impediments of legal procedures, decided to take things into its own hands, placing repression under the direct control of the executive. That was precisely the outcome that the jurists had tried to avoid, as the law they had proposed entrusted the matter to the judiciary and, ultimately, to the legislative assembly.

Because Merlin belonged to the *plaine*, the centre of the Convention (in 1791, with other moderates, he had left the Jacobins' club for the Feuillants'), it has been suggested that his collaboration on the drafting of the decree was obtained by threats and influenced by his fear of retaliation. Any sane man in his position had good reason to be scared in the summer of 1793 as the revolutionary factions were engaged in a bloody struggle to destroy one another; moreover, it is unlikely that he enjoyed having to work under the control of difficult and quarrelsome politicians. He did, however, share the obsession with conspiracy that haunted the revolutionary political class, and he was sincerely convinced that extraordinary means were needed to save the Republic, as he explained to a private correspondent: 'The measures [of the decree] were harsh but necessary and indispensable.'[15]

In 1791–2, as president of the newly established Criminal Tribunal of the North at Douai, Merlin had rapidly acquired a reputation for severity in the pursuit of ordinary criminals; he clearly felt no obligation to be more lenient towards political suspects. The differences between him and some of his colleagues were that he was not prepared to abandon his respect for legal forms, and that he made the effort of separating partisan sentiments and public vengeance from justice. Faced with the hysteria displayed by the Convention, he was at least guided by a clear purpose: that random violence by rebel crowds, civic militias or government agents must be stopped; and that the measures introduced to control the threat of domestic insurgence must be transparent, clearly defined and limited as to time. On 28 December 1794, reporting to the Convention on the reform of the Revolutionary Tribunal, Merlin articulated the necessity of abandoning the logic of revolutionary justice – with its ideological and moralistic undertones – for that of ordinary criminal law, denouncing the absence of proportion and nuance from the sentences meted out by the revolutionary magistracy and juries: 'Death, always death! Their penal code consisted of this simple word: *la Mort*!'[16]

The question resurfaced after Thermidor at the time of the prosecution of those Terrorist agents who became scapegoats for the previous government's policies, such as the former prosecutor of the Revolutionary Tribunal, Antoine Fouquier-Tinville. Robespierre and his associates had been executed without trial on the accusation of conspiring to overturn the Republic. In the case of Fouquier-Tinville – who underwent a protracted trial before being guillotined in May 1795 – a laborious attempt was made to disentangle the vague accusations of supposed counter-revolutionary activities from the specific ones of abuse of power and violation of legal procedures, such as depriving defendants of the right to speak or to consult their lawyers.[17] While the trial was clearly a political one involving the settling of old scores among the revolutionary political class, ordinary justice was now struggling to reassert itself.[18]

But how was it possible to return to the 'normal' exercise of justice when the Republic continued to be threatened by what Merlin called 'reptiles', the agents of conspiracy and counter-revolution? After Thermidor the Republic remained too unstable to allow a return to ordinary judicial practice. It was a difficulty experienced by the political class in different fields but felt more acutely by Merlin, for whom the law was not just one of the dimensions of government, but almost an end in itself, the pillar on which the entire edifice of the Republic must rest.

The machinery of justice

If the pressing constraints of the reason of state were a recurrent obstacle to the rule of law, the major (and unexpected) difficulty that emerged from the revolutionary experience was that of applying and enforcing legislation. As Merlin had observed about the abolition of feudalism, it was far easier to proclaim ambitious principles than to translate them into applicable rules. Following the intense activity of the Constituent and Legislative Assemblies in 1789–92, there was a growing gap between the overproduction of new laws and the capacity of both central and local authorities to interpret and enforce them. While emergency legislation could be seen as a temporary expedient, a practice that might be set aside once the political context became more stable, the ever-growing mass of unapplied legislation was not likely to go away under any circumstances; in time, it could only get worse, generating confusion and disobedience.

In the earlier phases of the Revolution, legislators were inclined to attribute the failed application of the law to the ill will and deliberate obstructiveness of the agents of executive power. In the words of Marie-Jean Hérault de Séchelles for the Committee of Public Safety, those agents must be called to answer for their 'crime of negligence' against the sovereign will of the people.[19] Indeed, the question of law enforcement became critical in the ongoing conflict between legislative and executive powers. However, the replacement of the old agents of the executive associated with royal power (*intendants* and ministers) with new ones strictly dependent on the legislative (deputies on mission, executive committees) made very little practical difference. The restoration of the executive that characterized the Directorial and consular regimes was intended to provide solutions to this pressing problem.

Merlin himself had never subscribed to the idea that the failure to enforce the law was caused by a conflict of powers. Nor did he regard it as the result of the hostility of some authorities, although of course there had been local resistance to the diktats of central government.

In his more pragmatic view, the causes of the difficulty were twofold. On the one hand, the laws themselves were often poorly designed, unclear in their formulation or imperfectly integrated into existing codes; in particular, the hierarchy of general and particular norms was no better established in the new legislation than it had been before 1789. Most of the time governmental agents were genuinely baffled by the confusing instructions they received, rather than deliberately disobedient.

The second major difficulty was the lack of adequate institutional structure to support the application of the law. While it was necessary to strengthen and reorganize the executive, judicial power was also an essential piece of the machine of government that must be rebuilt. At the beginning of the Revolution, the institutions of the judiciary had been the object of such radical interventions as the abolition of the *parlements* (generally seen as symbols of old-regime privilege and abuse) and of some existing tribunals. However, the comprehensive reforms that should have followed – notably the creation of a network of new penal and civil courts across the country – had not been carried out.

On the subject of the reform of the texts of law, providing France with a new penal code had been a priority of the Constituent Assembly, eager to suppress the judicial abuses of the past. The new code, inspired by the enlightened tradition of Montesquieu and Cesare Beccaria, was adopted in October 1791.[20] Apart from abolishing some of the most odious features of old-regime justice, it had been intended to leave as little as possible to the initiative of judges, requiring that crimes and punishments be defined very precisely so as to avoid arbitrary sentencing. The new text had failed to satisfy these requirements, calling for a complementary Code of Crimes and Punishments (*Code des délits et des peines*) in 646 articles, which was voted for by the Convention in October 1795. Apart from promoting some important novelties in the field of civil law (such as the introduction of divorce in 1792), the new civil code did not come fully into effect until 1804, under the Consulate.[21]

Merlin had not been a member of the committees that produced the new penal code, the Constitutional Committee and the Committee of Criminal Legislation (*Comité de constitution* and *Comité de legislation criminelle*). However, he did participate, with his fellow jurist Cambacérès, in the commission that worked on the definition of the hierarchy of norms and decrees, the Commission for the Classification of Laws (*Commission de classification des lois*). Since 1790 an unofficial Table of Laws (*Table des lois*), a kind of synoptic handbook, was available to guide the agents of the executive in interpreting the old and new legislation. Together, Merlin and Cambacérès produced a more comprehensive Code of Revolutionary Law (*Code du droit révolutionnaire*) that was designed to perform the same function. This document was never published, but there is evidence that it circulated as a manuscript until 1806, and that it was widely used.[22]

As a jurist, Merlin held fairly conventional views halfway between enlightened humanism and a traditional repressive attitude. For example, unlike some members of the Constituent Assembly, he was against the abolition of the death penalty, although he was in favour of reducing the number of capital offences. Even his readiness to contribute to Terrorist legislation can be seen less as the cowardly acceptance of radical policies than as the natural response of a disciplinarian confronted with the threat of social disorder. Equipped as he was with an encyclopaedic knowledge of the juridical background, it was not in the area of promoting legal innovation that he felt most at ease. But one domain in which he really came into his own – and proved extraordinarily effective – was the reorganization of the judicial institutions.

At the beginning of the Revolution, Merlin had been elected president of one of the six Parisian courts that had supplanted the old Tribunal of the Châtelet. In 1791, convinced that the Revolution had come to an end with the adoption of the new Constitution, he returned to Douai as president of the Criminal Tribunal of the North, which had been set up to replace the *parlement* of French Flanders (and was, in common with all old-regime *parlements*, a legal rather than a legislative body, as its name suggests). Later, on his return to Paris, he contributed to the reform of the Revolutionary Tribunal, the special court created to prosecute enemies of the Republic. Despite the different vocation of these institutions, the dysfunctional features they displayed were very similar. The competences within the courts were not properly articulated, especially considering that criminal and civil justice were now separated; there were residual venal offices that had been formally abolished but were still in place; judges were insufficient in number or not properly distributed (civil courts relied on rotating judges); the right of defence was not guaranteed; and the selection of jurors was not properly regulated.

It was only after Thermidor that Merlin had the opportunity to address these problems systematically. In November 1795 he was appointed minister of justice by the Directory. From the elegant premises the ministry had occupied under the monarchy, the Hôtel de Bourvallais in Place Vendôme (the building it still occupies today), he undertook a major overhaul of the entire judicial structure. An inquiry he conducted into the state of the courts across France confirmed his sense of disorder and lack of means. Judges were not always available; clerks and bailiffs were not paid, since they had never been properly engaged, only co-opted from previous institutions; archives were neglected; and even the necessary supply of writing paper was often missing. To complicate things, in 1790 the Constituent Assembly had abolished the bar together with all other professional corporations (it would be re-established under the Empire in 1810) and meanwhile any citizen, regardless of qualifications, could in principle act as lawyer at a trial.[23]

Under Merlin's supervision the ministry's competences were divided into three main sections: civil justice, penal justice and the bureau of reviews (*cassation*); an additional bureau of consultation, attached directly to the minister's office, dealt with the more complex cases. Recruiting the necessary personnel was not easy, and to find competent men Merlin had to turn to those who had previously served in the numerous defunct committees of the Assembly or were recommended to him on the grounds of what he himself regarded as the dubious qualifications of 'patriotism and diligence'. Even so, the ministry's employees grew rapidly from around fifty to nearly two hundred. The indefatigable minister personally supervised the correspondence for the entire department, and he even managed to find the time to establish a library, attached to the Court of Review, to collect juridical reference works.

In the new setting adopted by the Directory, the ministry of justice was also responsible for the police (they were later separated) and was thus divided into several sections: correspondence, commerce and public health, surveillance and security, customs and public opinion. Once he found himself in charge of public order, Merlin reacted with the rigour he had displayed all along, treating with equal severity the neo-Jacobins involved in Gracchus Babeuf's conspiracy, the ever-present royalist agents and the émigrés attempting to return to France. In September 1797 his promotion to the Directory, following the royalist coup of Fructidor and the eviction of Carnot, put an end to his eager bureaucratic scaffolding; however, the structures he had established were there to stay.[24]

Merlin's election to the Directory placed him in a position of power that he had never occupied before. For two years he shared with his colleagues Louis-Marie de La Révellière-Lépeaux and Reubell the main responsibility of government, but the experience was not a happy one. Unlike Sieyès and other more sceptical Thermidorians, Merlin considered the Constitution of 1795 adequate and dismissed all suggestions of constitutional revision. In a speech celebrating the anniversary of the Revolution on 14 July 1798, he argued that the Republic had now been established on solid grounds, offering a viable alternative to both absolute monarchy and revolutionary dictatorship. In practice, however, this was not true, and much of the government's energy was spent in keeping the executive politically afloat.

After the success of the Italian campaigns of 1796–7 and the occupation of Switzerland in 1798, the military fortunes of the Republic had taken a downturn. Faced with a second European coalition, the French armies were losing ground in all the countries they had previously occupied. Following the election of Sieyès to the Directory, carried by a Jacobin majority, the position of Merlin and La Révellière-Lépeaux was weakened. With the coup of Prairial (18 June) the assemblies, now led by the Jacobins, took their revenge on the two Directors whom they considered too conservative, and in particular on Merlin, who was guilty in their eyes of persecuting the *babeuvistes*. On 19 June 1799 the two men were summoned by the Five Hundred to answer a series of accusations. They were held responsible for the recent military defeats, and it was claimed that their supposed financial malpractice had deprived the armies of the necessary supplies; in addition, and inevitably, there were suggestions of dictatorial ambitions on their part. The deputy Antoine Boulay de la Meurthe was probably right when he declared that Merlin was better suited to running the office of prosecutor than to serving in government. There being no evidence to support the accusations, they were finally abandoned by the Council, but Merlin and La Révellière-Lépeaux were sufficiently disgusted to hand in their resignations.

The return of the jurists

A few months later, in a letter to Sieyès dated 13 December 1799, Merlin admitted that the Directorial government had turned out to be 'a poorly organized machine'.[25] Luckily for him, rescue was at hand; while he was confiding his misgivings about the machine of government to Sieyès, the latter's political miscalculations had already placed the very same machine in the hands of someone with a considerable ability to fix all manner of mechanisms: First Consul Napoleon Bonaparte. Given his removal from the executive, Merlin played no part in the coup of Brumaire, nor did he belong to the circle of Napoleon's early supporters, and he had no reason to expect a post in the new government. Whatever his real feelings, he was apparently quite happy to accept a middling position of magistrate in the Court of Review.

Yet Merlin's fortunes were about to change. The marked presence of men of law in Napoleon's entourage was not coincidental but rather signalled the commitment of the new regime to the pursuit of those legal reforms that the Revolution had left unfinished.[26] On 18 April 1800, a few days after his return to the magistracy, Merlin addressed to the Institute a report entitled 'Memoir on the Necessity of a Universal, Uniform Code for the Whole Republic', in which he denounced the fact that the 'indispensable codification of civil laws, promised to the French since 1790', had made no decisive progress. On the contrary, 'the vicious organization of the legislative body' had increased confusion in the administration of justice, so that it was still necessary to combine '30 or 40,000 new laws with the debris of the ancient ones'. This dismal account of the situation was fully in tune with the new government's agenda.[27]

Merlin was not part of the small team of jurists who worked, under Cambacérès' direction, to draft the new civil code that was finally adopted on 21 March 1804, a document destined to exercise a major influence across Europe and beyond. The group included several seasoned lawyers and magistrates, whose political past was less charged and controversial than Merlin's own (two of them, Félix Bigot de Préameneu and François Tronchet, had defended Louis XVI at his trial in December 1792). But while he was not one of the authors of the code, Merlin did contribute significantly to the conditions for its application. Once again it was essential to ensure that the new principles were properly connected to the existing norms, to avoid ambiguity and conflict. Merlin was able to pursue his favourite activity of clarification and reordering in the framework of a new institution created by the Consulate, the Council of State.

The Council of State – a novel institution, often inappropriately compared by historians to the royal councils of the monarchy – was introduced discreetly, almost surreptitiously, in the Constitution of 1799 (Year VIII) under Heading IV, 'Government'. The somewhat laconic Article 52 stated: 'Under the direction of the consuls, a Council of State is charged to draft the projects of laws and the rules of public administration, and to solve the difficulties that should emerge in any administrative matter.'[28]

Mainly inspired by Cambacérès, the Council completed the design of the Consular Constitution of 1799 (Year VIII), which entrusted all legislative initiative to the executive. The legislative assemblies (Legislative Body and Tribunate) could debate and vote on only those laws that were proposed by the executive (namely the three consuls and their ministers). However, the government took the advice of legal and administrative experts in formulating their proposals, to make sure that the new laws would not prove incoherent or inapplicable and therefore fall into the impasse they had experienced during the Revolution: advising the government was the specific function of the Council of State. To some extent the Council's function of 'verification' of the form of the laws was similar to that of the old parliaments; however, rather than being part of the judiciary, the Council was a component of government, though with merely consultative functions.

The growing importance of this institution is attested by the Constitutions of 1802 (Year X) and 1804 (Year XII), which amplify its role, describing it in greater detail than the early formulation of 1800, specifying the number of its members (no more than 50, no fewer than 25) and subdividing it into six sections: legislation, interior, finance, war, navy and commerce. Regarded with suspicion and marginalized after the Restoration, the Council of State was revived in 1848; today it continues to occupy an important place among the institutions of the 5th Republic.

It was at the meetings of the Council of State, where – according to witnesses – discussions were free and animated, that Merlin's erudition and competence could shine and impress the First Consul. His performance as counsellor was the first step in his new, brilliant legal career. Appointed attorney general in 1801, he was made a life member of the Council of State and received the title Count of the Empire and other official distinctions, accompanied by suitable compensation. Unlike Carnot, he does not seem to have been troubled by the transition to the Empire and hereditary rule in 1804; it is also reasonable to assume that his love of order reconciled him to the authoritarian penchants of the imperial regime. After all, he had seen much worse.

Merlin was loyal to the man who, besides showering him with honours, had (as he saw it) contributed to the establishment of the rule of the law, and remained faithful to Napoleon during the Hundred Days. Because of this, in 1816 he was excluded from the amnesty granted by Louis XVIII to former dignitaries of the Empire and, like Sieyès and Cambacérès, chose Brussels as his place of exile. It was only in 1830, at the advent of the July Monarchy, that he was finally able to return to France. The long years of exile allowed him to accomplish the work of legal systematization that he had begun in the 1780s but inevitably neglected while in office; he completed a *Répertoire de jurisprudence* (Directory of Case Law; 1812–24) in eighteen volumes and a *Récueil alphabéthique des questions de droit* (Alphabetical Collection of Legal Questions; 1827–8) in eight. On matters of general principles, such as popular sovereignty and the social contract, the content of these compilations was not very different from the versions drafted before the Revolution.

In 1832 the contributor to a multi-volume handbook for lawyers commented that 'Merlin's works have been criticized by those who disliked his person. But they are in all libraries, they are cited at all trials, and they continue to be secretly and profitably consulted by the same men who are reluctant to acknowledge them in public.'[29]

THE OVERWHELMING PRESENCE of men of law within the political class has generally been regarded as the cause of an excessively 'philosophical' approach to government by the French revolutionaries, a preference for abstract principles over political reality. This view, mainly the product of entrenched prejudice, was originally set forth in the writings of Edmund Burke and Alexis de Tocqueville and has remained a commonplace in the historiography of the Revolution. It is questionable whether the penchant for abstraction was the prerogative of jurists as such, or a broader cultural trait of the generations formed by the writings of the Enlightenment.

Whatever their commitment to philosophical ideals, anyone pursuing a successful career as a private lawyer, before or after the Revolution, had to possess an excellent grasp of practicalities. Merlin's career illustrates how an attachment to the principles of 1789 was compatible with a substantial dose of political realism. This did not mean simply the opportunistic capacity to compromise and adjust to unstable circumstances; it involved the distinctive ability to identify the instruments necessary to defend and consolidate those principles over time. The rule of law may not have been the shining kingdom reflected in the gilded mirrors, bronzes and lustres of the Hôtel de Bourvallais, but it was inscribed in the imperishable bronze of legal codes, administrative regulations and bureaucratic routines.[30]

5

Voltaire's Eclectic Heir: Nicolas François de Neufchâteau (1750–1828)

The first forty years of Nicolas François de Neufchâteau's life read like the plot of an adventure novel: the colourful career of an aspiring man of letters with fanciful disposition and uneven fortunes. He was a published poet at the age of sixteen, and his literary vocation was encouraged by a grand aristocratic patron who may have been his natural father, the *bailli* of Alsace (the king's representative in the region), Pierre-Simon de Hénin-Liétard.[1] It was also blessed by an indulgent Voltaire, who received him at his château at Ferney (now Ferney-Voltaire) in 1766 and saluted him graciously as his heir.[2]

In homage to his patron's residence and to the place of his early studies – a commune in Lorraine – the young writer added 'de Neufchâteau' to his too-ordinary surname François. However, coming from an impecunious family (his legal father was a schoolmaster), the budding poet half-heartedly chose the law as a way to make a living. At the same time he declined the opportunity of a career in the Church offered by the sympathetic Bishop of Toul because of a lack of religious vocation, anticipating the uncompromising anticlericalism he professed consistently throughout his life. Counsel (*avocat*) at the *parlement* of Paris since 1772, he never practised the law, instead writing extensively on current legal affairs and canvassing for a string of administrative offices in line with his legal qualifications.

The most exotic of these postings – the office of general prosecutor of the French colony of Saint-Domingue (now Dominican

Republic), which Neufchâteau held between 1783 and 1787 – ended dramatically with a serious illness caused by the tropical climate, and with a shipwreck in which he lost, among other things, the manuscript of his translation of Ludovico Ariosto's *Orlando Furioso*. By the time the Estates General met in 1789, he had also gone through two marriages contracted essentially for financial reasons (two more were to follow), and a liaison with a well-known actress.[3]

Predictably, as was the case for many in his generation, after the summoning of the Estates General Neufchâteau's uncertain professional progress was swiftly redirected from the stagnating waters of old-regime patronage and venal offices to the more promising navigation of revolutionary institutions. In 1789 he drafted the *cahiers de doléances* for Vicherey, a commune in the *bailliage* of Toul; it was a document that, published and widely circulated, became a model of the genre for the entire region. Although he failed to be elected deputy of the Third (he made it only as replacement for Lieutenant General Claude-Pierre Maillot), in September 1791 he was elected to the Legislative as a representative of the newly created *département* of the Vosges.[4] After serving as secretary and president of the Legislative, he was re-elected to the Convention a year later, in September 1792. This time he resigned quickly on account of alleged ill health, declining the position he was offered of minister of justice; clearly, as mob violence and factional struggle escalated in Paris, he thought it safer to retire to the backwaters of Lorraine. His absence from the Convention meant that he did not vote at the trial of Louis XVI, and therefore at the Restoration he avoided the sanctions against regicides.

Despite such prudence in his political life, Neufchâteau was not equally careful in the pursuit of his literary ambitions and of attractive leading ladies. In August 1793, in what was already a climate of Terror, he staged at the Théâtre de la Nation (the former Comédie Française) in Paris a play entitled *Paméla, ou la vertu récompensée* (Pamela; or, Virtue Rewarded), his own adaptation of Samuel Richardson's novel *Pamela* (1740) and Carlo Goldoni's stage version of the same. The play

Philippus Velijn, after Marie-Thérèse de Noireterre,
François de Neufchâteau, 1814, woodcut.

ran successfully for several weeks yet, despite being of no imaginable political significance, aroused the suspicions of the revolutionary government on account of some lines praising the virtue of clemency. 'The play', stated the report submitted to the Committee of Public Safety, 'aims at re-establishing, or at least expresses attachment to, the order of nobility.' Accused of promoting counter-revolutionary views, the author was arrested along with the whole cast; detained in the palace of the Luxembourg, he was held for several months until the beginning of August 1794, shortly after the coup of Thermidor.[5]

Neufchâteau's imprisonment and low ideological profile made him one of those survivors who could safely be recruited for the post-1795 institutions, since he was not compromised by association with the Terrorist regime. Consistently moderate in his political action, he had shown great severity only when dealing with ministers of cult, whether refractory priests in France or sorcerers in Saint-Domingue. But while his promotion within the Thermidorian political class corresponds to a common pattern, the point of arrival of his career is more surprising. In a disconcerting *coup de théâtre*, the former playwright emerged from his diverse experiences as one of France's most effective and creative administrators, a legendary minister of the interior who practically invented the function for future governments. It was on the strength of this performance that he made his second entrance into the Luxembourg only three years after being kept there as a political prisoner. On 9 September 1797 he was appointed to the Directory as the replacement for Lazare Carnot, who had been evicted after the coup of Fructidor. As a Director, he found himself back in his former prison, now restored to its original palatial status and promoted to official residence of the government.

The useful writer

Unlike other men who served on the Directory, Neufchâteau did not possess a solid professional background; all he had was some basic legal competence that he had acquired when he was studying (probably at Reims) to qualify as counsel, and some experience as a local administrator. He was neither an expert legal advisor nor a learned jurist or constitutionalist. His most distinctive quality was less an acquired skill than a natural talent: the ability – shared with his role model, Voltaire – to write fluently and effortlessly in a variety of forms and on a wide range of subjects. His gift is attested by the impressive mass of heterogeneous publications he produced throughout his life, ranging from poetry and literary compositions to essays, pamphlets, manuals, educational texts and tables, statistical compilations and ministerial circulars. Having realized early in life that his dreams of literary glory were unlikely to come true, he applied himself to the task of becoming what he called 'a useful writer': someone who could serve the common good by explaining, illustrating and making accessible to his readers issues of public relevance.[6]

Helpfully, Neufchâteau's range of interests was very large by any standards, encompassing fiscal and monetary subjects, commerce, local history, education, the arts, industry and everything connected with agricultural improvements. He was especially attentive to economic questions, and at the time of his colonial adventure he published an essay entitled *Sur la disette du numéraire à Saint Domingue et sur les moyens d'y remédier* (On the Cash Shortage in Saint-Domingue and Ways of Resolving It; 1788), which was generally well received. The question of the scarcity of coinage – a major one at the time – continued to occupy him during his ministerial mandates. His broad interest in the new doctrines of political economy is documented by the presence in his library of two different translations of Adam Smith's *Wealth of Nations*. In time, however, agriculture emerged as his favourite domain, leading him to produce works on such subjects as the techniques of harvesting, the mechanics of ploughs, the quality of seed, the importance of prunes and dried fruit in general, and the planting of *Robinia*. Although there is an amateurish, indeed almost comical element to the encyclopaedic range of his intellectual curiosity, he was not satisfied with acquiring superficial notions with which to embellish his speeches; instead he applied himself diligently to the study of those problems that seemed to be of real practical importance.

The task of communicating openly and clearly on all subjects of public interest became the focus of Neufchâteau's political commitment. In 1790, in an open letter addressed to local administrators, he argued that one of the greatest abuses of the old regime had been to prevent the public from learning about, and discussing openly, all matters of common concern. He himself, he explained, had been stopped in his attempts to inquire about fiscal practices by the injunction to respect 'the mysteries of bureaucracy'.[7] At the time of the drafting of the *cahiers* in 1789, he had been briefly arrested, with a few others, on the accusation of conspiracy because he had requested a full account of the fiscal revenues of the *bailliage*, a demand that stood out from the list of somewhat vague grievances set forth in the *cahiers de doléances*.[8] Later, in his quality of minister of the interior, he was confronted with the practical consequences of the absence of transparency, which not only affected relations between the governing institutions and the public, but represented a major problem within the institutions themselves.

Naturally Neufchâteau subscribed to the obligatory revolutionary principles of the abolition of privileges, the sovereignty of the nation and the limitation of power, as is shown by his unimaginative commentary on the Constitution of 1791: *L'Origine ancienne des principes modernes* (The Ancient Origin of Modern Principles; 1791).[9] In this respect, his commitment to the new political order was sincere enough, in line with the aspirations to change and reform that he had advocated from the beginning of his public career. However, he was not especially preoccupied with the form of the Constitution, or with any of the ideological divisions that had torn leaders and factions apart within the revolutionary assemblies. The easy opportunism that led him, in later years, to endorse Napoleon's imperial ambitions, or to be reconciled with Louis XVIII's restored monarchy, is explained partly by the fact that he attached only a secondary importance to the *form* of any regime, provided that it satisfied basic requirements of equality, rationality and stability.[10]

Neufchâteau's vision was close to that originally expressed by Emmanuel Sieyès in his writings of 1789 on privileges and the Third Estate: the ideal of a nation of productive, useful individuals, shareholders in the enterprise of ensuring general progress and prosperity. In Neufchâteau's view, public powers had the duty to promote competence and merit, to modernize the administration and to keep citizens informed about their actions. Only insofar as the administrative order was reorganized on the principles of a free constitution was it possible to claim that a love of the public good was no longer the chimera it had been in the past.[11] Serving this ideal was his own contribution to the revolutionary cause, one he continued to work for in the context of the institutions that took shape under the Directory.

Reinventing the executive

Personal experience gave Neufchâteau some insight into the functioning of all three constitutional powers, both nationally and locally. Before his arrest in 1793, he had been a magistrate, a local administrator and a member of the Legislative and the Convention. After his liberation, he was first appointed judge at the Court of Review; then, with the advent of the Directorial Republic, he became 'commissioner' of the Directory, the new term for agents of the executive in the *départements*. In that capacity, on 22 September 1796 he organized the festivities for the fourth anniversary of the Republic at Épinal, capital of the Vosges. On that occasion he presented his poem 'Les Vosges', a lyrical celebration of the local mountains modelled on Albrecht von Haller's classic 'Die Alpen' (1729).[12] Finally, in July 1797 his former fellow deputy and friend Joseph-Clément Poullain de Grandprey recommended him to the Director Jean-François Reubell for the post of minister of the interior. He served in the same ministry twice, once briefly, between July and September 1797, and the second time between July 1798 and June 1799. In between he was elected to the Directory; deselected by lot, he was quite happy to return to his ministerial department.[13]

Since the beginning of the Revolution, the executive, being the most controversial of the constitutional powers, had been systematically undermined by a part of the political class, and its organization had been subject to endless transformations and adjustments. The Constitution of 1795 had restored, to some extent, its essential role within the balance of powers, but had left several questions of competence and internal structure essentially unresolved. While the most contentious issue was the relationship between the Directors and the two legislative Councils, another source, if not of conflict, at least of confusion over competences was that between the Directors and the ministers working under them. During the Revolution ministers had seen their power gradually diminished, until in 1793 they were finally replaced, on Lazare Carnot's suggestion (see Chapter Three), by twelve executive committees issued from/dependent on the Legislative Assembly.

With the Constitution of 1795 the ministerial function was restored. Six ministers were placed at the head of their respective departments: foreign affairs; finance; war; navy and colonies; interior; and justice and police. In 1796 the police became a separate ministry, bringing the number of departments to seven. Each ministry's specific area of competence had to be redefined, untangling the murky practices inherited from the past, since under the monarchy a minister's sphere of action had often depended on his personal initiative, rather than being defined independently from the individual who occupied the post. The staffing of ministries also had to be reorganized. Many posts – as in the judiciary – had originally been venal offices, sold whenever the Crown needed ready cash, or sinecures, so there were no procedures for recruitment and no budget to pay stipends and pensions.

An additional difficulty was the widespread mistrust of the Directory's paper money. Even after the suppression of the *assignats* and their replacement by the territorial mandates, many clerks simply refused to work in public services for an emolument that was not paid in metallic money. Like Merlin de Douai at the ministry of justice, Neufchâteau took it as his mission to remedy all these deficiencies, and he undertook the task with managerial brio. He had written wistfully a few years before that public officials must be 'prudent, virtuous, efficient and distinguished by talent rather than fortune'; in practice this meant that they should be chosen by public competition, to ensure that only the most able and deserving would be recruited.[14]

In the executive created by the Constitution of 1795, each Director oversaw one or more ministerial departments. In practice the Directors constituted a kind of cabinet, while the ministers depended individually on one or other of the Directors, without forming a council (Article 151). In the only surviving example of this historical model of collegial government – the Federal Council of the Swiss Confederation – there are no ministers; the seven members of the Council divide the various ministerial portfolios between themselves, instructing and supervising the civil servants who run the departments for which they are responsible.

Apart from keeping the traditional term 'minister', the functioning of the Constitution of 1795 was probably quite similar. Directors made the policy decisions, while ministers were simple executors; their appointment was not decided collegially, but they were nominated individually by one or other of the Directors.[15] However, Neufchâteau's easy switch from the position of minister of the interior to Director, and back again, suggests that the separation of roles was flexible, and largely dependent on circumstances and personal initiative. While the competences of the ministry of the interior were exceedingly large by modern standards, they mostly concerned matters of domestic governance. Neufchâteau took advantage of this state of affairs. Since the main areas of conflict within the Directory were the conduct of the war and foreign policy, he was left free to pursue his own projects without much interference from the rest of the executive or the Councils.

A vast interior

Luckily, the broad yet surprisingly heterogeneous scope of action of the minister of the interior included various areas that Neufchâteau was already familiar with, partly from his administrative experience, but also because they were the objects of his intellectual pursuits. His ministry was responsible for agriculture, commerce and supplies, industry, roads and canals, the arts and education, among other things. It was a vast agenda to which he applied himself with characteristic energy and enthusiasm, bringing tangible results in a short time. The terms 'to revive' and 'to resuscitate', applied to his different fields of intervention, became recurrent themes of the new ministerial programme.

The old agricultural academies had disappeared during the Revolution together with the other Royal Academies; Neufchâteau contributed to re-establishing them as an essential means of promoting improvement and innovation. The confiscation and sale of Church and émigré lands had brought about an important transfer of agricultural property, but many of the new owners had simply seized on a profitable investment. Although generally quite prosperous and often well educated, they were not necessarily concerned with or well informed about new techniques and improvements in cultivation. To stimulate and guide their interest, Neufchâteau created a journal, the *Feuille du cultivateur* (Farmer's Pages), dedicated to such questions; he also proposed that agriculture should feature among the basic subjects taught in schools. A major problem at the time was deforestation. Already denounced in many of the *cahiers* of 1789, it had worsened during the years of financial crisis. Cutting down woods was a quick way to get ready cash, and the value of the Directory's unsuccessful territorial mandates rested largely on the easily disposable resource represented by forests. Neufchâteau promoted a national campaign to replant trees, engaging his poetical vein in the celebration of woods as 'natural temples' that the Republic must raise to liberty all over France.

The development of the system of internal navigation on rivers and canals – essential for the growth of trade – was another important objective. The project of a network of waterways across the whole of France had been conceived in the 1770s under the monarchy. Entrusted to the École Royale des Ponts et Chaussées (Royal School of Bridges and Roads), it implied a major engagement on the part of the State both in financial terms, and in order to overcome boundaries and regional claims. During the Revolution the technical difficulties caused by the war, such as the lack of materials and workforce, had been aggravated by administrative confusion over who was in charge (the École Royale had been replaced by the new École Polytechnique in 1794) and what legislative measures were needed. By the time Neufchâteau took over the dossier, the obstacles were more formal than technical. The minister found himself engaged in a fierce legal battle against a maze of rights of passage, unauthorized constructions, local regulations and all manner of bureaucratic constraints.[16]

On 7 April 1799 Neufchâteau inaugurated the Museum of the Louvre. It had been established on 10 August 1793 (the first anniversary of the fall of the monarchy) as the Musée Central des Arts to make the artworks previously collected in royal palaces available to the public. Unfortunately, only a few months later the building had had to be closed, since water was seeping down from the roof into the galleries. In 1796–7 the Italian campaigns brought to Paris an additional mass of antiquities, statues and paintings requisitioned from the occupied territories, and soon afterwards more archaeological finds and treasures arrived from Egypt. Neufchâteau struggled to secure funds for the restoration of the museum but succeeded in reopening at least some of the galleries (the rest were finally opened to the public two years later, on 14 July 1801).[17]

Another important task was the reorganization of schools. Revolutionary legislators had aimed to create a national network of State schools, accessible to all and free of charge, to replace those once provided by various religious orders. This ambitious project had been subsequently scaled down to the establishment of a semi-private system in which the State paid the teachers' wages while the upkeep of schools was financed by fees charged to the pupils' families; the result was, inevitably, the emergence of considerable inequality in the educational provision across the country.

Neufchâteau tried to reorganize the hierarchy of schools – primary, general and special – improving buildings and supplies, and creating bursaries to allow gifted pupils from poor families to progress through the different levels of education. He was convinced that access to the sciences and the arts should no longer be reserved for the wealthy. All this yet again required additional resources, with the complication that schoolteachers were among those who were unwilling to work for paper money. At the end of his mandate, the minister had not only succeeded in financing his various projects, but left in the public coffers a large sum in 'secret funds' that he might legitimately have kept for himself.[18]

While the mandate of the interior ministry encompassed diverse fields, a common problem – and one that Neufchâteau readily identified – was the difficulty created by poor communication at all levels of the administration. Existing regulations as to what sort of buildings were allowed to stand on the banks of waterways (such as mills, locks or sheds) were obscure and contradictory, generating complaints and litigations. Books supplied to primary schools were beyond the reading capacity of most pupils, and he was happy to design himself suitable didactic tables to be displayed on schoolroom walls. The protection of the interests of playwrights – a cause naturally close to his heart – was poorly served by murky and incoherent legislation on copyright. The old regime was over, but the fog associated with the mysteries of bureaucracy lingered, impeding the 'simple and regular march' necessary to the functioning of republican institutions.

Neufchâteau soon realized that the reason for local administrations failing to obey the government's instructions was often that they could not understand them, and that, conversely, ministers often lacked basic information on the specific conditions of the *départements*. As a remedy, he took pride in drafting circulars of great clarity and precision. In parallel, he promoted a system of regular inquiries, sending off questionnaires on such subjects as demography, the supply of agricultural products, manufacturing, schools, hospitals and the financing and taxation of communes. The exercise had already been attempted by his predecessor, Pierre Bénézech, without any results. The more persistent Neufchâteau introduced a system of incentives and rewards to encourage the local authorities to respond. In 1799 the former Place Royale in Paris was rechristened Place des Vosges to honour the first *département* – his own *département* – that had been able to complete its tax returns.[19]

Neufchâteau is generally credited with having introduced a form of 'descriptive statistics' in French public administration. Thanks to him, regular inquiries were generalized and became standard practice.[20] It is easy in retrospect to ridicule the ambition that led him to publish the collection of his ministerial circulars (in three volumes), as if they were a serious literary work. The former poet was indeed happy to put his signature in 1799 to a collection of writings which included a *Manuel républicain*, with instructions on the new system of weights and measures; a *Méthode pratique de lecture*; and a handbook of mnemonic techniques for schoolchildren. In his mind, nothing was beneath a minister's attention in the service of the public good.

In the Temple of Industry

An episode that provides a more vivid illustration of the philosophy behind Neufchâteau's ministerial activities is the inauguration of the first 'Exhibition of the Products of French Industry' ('Exposition publique des produits de l'industrie française') in September 1798. The minister of the interior was responsible for organizing the celebrations for the anniversary of the Republic, and in Paris these were on a grand scale. The occasion generally combined the usual features of popular festivals – food, music, games and dancing – with patriotic celebrations including speeches, recitals and allegorical masques. While some detachments of infantry and cavalry animated the scene to the sound of trumpets and drums, the general tone of the events was civic rather than military, without the exhibition of weaponry characteristic of today's 14 July parades.

In 1798 Neufchâteau decided to exploit the festivities for the sixth anniversary of the Republic, turning them into a major promotional event for French industry and trade. The choice was not a casual one, since the difficult situation of French commerce, and its consequences for the national economy, was at the centre of his preoccupations, as is shown by the report he addressed to the Directory on 6 August 1798 (19 Thermidor Year VI).[21] Predictably, French trade had been negatively affected by the war and by the decline of luxury consumption (luxury goods being the most important French exports) brought about by the Revolution. The diminished balance of trade in France's favour, the report argued, was a major cause of the persistent scarcity of coinage, and factories, deprived of their usual outlets, had also suffered. Now that durable peace was finally in sight – Napoleon had recently signed the peace treaty of Campo-Formio with Austria – Neufchâteau thought it time to boost production, giving French factories a new impulse. He was convinced that the Republic's success was crucially dependent on its capacity to compete with its great rival, England, in the international markets.

To meet the anniversary deadline, the exhibition had to be set up in a hurry. Neufchâteau recruited the architect Jean-François-Thérèse Chalgrin and 68 arcades were erected hastily all around the grounds of the Champ de Mars – the traditional location of republican events – to display the products.[22] At the centre stood the Temple of Industry, a neoclassical structure supported by columns, which served as a stage for official speeches and prize-giving ceremonies. Because of the short notice, only about 110 artisans and manufacturers were able to take part in this first iteration of the exhibition, although their numbers would increase considerably once the event became a regular occurrence. The trade exhibitions continued, under different regimes, until 1849, growing considerably in scale and anticipating the 'universal' exhibitions of the second half of the nineteenth century.

The products on display included clocks, mathematical and medical instruments, chimneys and stoves, porcelain and pottery, cutlery, blades, filigree jewellery, leather goods and various types of cotton cloth and lace. An eccentric inventor, Nicolas-Jacques Conté, presented the first ever coloured pencils, and visitors could admire the *keratome* (an instrument for performing cataract operations), the wonderful metronome-clock by the famous clockmaker Abraham-Louis Breguet (the firm had recently acquired a prestigious customer, Napoleon), and an unnamed mechanical device that showed 'the divisions in the new republican system of measures'. Medals were given in recognition of exceptional exhibits – Breguet received one – but in principle prizes were reserved for inventions and new technology that could be reproduced for further use.[23]

The opening ceremony was marked by a curious procession in which the centrepieces, among the usual military bands and civil authorities in their tricoloured feathered hats, were the artworks – antique statues, paintings by Italian masters and suchlike – captured during the recent military campaigns. It was a peculiar version of a Roman triumph, where the victorious generals were notably absent while the spoils of conquest marched, as it were, by themselves (carried on carts), under the vigilant guard of distinguished members of the Institute. In his opening speech Neufchâteau set forth his views on the meaning of the event. He praised the merits of a 'free government founded upon virtue and industry'. The old regime had set all manner of obstacle to the progress of industry, protecting privileged corporations and imposing restrictions. The Revolution, on the contrary, had 'proclaimed the freedom of work, and opened the path to man's genius'. Naturally there had been difficulties, but these had been overcome: 'political troubles, inseparable from circumstances, domestic and foreign wars [had] in vain opposed themselves to the progress [of industry]: industry had triumphed over factions, over circumstances, over the war . . . All over France numerous workshops had stood firm among the storms.'

Then the minister took inspiration from the display of ancient artworks to explain that the traditional distinction between 'liberal' and 'useful' arts should be abandoned, following in this the teachings of Francis Bacon and Denis Diderot. The old regime had humbled and despised those who practised the mechanical arts, while workers (*ouvriers*) and artists must be equally honoured and rewarded. Human activity satisfied basic human needs – food, clothing, housing – but the arts could not confine themselves to what was strictly necessary, or life would be 'sad and savage'. Instead they expanded the scope of human needs: 'they embellish their products; they exploit the three kingdoms of nature and the four parts of the world; they combine elegance and convenience, enjoyment and riches'.[24]

In conclusion, Neufchâteau stressed the direct connection between Revolution, the arts and liberty. The arts – agriculture, industry and commerce – could flourish only in a climate of freedom, such as the one the Revolution had strived to create. Conversely, the arts were necessary to consolidate victory and peace, making the conquests of the Revolution secure, because 'industry [was] immortal'. The minister's personal interpretation of modern liberty had a distinctively Smithian flavour to it. He endorsed the broad liberal view that held that political freedom and economic progress depend on each other. For him, progress was identified mainly with technological innovation, and freedom with the enjoyment of consumption. Under the arcades of the Temple of Industry, republican virtue revealed its new, post-revolutionary identity: a force in the service of commercial society, of the capacity to fulfil a higher level of collective needs.

Balancing acts

While most of Neufchâteau's tentacular activities could be carried out, as it were, under the radar of Directorial politics, in the long run it was impossible for him to escape the crossfire between the Directory and the two Councils. Between 1797 and 1799 the Directory found it increasingly difficult to function without coming into open conflict with the legislative Councils. The inevitable tension between the two powers was aggravated by the persisting divisions between royalists and Jacobins within the Councils and in public opinion. The elections of 4 September 1797 (18 Fructidor Year V) produced a royalist majority, while those of 18 June 1799 (30 Prairial Year VII) returned a Jacobin one. The swing from right to left threatened the precarious balance of the government, which applied itself to suppressing the electoral results. The impact of the elections was amplified by the constant menace of insurrection and conspiracy hatched by both political sides to overturn the regime, a threat that provided the opportunity for the executive to 'purge' the Councils.[25]

In this unstable context, Neufchâteau found himself in a vulnerable position. Even during his brief mandate as Minister of the Interior (between September 1798 and July 1799), he was never a strong political player when compared to such personalities as Paul Barras, Reubell or Sieyès; as a result, he was generally sidelined by his colleagues in their ongoing competition to control the government. The reason for this may have been lack of ambition on his part (at least in this area), but also the fact that he did not have the support of either of the dominant parties. He was neither a former Terrorist nor a true regicide; persecuted by Terror, he had never belonged to the Jacobin or Girondin factions. At the same time, he felt no sympathies for the monarchical cause, and, in particular, he was strongly opposed to the royalists' pressing demand for pardon on behalf of refractory priests.

It was during his second ministerial mandate that Neufchâteau had to face the full hostility of the Councils. The ministry of the interior was, as it is today, responsible for organizing elections. In preparation for those of June 1799, he addressed a circular to the central administrations, urging them to support the government against the threat of royalist conspiracy. This initiative – a clear abuse of his prerogatives – was predictably attacked in both Councils. However, by an odd coincidence, it was not this questionable political intervention, but rather his promotion of a contested theatrical performance, that led to his resignation.

The object of contention was the (now largely forgotten) opera *Adrien, emperor de Rome* (1791) by Étienne-Nicolas Méhul, which was performed in Paris on 4 June 1799. Based on a subject by Pietro Metastasio, it had a similar plot to the contemporary *La clemenza di Tito* by Mozart: a potentially despotic ruler refrains from abusing his power, bending to the claims of friendship, love and clemency.[26] Originally scheduled to be staged in 1792, *Adrien* had been censored by the monarchy. In 1798 the author tried once again to have it performed; hoping to make it less controversial, he demoted Hadrian from emperor to mere general, and a 'triumphal march', originally in the score, was also prudently set aside.

However, in the circumstances, the switch from emperor to military commander was not an especially astute choice, since – six months before Brumaire – victorious generals were a greater source of concern in France than emperors. The Councils claimed they recognized an allusion to Napoleon, and Neufchâteau was attacked (once again) for sponsoring a performance that promoted 'anti-civic' sentiments. Accused, unjustly, of having embezzled public funds to satisfy his questionable operatic taste, he was finally forced to resign.

Just as had happened with *Pamela*, it seems unlikely that Neufchâteau had sponsored the opera with a specific political agenda in mind, or indeed that the Councils really believed their own accusations. As in the case of Reubell and Merlin, denouncing members of the executive for corruption was a standard move in the ongoing fight between legislative and executive. Possibly Neufchâteau was only paying the price for his too visible and ambitious cultural policies and independence from parties. At the time, although Napoleon's celebrity was growing and the ghost of Oliver Cromwell was being agitated, the project of the coup of Brumaire with the general as its military pivot had not yet taken shape. When it did, Neufchâteau was out of office and played no part in the conspiracy. On the other hand, he had already met Napoleon and, predictably, had fallen under his spell.

The price of fidelity

Towards the end of 1797 Napoleon returned incognito to Paris, avoiding any popular acclaim for his victories in Italy. A few days after his arrival, the Directors held a grand reception in his honour at the Luxembourg. There are several accounts of this event from those who were present, including a distinctively lukewarm one by Germaine de Staël.[27] By contrast, only one newspaper reported on the private dinner hosted by Neufchâteau; carried away by the general excitement, the author of the article claimed that Napoleon had discussed mathematics with the scientist Pierre-Simon de Laplace, metaphysics with Sieyès, poetry with Marie-Joseph Chénier (brother of André Chénier, the poet guillotined in July 1794), legislation with Pierre Daunou, and culture with his host. While it is difficult to imagine such dinner conversations in real life, the report shows at least that Napoleon and Neufchâteau had met privately before the end of the latter's ministerial mandate.

Shortly after the coup of Brumaire, Neufchâteau was appointed to the Senate, the new council of lifelong nominees created by the Constitution of 1799 (Year VIII). It was a prestigious and well-remunerated position, albeit one that put an end to his frenetic ministerial activism. In the circumstances, he was probably relieved to be out of the way of further political infighting. He held the post, with varying responsibilities, until Napoleon's abdication in 1814.

On 2 December 1804, in his capacity as president of the Senate, Neufchâteau was responsible for presenting to the First Consul, 'now that he had brought the ship of the Republic into port', the request to turn his lifelong magistracy into the hereditary position of 'Emperor of the French'.[28] A full account of the circumstances leading to this transition from Consulate to Empire is beyond the scope of this book. A series of attempts on Napoleon's life had focused public attention on the fragility of a regime that rested almost entirely on his person, promoting the idea of hereditary rule. Although the declared model was that of England's Glorious Revolution of 1688, the notion of 'empire' was preferred to that of 'monarchy' since it marked a clear discontinuity from the old regime. The term 'empire' belonged to the republican tradition and had been used since 1792 to describe France's position as an international power, expanding its dominion over its colonies and over other nations.

In the text of the oath agreed between the Senate and Napoleon, the latter engaged himself to respect the integrity of French territory, the freedom of religion, the equality of rights, and political and civil freedom, while a reference to the liberty of the press present in an earlier draft was dropped. The acquisition of national properties (*biens nationaux*) was declared irreversible, and taxes could be imposed only 'within the terms of the law'. The emperor governed in view of 'the interest, happiness and glory of the French people', and by their consent. He was, in republican terms, a magistrate and a constitutional ruler. To the official text of the oath, Neufchâteau added: 'It is at this price that the nation promises to be faithful to you; her vow and yours reflect and guarantee one another' – a comment that stressed the contractual dimension of the new regime.[29]

There were predictable objections to this interpretation, such as that set forth by Carnot at the Tribunate: that republican magistracies were, by definition, non-hereditary, and the notion of a republican empire could well be regarded as an oxymoron.[30] The analogy with the Glorious Revolution might have worked for someone belonging to a collateral line of the Bourbons (such as the Orléans), but not for a general with no connection whatever to the legitimate royal family; Napoleon was inevitably more Cromwell than William of Orange. Overall, however, the political class rallied around the Empire as the inevitable consequence of the choice they had made collectively at Brumaire.

As a tepid republican, Neufchâteau had no reason to be troubled by the new regime. Indeed, for a few years he was genuinely enthusiastic about the hero Napoleon, whom he judged 'superior to any consul or king' of the past. In his honour Neufchâteau returned to his early vocation of court poet, composing verses for such public occasions as the celebration of the victory of Austerlitz with the capture of 360 Prussian flags and of Frederick the Great's sword, brought back in triumph to the Invalides from Berlin. Neufchâteau meanwhile accumulated honorary titles: member of the Académie (he was already a member of the Institute), Chevalier of the Légion d'Honneur, Count of the Empire. Aware of his past as a playwright, the emperor graciously entrusted him with the reform of the Comédie Française, the theatre that had been the stage of Neufchâteau's arrest in 1793.

This phase of hero worship, during which Neufchâteau engaged in what an acid observer described as '*les affaires laudatives*', lasted until about 1807. After that, however, he seems to have lost heart. 'The hero', he observed cryptically, 'has changed. I remain silent.'[31] Although he retained his senatorial post, he withdrew gradually from the political scene, concentrating his efforts on the activities of the various learned societies to which he belonged. He also focused on cultivating his garden – literally, rather than in the metaphorical sense of Voltaire's *Candide*. Within the grounds of his *hôtel particulier* on rue Saint-Honoré, he created a vegetable garden with a special place for potatoes: a new addition to the French diet promoted by his friend the pharmacist Antoine-Augustin Parmentier. By the time Louis XVIII returned to Paris, Neufchâteau was able to meet him, quite innocently, in his capacity as president of the Société Générale d'Agriculture, presenting him with the sixteen volumes of the society's proceedings.

From Voltaire to Victor Hugo

For all his hard work and goodwill, Neufchâteau had never become the new Voltaire, and he was clever and modest enough to recognize this fact. He did not possess Voltaire's genius and vision; he had not set France on fire with his writings, gaining the admiration or the hatred of the whole of Europe. His struggle against the old regime had been sincere, but prudent rather than heroic, in the spirit of the times rather than original. Today his diligent, solid contribution to the shaping of modern French institutions is largely forgotten, even by historians. He had successfully penetrated the mysteries of bureaucracy, but – as in the case of the masonic rites he practised – the price he paid was the impossibility of revealing them to the public, who would never be able to appreciate their depth.

In 1817 the fifteen-year-old Victor Hugo, a candidate in a competition set by the Académie, addressed some flattering verses to Neufchâteau, recalling the Voltaire connection of his distant youth. The two exchanged epistles in rhymes; Neufchâteau invited the young poet to dinner and offered help, but declined the flattery. He had come to see Voltaire's endorsement – Neufchateau wrote – '*sans vanité*', without vanity, as a tribute to his precocity rather than to his talent. He hoped the same would not be true of young Hugo.[32] Over the following years, until the time of his death in 1828, he continued to publish profusely, producing, among other titles, works connected with the Société d'Agriculture, a translation of William Robertson's *History of Charles V* (1769), essays on Pierre Corneille, Blaise Pascal and Alain-René Le Sage, an ode to criminal justice, a study on the invention of a new type of windmill, and a poem in three parts entitled *Les Trois Nuits d'un goutteux* (The Three Nights of the Gouty), inspired by his experience of the complaint. He never ceased to pursue his vocation as a useful, as well as less useful, writer.

6

Unsuited to the Post: Emmanuel Sieyès (1748–1836)

Emmanuel Sieyès was elected twice to the Directory. The first time was in October 1795, when the new executive was first established; on that occasion he came fourth on the list of five names chosen by the two Councils, the ranking being based on the number of votes each candidate had received. He declined the appointment, however, claiming cryptically that he was 'unsuited to the post'. The tone of the letter he addressed to the president of the Elders to announce his refusal was somewhat frosty; he could not serve his country as Director, he wrote, because the position required the confidence of all parties, while he had since the beginning of the Revolution been the target of their combined hostility.[1]

Some contemporaries, such as Paul Barras, believed that Sieyès' gesture was motivated by his implacable dislike of his designated co-Directors, especially Jean-François Reubell. Other commentators have stressed his disapproval of the Constitution of 1795, which was drafted without his own proposals being considered, let alone adopted. It is true that when he was elected to the Directory for the second time, in May 1799 after Reubell's deselection, Sieyès accepted the post because he apparently expected imminent changes to the Constitution. Since the text of 1795 stated that constitutional revision was possible only after nine years, any such changes would have involved the violation of this disposition.[2] All things considered, Sieyès' association with the Directory had a negative connotation from the start, and by claiming that he was unsuited to the position, he really meant that the new collegial executive was inadequate: not good enough for him, not good enough *tout court*. Yet his joining it, only months before the coup of Brumaire, represented his last chance to exercise a significant impact upon the evolution of the revolutionary process.

Historians have been intrigued by the gap between Sieyès' towering reputation as political theorist, pioneering constitutionalist and inspirer of 1789, and his relatively marginal role in revolutionary politics, where the chance to exercise his leadership constantly eluded him. But the first to be puzzled by this imbalance between fame and power, prestige and influence, was Sieyès himself. Throughout his career he nourished a scarcely hidden resentment for what he saw as a deplorable lack of recognition of his own unique contribution and superior abilities.

Various explanations have been provided for Sieyès' failure to play a relevant role in the different revolutionary regimes: his inability to dominate the assemblies for lack of a powerful voice or imposing physique; his taste for backroom arrangements; his fear for his life and the consequent avoidance of open confrontation; his preference for abstract schemes over pragmatic compromises. While there is some truth in all these suggestions, none of them seems conclusive. For all his love of philosophical speculation, Sieyès was seriously interested in the practice of government, not just in formulating principles, or he might have retired, as others did, after the dissolution of the Constituent Assembly in 1791. So what went wrong in his repeated attempts to achieve power? How did he finally find himself in the role of liquidator of the Directorial Republic?[3]

A path contrary to nature

Sieyès was the only one of the Directors to have followed a career in the Church. The son of a postmaster with a large, devout family of limited means, he was expected from a young age to become a priest.

Jacques-Louis David, *Emmanuel Joseph Sieyès*, 1817, oil on canvas.

Placed in a similar position, Merlin de Douai – also intended for the clergy by a pious family – refused to comply and instead qualified for the bar (see Chapter Four). Perhaps Sieyès' parents were more insistent (there were tearful scenes with his mother), or perhaps he lacked the determination to oppose their authority. His frail constitution – nobody imagined that he would live as he did to his late eighties – probably contributed to the choice. The biographical *Notice* that appeared at the beginning of 1795, largely inspired if not actually written by Sieyès himself, describes a naive fourteen-year-old forced to follow 'a path contrary to his own natural inclination': a painful situation that led the boy to develop 'a savage melancholia' and to seek refuge in the study of philosophy.[4]

Whatever the pressure exercised upon him, Sieyès' acceptance was not sustained by any religious sentiment. Even before he could refer openly to religion as 'superstition', he clearly considered the positions he occupied in the clerical hierarchy as mere administrative offices, never showing the slightest interest in the sacramental or pastoral sides of his functions. When he surprised the Constituent Assembly by speaking in defence of ecclesiastical property rights, his view was dictated by juridical and political considerations, rather than by any respect for or attachment to the Church.

Setting aside the question of their impact on his character and intellectual make-up, Sieyès' years as a priest – from the early 1770s to 1788 – gave him an acute sense of the frustrating nature of patronage, a sentiment of injustice that he seems to have felt more vividly than the rest of his future colleagues. Naturally, anyone growing up under the old regime must have been aware of the weight of privilege; however, some careers, such as the legal profession, offered greater independence and gave wider scope to individual talent. Although in time Sieyès acquired a reputation as a theorist of constitutional law, he was not a jurist in the technical sense of the term, having neither trained as a lawyer (indeed, he despised lawyers) nor occupied any office in the magistracy. Within the clergy his advancement was entirely dependent on the goodwill of his patron, Bishop Jean-Baptiste-Joseph de Lubersac.[5] The young cleric's correspondence is filled with bitter remarks whenever his expectations for promotion were frustrated or disattended. His unsuccessful pursuit of a position in the service of Mme Sophie (one of the king's aunts) dragged on for years until her death in 1782.

On the positive side, Sieyès' ecclesiastical posts offered him an experience he could not have acquired otherwise, that of the pre-revolutionary ecclesiastical assemblies.[6] In the late 1770s, when attached to the diocese of Tréguier, he was one of the delegates of the clergy to the Estates of Brittany. Inherited from the ancient duchy, this assembly was summoned twice a year to discuss financial and fiscal issues; interestingly, the vote was by head rather than by order as in the Estates General. In any case, the nobility had an overwhelming majority, with 1,300 delegates against fifty each for the clergy and Third Estate. Following his promotion to *grand vicaire* of Chartres in 1780, Sieyès was chosen by his bishop to represent the clergy at the Assembly of the Orléanais, one of the provincial assemblies established in 1787 in an attempt to increase regional participation. He served on various committees, especially the Comité pour les Vingtièmes, which dealt with fiscal reform, the subject at the very heart of the political debate.[7]

These activities, however instructive, were only the exterior side of Sieyès' engagement. The other side was the mass of readings and commentaries on both classic and contemporary works that he continued to accumulate over two decades and that led him to develop his own theory of the principles of political authority. Somehow the financial crisis faced by the monarchy in the late 1780s acted as a catalyst, bringing together the speculative and the political dimensions of Sieyès' vision. The result was the production of the two pamphlets that made his reputation: the *Essai sur les privilèges* (1788) and *Qu'est-ce que le Tiers Etat?* (1789), in which he expressed in vivid and accessible terms his rejection of aristocratic privilege, and elucidated the new doctrine of national sovereignty and representative government.[8]

Mahomet at the Constituent Assembly

At the mature age of 41, Sieyès saw his life entirely transformed by the success of these works. Suddenly he was famous, his opinion solicited, his views commented on, and he was received in the most prestigious political salons, including those of the ladies Condorcet, Necker, Helvétius and Genlis. His name has been associated with various masonic lodges bearing such suggestive names as the Confédération des Amis de la Vérité or the Club de la Propagande; he became a member of the Club de Valois, which gravitated around the Duke of Orléans, and was later accused of having contributed to the production of pamphlets commissioned by the duke through the intermediary of his secretary Pierre-Ambroise Choderlos de Laclos, allegations Sieyès always refuted. More crucially, he was elected to the Estates General, although for the rest of his life he maintained that he had not wished to be chosen and had done nothing to obtain the position. Unlike other deputies, Sieyès had no local constituency to support him. He had left his native town of Fréjus in southeastern France in his early teens to study in Paris, first at the Seminar of Saint-Sulpice, then at the Sorbonne; after that his duties had taken him to Brittany and Chartres. His newly acquired fame was not such as to favour his designation as representative of the clergy by his superiors. Instead, he was elected one of the twenty delegates of the Third for Paris.

In his *History of the French Revolution*, Jules Michelet recalled how the man who had 'seen, formulated and calculated' the new 'great movement' arrived at Versailles several days after the opening of the Estates on 5 May 1789, because of delays in verifying the election of the large Parisian contingent.[9] Even as a late arrival, Sieyès made his mark by proposing, on 16 June, that the Assembly of the Third should style itself 'Assembly of the Representatives of the Nation', inviting the delegates of the nobility and clergy to join it. In evoking this episode, the *Notice* stressed the fact that the Revolution did not begin – as many seemed to believe – as a revolt, a 'popular explosion'; instead, it was pronounced *d'office* by the National Assembly. In other words, by his initiative Sieyès was really its author. Sieyès made his entrance into the Constituent Assembly haloed by the glory of his founding gesture. Even the prestigious leader of the Third, the Count of Mirabeau, addressed him with deference, calling him in his letters 'Mahomet', an allusion to his role of prophet of the revolutionary movement. Sieyès reciprocated by naming the count 'Hercules of liberty'.[10]

As time went by, however, Sieyès appeared increasingly isolated and faded gradually from the centre of the political stage. Was this because of his political views, as they emerged from the debates, or because of his personal attitude? It is true that the outcome of the deliberations of the Constituent Assembly did not reflect Sieyès' own vision of the new French nation, only partial elements of it; but then, nobody else's project can be said to have prevailed. The constitutional monarchists led by Jean-Joseph Mounier – the most influential group in 1789 – were defeated in their attempt to establish a bicameral legislative modelled on the English system; they were also forced to compromise on the nature of the royal veto, giving the king the right to suspend only temporarily the measures voted for by the assembly, not to block them altogether. Sieyès had been in favour of bicameralism, but not in the version proposed by Mounier with a hereditary senate modelled on the English House of Lords. He was also opposed to any form of royal veto, be it suspensive or absolute; although at this stage he was not against the monarchy, he considered the king simply as an element within the Constitution, not as an individual invested with special prerogatives. Pressure exerted on him by Antoine Barnave to vote for the suspensive veto failed.[11]

According to witnesses, when Sieyès presented to the assembly his draft for the Declaration of Rights in 32 articles, which included the question of the exercise of sovereignty and representation, his text sounded 'dry, metaphysical, obscure and fatiguing' and failed to gain support.[12] His design for the division of the territory into *départements*, another element in his project of a structure for national representation, was adopted, but with several correctives of which he disapproved. On two issues – compensation for the loss of the tithe (or *dime*, the tenth part of landed revenues paid to the Church) and the confiscation of ecclesiastical property – Sieyès' position in defence of the Church's prerogatives was misinterpreted. He believed in preserving property rights in all circumstances and thought that starting a crusade against the Catholics, after acknowledging the rights of

Protestants and Jews, made no sense and would prove counterproductive. Instead, the impression he conveyed was that of a priest (he was, after all, still addressed as *abbé*) anxious to defend the privileges of his own corporation.[13] He took another unpopular stand on the question of the liberty of the press. He was in favour of abolishing censorship but argued that writers should be responsible by law for any calumnies and false allegations, a position that was unacceptable to defenders of the unlimited freedom of the press, such as the radical journalist Jean-Paul Marat.[14]

On balance, some of Sieyès' views were clearly more moderate than those of the majority, inviting accusations of 'bourgeois liberalism' from later Jacobin historiography. Others, such as his ideas on constitutional control, were more advanced, to the point of proving unintelligible to those who looked to him for guidance. But it is not from the degree of success of his proposals that one can measure Sieyès' actual influence. On that front there were no obvious winners in the Constituent Assembly. The relevant factor was rather his incapacity or unwillingness to acknowledge the dynamics of the assembly itself – a large body representing a variety of interests and ideological positions – once it got under way.

In her *Considerations on the French Revolution* (1818–20), Germaine de Staël, a direct witness to the functioning of the Constituent Assembly, lamented the divisions present even within the large majority of the deputies who were favourable to constitutional monarchy. Divided by individual ambition, personal vanity and factional rivalry, the 'elegant leaders of the popular party' were unable to work together to achieve their common objective and finally succumbed to the better-organized and more disciplined Jacobins.[15] In this fluid and unstable setting, Sieyès, who was initially close to Mirabeau despite their obvious differences, failed to find either associates or followers.

His strong anti-aristocratic prejudices were directed from the start against the 'minority of the nobility' who sided with the Revolution, among them the various Gilbert de Lafayette, Stanislas de

Clermont-Tonnerre, Louis de La Rochefoucault, Alexandre and Charles Lameth and Boniface de Castellane, who seemed to dominate the audience with their dashing presence and brilliant speeches. 'Nobody', Benjamin Constant recalled, 'detested the nobility as much as he did.'[16] Soon Sieyès' hostility was extended to those whom he called 'representatives of the lawyers': Mounier, Antoine Barnave and Adrien Duport. Somehow he convinced himself that these men were conspiring, singularly or collectively, to discredit him. While he mistrusted aristocrats and lawyers, he was of course far from feeling sympathetic towards the Jacobins, whom he regarded as vulgar and dangerous demagogues, although on some questions they may seem to have been closer to his own position.[17]

There can be no doubt that Sieyès' prejudices and diffident attitude towards these groups gained him few friends. Indeed, on some occasions he seemed determined to alienate his colleagues. When, for example, on 4 June 1790 he was elected president of the Constituent Assembly, he made a resentful speech in which he begged to be replaced, claiming that he had been appointed only in virtue of some procedural rule, rather than by a free choice of the deputies. Yet, for all his touchiness, he was not generally unwilling to take part in discussions and exchanges; on the contrary, his frequenting of clubs and salons had allowed him to develop a sociable, worldly side to his personality that might have proved politically helpful.

The problem was that Sieyès' conception of the role of representatives was distant from the reality of ordinary parliamentary politics. His vision (originally derived from his readings of Thomas Hobbes and Jean-Jacques Rousseau) did not include the presence of rival parties and failed to recognize the necessity of accommodating the different interests and opinions present in the assembly. Historians have sometimes attributed to Sieyès a taste for backroom agreements, yet every time he was involved in such negotiations and compromises, he ended up finding them unacceptable. The experience of the pamphlets that had launched him into politics confirmed his idea of a direct, immediate relationship between the electors and the individuals who represented them, without the dense and distorting filter of negotiations and alliances between parties. He even considered that all preliminary agreements on a given vote between parliamentary groups were contrary to the principle of representation.

In this spirit, during the debates in the Constituent Assembly Sieyès produced and made public texts illustrating his own views on the various questions – such as the Constitution, the Declaration of Rights, ecclesiastical property and administrative divisions – possibly hoping that they would meet with unanimous approval and re-create a direct bond between himself, the assembly and public opinion. None of them made an impact either inside or outside the house, however.[18] Paradoxically, after having invented and popularized the modern notion of national representation, Sieyès could not accept the way this worked in practice, and he resented all adjustments and deviations from his original ideal.

Into an unknown world

As time went by, Sieyès' participation in the Constituent Assembly's debates became more irregular, his health complaints more frequent, his attitude more distant. Similarly, he seemed to lose interest in the Société de 1789, which he had promoted to offset the influence of the Jacobins' club. After the dissolution of the Constituent Assembly at the end of September, in October 1791 he retired to Auteuil, giving the impression that he meant to quit politics. But this retirement did not last for long; the 'superstitious respect' that surrounded him worked once again, and on 6 September 1792 he was elected to the Convention for the *département* of the Gironde, with a large majority.[19] In his manuscript *Bases de l'ordre social* (The Foundations of Social Order; *c.* 1795), Sieyès provided the following account of his conduct during the last phase of the Constituent Assembly, and of his passage to the Convention: 'It was necessary to seek refuge in silence, a happy choice if deceptive hopes had not led me to get out of it on various occasions, even happier had I refused to join the Convention.'[20]

Just as he had done for the Estates General, Sieyès presented his election to the Convention as a burden that he had not solicited, forced upon him against his better judgement. In the *Notice* he described the new assembly, the Legislative, as 'an unknown world' in which he felt completely alien – although in fact more than ninety former constituents who had been ineligible for the Legislative were re-elected with him. It was, he claimed, a barbarous environment in which vulgar behaviour, corrupt language and brutal appetites were taken as signs of patriotism. For the members of the new legislative, 'revolution' meant no longer 'a change of government or of constitution', but rather 'a general upheaval, the complete ruin of all those relations that bound men and things together in the civil and economic order'. Even the people, in whose name the deputies pretended to act, were 'fake': not the real people of France, but 'unruly hordes of barbarians'.[21]

Despite his retrospective efforts to distance himself from the Convention, Sieyès moved among the 'barbarians' and their 'politics of the caves' very much as he had done in the Constituent Assembly: by trying to lead on the subjects that mattered to him, and occasionally baffling the deputies with some unexpected stance. At the same time, he kept away from both the Girondins and the Montagnards (although he had friends in both camps), sticking to the safer ground of the *plaine*. He was as a matter of course elected to the Constitutional Committee in charge of developing the new republican constitution, although it was the Girondin Marquis de Condorcet who became rapporteur and imposed his views. Sieyès felt the latter's project for the Constitution of 1793, by establishing universal male suffrage, would create a form of direct, rather than representative, democracy, and disapproved of it strongly. In the end he preferred for himself the role of chairman of the less controversial Committee of Public Instruction.

Sieyès intervened in the debate on the urgent matter of the reorganization of the ministry of war, presenting to the assembly an elaborate (and obscure) project that separated the activity of 'direction' from that of 'administration' of the department. His main concern, he explained, was to make sure that civil government retained full control over the conduct of the war, preventing some victorious general from becoming a dictator – a widely shared view at the time, and one that casts an interesting light on Sieyès' subsequent search for military support in view of the coup of Brumaire. When the question of the king's fate was discussed, Sieyès once again surprised his colleagues by declaring himself against holding the trial. While there is evidence that he considered Louis XVI guilty of perjury and treason – he voted for the king's culpability and death without any hesitation – his objections, in common with those of other jurists, were focused on the legitimacy of the procedure, and he may also have feared the political backlash of a trial on the Convention. After the king's death, as the assembly sank into factional conflict, Sieyès kept a very low profile in order to ensure, as he famously recalled, his own survival.[22]

In any case, Sieyès' 'colossal reputation' pursued him. The royalist propaganda accused him – largely on the grounds of fake documents – of being behind the whole politics of Terror. He was, for example, widely held responsible for the special law introduced on 17 September 1793, the Law of Suspects, although he had not served on the committee that drafted it.[23] Similarly, there was fanciful and totally unfounded speculation about his role in the liquidation of Jacques-René Hébert's and Georges Danton's factions. In the eyes of the enemies of the Revolution, he remained 'the invisible cause that directed everything'.[24] Sieyès has often been described as excessively cowardly, even by the standards of those moving in the dangerous environment of the Convention, yet one can see why his extreme prudence was justified. While the royalists saw him as a bloodthirsty revolutionary, the Jacobins suspected him of conspiring against them all along, and his natural haughtiness, convoluted interventions and protracted silences helped to feed this legend of him as the worker of mysterious designs. In fact, he had no notable relations, good or bad, with Maximilien Robespierre and his circle, and he played no part in the events of Thermidor.

Even after the fall of Robespierre, Sieyès did not feel quite safe and kept out of the limelight, no doubt fearing accusations of complicity in the previous regime. In December 1794 he was chosen by ballot to preside over the trial brought by Merlin against four members of the Convention and of the former Committee of Public Safety, who stood accused of 'Terrorism': Bertrand Barère, Jacques-Nicolas Billaud-Varenne, Jean-Marie Collot d'Herbois and Marc-Guillaume Alexis Vadier. He tried desperately to avoid the responsibility, first resigning, then claiming his name had been placed in the urn through some irregularity of procedure, but he was finally forced to accept by the protests of his colleagues; the accused were sentenced to deportation to French Guiana.[25]

A few months later, in March 1795, Sieyès was elected with Reubell and Merlin to the Diplomatic Committee, a subsection of the Committee of Public Safety. France had by then concluded the negotiations over the Treaty of Basel, the peace agreements with Prussia and Spain that would be signed in July; instead Sieyès was responsible for discussing the establishment in Holland of the Batavian Republic, a negotiation he conducted in very exacting terms. Much as he disliked Reubell, he agreed with him fully on the defence of France's frontiers and the consolidation of the Republic's territorial conquests. In matters of international politics, at least, there were no significant differences between him and his hated colleague.[26]

Between constitutions

The issue that really mattered to Sieyès, the one for which he had probably prepared his political comeback with the publication of the *Notice*, was the new Constitution. The Thermidorian Convention was called to decide on the status of the Constitution of 1793, suspended on account of the war: should it come into force or be replaced by a new one? Most deputies regarded that constitution as far too democratic and radical (even though they had voted for it two years earlier), but they feared popular protest if they set it aside. Once again, Sieyès confused the assembly by defending the legitimacy of the text of 1793. That constitution, he explained, had been approved by the people by referendum; it was 'respectable' and in any case the Constitution was the supreme law. Since his strong opposition to the late Condorcet's design was well known, his defence of it puzzled the deputies.[27] Cambacérès pointed out with some irony that what Sieyès said was not always easy to understand.[28] It is difficult to tell whether he was truly in doubt as to the legitimacy of the procedure, or whether he was just playing for time, waiting for the Convention to take the initiative.

Following the invasion of the assembly by an angry crowd demanding the application of the text of 1793, Cambacérès proposed – as a delaying tactic – the creation of a committee, the Commission of the Eleven, to 'examine' the question. This Commission was clearly expected to write a new constitution, rather than reviving the old one, yet Sieyès declined to be part of it, using as a pretext his mandate at the Committee of Public Safety and claiming that the two offices were incompatible. In his *Memoirs* the future Director Louis-Marie de La Révellière-Lépeaux accused Sieyès of having deliberately kept out of the Eleven so as to draft and present his own project without sharing or discussing it with his colleagues. Sieyès probably thought the Eleven would produce no new ideas, and that the crucial development of the Constitution would occur during discussions in the assembly; indeed, Merlin and Cambacérès – generally keen to offer their expertise – made the same choice.[29]

But how distant were Sieyès' views on the new Constitution from those outlined in the draft by the Commission? From a broad political perspective, the positions were quite similar. Their common objective was to bring the Revolution to an end while preserving the principles of 1789. In practice this involved acknowledging individual rights and the sovereignty of the nation; it also implied limiting the right to vote to property owners as the true stakeholders in the Republic's fortunes, and making it clear that 'equality' meant the abolition of hereditary privileges, rather than any form of economic redistribution.[30] Another essential point was ensuring the division of powers to avoid the kind of 'dictatorship' exercised by the legislative assembly through its committees during the Terror.

On all these points Sieyès could only agree. As in the case of other Directors, it has been said that after Thermidor his position became more conservative, yet, quite apart from the fact that he abandoned the provocative tone of his early pamphlets, there were no significant changes to his understanding of citizenship and property rights, or his view that 'perfect equality' was a chimera. The only real alteration was an increased awareness after the Terror of the risk represented by insufficient limitation of constitutional powers, of the danger – in his own terms – that the *ré-publique* might become a *ré-totale*.[31] Rather, the point on which his views did significantly differ from those of the Eleven involved the means that would be necessary to ensure that limitation.

The structure designed by the Commission and finally adopted in the Constitution of 1795 was the traditional model of the horizontal separation of powers, to obtain the desired 'checks and balances' effect. However, the articulation of the competences of the two legislative Councils and the Directory proved poorly designed and inadequate. Instead of the balancing of weights and counterweights, the result was either open conflict between legislative and executive, or at best the separate and uncoordinated action of the two. Sieyès was in any case strongly opposed to this model of horizontal separation of powers, since he believed from the start that it would lead to paralysis and inaction.

What he imagined instead was a system of vertical control. In his project this was exercised by a third council, called the constitutional jury (*jury constitutionnaire*) and placed above the two legislative Councils, with the power to annul by decree any measures it considered to be against the Constitution. In Sieyès' design the jury was formed of 108 members, originally elected by the Convention, subsequently partly co-opted and partly elected; it would intervene directly in the legislative process, more than a modern constitutional court. What was unclear, however, was what relationship the jury might have with the executive, an ambiguity that resurfaced in the Constitution of 1799 (Year VIII).[32]

According to Antoine-Claire Thibaudeau – rapporteur for the Commission – the Eleven made sure that only the section of Sieyès' project concerning the formation and functioning of the jury itself was presented to the Convention. Unsurprisingly, taken apart from the rest of the constitutional design, the idea of the jury did not make much sense. While Sieyès had succeeded in bringing it to the attention of the assembly, the introduction of a third council seemed a redundant and unnecessary complication and was rejected unanimously. Once again, forced to defer to the 'first political architect', the legislators took great care to avoid following his advice. In the debate La Révellière-Lépeaux said he was afraid of those men who, 'believing themselves great, were in fact just bizarre', and who might lead the assembly into 'unknown paths' where they would all lose themselves. Bypassing the Commission had not increased Sieyès' influence, but merely placed him in a false position.[33]

The ever-present outsider

Defeated once again in his quest for the perfect constitution, Sieyès unsurprisingly declined to join the Directory, an institution, in his view, designed to express the influence of those forces that were always hostile to him, namely political parties. Having refused the top executive position, he was obviously uninterested in one of the lesser ministerial posts that other Directors occupied at various stages in their careers, but he did keep his seat on the Five Hundred. Renewing his usual posture of maintaining his own visibility at some distance from the exercise of power, he established his presence in the intellectual and political circles that gravitated around the Directory. He was elected to the Institute in the Class of Moral and Political Sciences; he frequented the salon of de Staël (where he found an admirer in the young Constant) and joined the Club de Salm, the political club formed by the left-leaning deputies as a counterweight to the royalist Club de Clichy.

Sieyès' fame was heightened by the drama of an assassination attempt. Early in the morning of 11 April 1797 a deranged man, a certain *abbé* Poule, presented himself at Sieyès' house to demand a pension or money on grounds that are not clear. When Sieyès tried to send him away, Poule took out a pistol and fired a shot that caused only superficial wounds to his victim and to himself, before he was overpowered by some of Sieyès' neighbours, alerted by the noise. Sieyès was gratified to learn that the Five Hundred were solemnly informed that afternoon of his tragic 'assassination' and celebrated his memory in suitably flattering terms, although he must have considered the possibility that on balance his colleagues preferred him dead rather than alive.[34]

Always biding his time from a distance, in May 1798 Sieyès accepted from the minister of foreign affairs Charles-Maurice de Talleyrand, with whom he entertained semi-friendly relations, the position of extraordinary ambassador of the French Republic to the court of Prussia. Although initially reluctant to take up a post abroad, Sieyès was attracted by the prospect of meeting those German intellectuals who had shown an interest in his constitutional ideas and who had in some cases become his correspondents and his friends. A translation of his political pamphlets by his biographer Konrad Oelsner had appeared in Germany in 1796, and he was especially keen to exchange ideas with the philosopher Immanuel Kant, whose writings were partially known to him through the accounts that had been published in French journals.[35]

In the earlier phase of the Revolution Kant had expressed positive views on the political developments in France. However, attempts to promote the authoritative German philosopher to theorist of the French constitutional model (partly based on a misunderstanding of his position) were unsuccessful; similarly, the project of obtaining Kant's election to the Institute in the Class of Moral and Political Sciences – to which Sieyès also belonged – was not successful. Contrary to what has sometimes been suggested, there was no direct epistolary contact between him and Sieyès, and the two theorists never met, depriving Sieyès of his hoped-for opportunity to elucidate Kant's views on the Constitution of 1795. The publication of a pamphlet entitled 'In Response to the Abbé Sieyès', allegedly by Kant but in fact an anonymous fake, must have induced the Königsberg professor to be especially cautious in his foreign contacts so as to avoid being politically compromised.[36]

On his arrival in Berlin in June, Sieyès was greeted warmly by a small crowd of revolutionary sympathizers, enjoying once again his role of oracle of 1789. By contrast, his reception at the court was predictably frosty. King Frederick William III did not share the intellectual and Francophile leanings of his predecessor, Frederick II, and considered the choice of the famous revolutionary as French ambassador to be little short of an insult. Since the Directory would not countenance Sieyès' recall, both parties managed to smooth over their differences. They went through the motions of a correct formal reception, with the ambassador making a polite speech about the good relationship between France and Prussia and praising the memory of the 'Great Frederick'. Sieyès did not, however, wear the sword as demanded by protocol.

After the peace settlements of Basel, there was no particular tension between the two countries. Still, Sieyès must have been relieved to be called back to Paris when Talleyrand informed him of his re-election to the Five Hundred in April 1799, in view of his appointment to the Directory. The minister advised him to take a military escort on his return journey to France, since two French deputies, delegates to the Congress of Rastatt, had been murdered on their way back by a squad of Hungarian hussars (see Chapter Two). Sieyès' relief must have been shared by the king of Prussia, and the ambassador's departure was marked more warmly than his arrival, with the king graciously offering the customary gift of a diamond-studded gold snuffbox carrying his portrait.

Coups d'état

When did Sieyès' partially detached observation of the French political scene turn into an active project to end the Directorial Republic? Why, when the opportunity finally presented itself in November 1799, did he fail to see that the consequences of the coup might spiral out of control? Did he really misjudge Napoleon's personality and intentions? These questions can be asked about other actors in the coup of Brumaire, but Sieyès' case is especially significant because he played a crucial role in events, lending his prestige to the operation, and because his aim was not simply to stay in power, but to promote a better, more stable constitutional order.

Sieyès' somewhat short-sighted, hazardous sponsoring of the coup has generally been explained along two main lines. The first argues that he was the victim of his own metaphysical disposition, which blinded him to the power games being played all around him, in particular by Napoleon. The second suggests that, after ten years of struggle to impose the principles of 1789 on an ungovernable political context, he had become disillusioned and simply opted for the solution that offered him the greatest personal advantage. The first reading presents him as politically naive, despite his experience, and the second as discouraged and cynical; both probably contain a part of the truth.

Most historical accounts of Brumaire are somewhat distorted by the knowledge of its final consequences: the end of the revolutionary Republic and the advent of Napoleon's personal rule. But for those who took part in or witnessed it, the coup did not represent a historical watershed, even less the prelude to some future empire. It was just one episode in a sequence of interventions designed to protect the Republic by stretching or forcing the framework of the Constitution. The implication was that once the Republic was secure, legality would be fully restored; meanwhile the constant threat of military defeat, insurrection or conspiracy kept pushing forward the horizon of this desired outcome.[37]

For all his professed respect for constitutional legitimacy, Sieyès had already played a role in two of these episodes: Fructidor in September 1797 and Prairial in June 1799. At Fructidor the result of the elections in the Year V that gave a majority to the right was annulled following the discovery of a royalist conspiracy. While it was true that some plot had been in the making, its discovery was used as a pretext to get rid of scores of political opponents who had nothing to do with it. Several deputies and two of the Directors – Balthazar François de Barthélemy and Lazare Carnot – were arrested and sentenced to deportation or fled into exile. Sieyès had not taken part in this anti-royalist purge, which was carried out by the majority of the Directory; afterwards, however, he was appointed to the committee charged with proposing 'the measures necessary to guarantee public safety', and was elected president of the Five Hundred to replace General Charles Pichegru, who stood accused of being a royalist agent.[38] As always on such occasions, military support (entrusted to General Charles-Pierre Augereau) was deployed to prevent public disorder in Paris.

The coup of Prairial was a somewhat different occasion, the reaction of the Councils against what they saw as the executive's abuse of power. Two Directors – Merlin and La Révellière-Lépeaux – were accused of various misdeeds and forced to resign. This time at least constitutional forms were preserved, although the charges were clearly a pretext; as in the case of other accusations of Directors by the assemblies, no evidence of their guilt was ever produced. By shifting the balance of the assemblies to the left, Fructidor had helped to prepare Sieyès' access to power; now Prairial gave him effective control of the Directory. However, if on the seventh anniversary of the Republic, held on 23 September 1799, Sieyès was celebrated as its 'first founder', Jacobin propaganda had already begun an aggressive campaign denouncing him and Barras as 'oligarchs' and enemies of the people. Once again, the Directors and their entourage thought it necessary to stage yet another coup to redress the balance and defend their political line of moderation.

Up to a point, preparations followed the well-practised script. A conspiracy against the Councils – this time supposedly orchestrated by the Jacobins, but in fact entirely fictitious – was denounced. At Napoleon's insistence there were no arrests, but the Councils were transferred, allegedly for reasons of security, to the château of Saint-Cloud outside Paris. The usual military back-up to control the capital was on hand. Sieyès' hesitation to identify his 'sword' during the previous months, namely the general ready to provide military support to the operation, has often been recalled; his choices included Generals Barthélemy-Catherine Joubert (who was killed in action at Novi during the summer), Jean Bernadotte (who refused: 'not an eagle but a blackbird', was Sieyès' acid comment) and finally Napoleon, despite or because of his obvious popularity.[39]

This time, however, plans went beyond the usual purging of undesired political opponents from institutions. All five Directors signed letters of resignation: Sieyès and Roger Ducos because they were party to the conspiracy; Barras, Louis-Jérôme Gohier and Jean-François Moulin, who were not, because they were given no choice. Following the dissolution of the Directory, the Councils were asked to vote for the abrogation of the Constitution of 1795. After a stormy confrontation between the Five Hundred and Napoleon at Saint-Cloud, the abrogation was finally endorsed by a motley group of deputies from the two Councils and by the three newly appointed Provisional Consuls: Sieyès, Ducos and Napoleon himself.

Interestingly, Sieyès, who had obviously been engaged in the preparations for the coup, had failed to draft a constitution to replace the existing one. While Napoleon faced the angry and aggressive Five Hundred gathered in the Orangerie of Saint-Cloud, Sieyès had been waiting in a room upstairs for news of the outcome. When it was all over, as they travelled back to the Luxembourg, his friend Antoine Boulay de la Meurthe was surprised to find that there was no text; in the coach Boulay took dictation of a few annotations limited to some general comments about rejecting 'brute' democracy and the necessity of representative government. In his satirical pamphlet *Letter to a Noble Lord* (1796), Edmund Burke had claimed that the *abbé* had 'whole nests of pigeon-holes' filled with ready-made constitutions of all kinds, including one in which the electors choose their representatives, and another in which the representatives choose their electors; yet on this crucial occasion it turned out that this was not the case.[40]

In the end the 'short and obscure' Constitution of 1799 (Year VIII) was drafted by two Executive Consular Commissions formed of 25 members each from the Five Hundred and the Elders. The result adopted some of Sieyès' suggestions, and his cherished jury of 1795 was resurrected as the Senate (*Sénat conservateur*). In addition to verifying that laws and decrees conformed to the Constitution, the Senate also had the task of validating the lists of those eligible to serve on the legislative Councils. Yet despite this Napoleon disliked Sieyès' design for the executive, which included a magistrate, the Great Elector, entrusted with all appointments, and two 'operative' consuls.[41] Instead, the Constitution placed three consuls at the head of the executive, with the First Consul holding the most extensive powers. An important novelty was the creation of an executive body, the Council of State, a committee of nominees in charge of coordinating legislative and executive action. It would play a crucial role during the Consulate and the Empire.

The old man in the clouds

By the beginning of 1800 Sieyès, at the age of 52, had finally arrived at the top of the political institutions, only to discover that these were now being divested of all substantial power. His role of Provisional Consul was soon over and he was replaced in the Consulate, to his great surprise, by his former minister of justice Cambacérès, whom he had always regarded as a marginal actor in his own plans. Instead, Sieyès was appointed senator and then president of the Senate, thus finding himself back at the Luxembourg, now converted from the executive's place of residence to the seat of the new council.[42] In addition to this prestigious and lucrative, if uninfluential, position, he received the gift of three substantial estates (two of them in Paris) from among the national properties, and in time various other distinctions and decorations, including the title Count of the Empire. He was to all effects 'buried in honours' by Napoleon, who was anxious to get the 'old man in the clouds' (as he described him) out of the way.[43]

The mystery of Sieyès' ambiguous attitude towards the end of the Directory, with its odd combination of careful preparation and deliberate omissions, of a craving for control and resigned impotence, remains unsolved. Convinced that the Directorial Republic was dysfunctional, he felt no compunction in destroying it. His lasting fear of a possible return of the Jacobins also played a part, and after the coup some thirty Jacobin opponents were deported (the only political casualties of the conspiracy) at his personal insistence. But what did he expect the new regime created by the Constitution of 1799 to be like? Did he really imagine that Napoleon, placed at the top of the executive, would be happy to occupy an honorary position, however lucrative that might be? The evidence does not allow us to answer these questions with any clarity or confidence.

While most Thermidorians were convinced by the circumstances to seek safety in a strong executive, Sieyès' case is unique, since it was not the executive that he wished to place at the top of the pyramid of constitutional powers to ensure their stability. For him the executive remained – as he had shown at the time of the debate on the royal veto in 1789 – a mere cog in the constitutional machine. The dominant power, in his view, was always the legislative, but instead of the representative assemblies, subject to the vagaries of elections and to the pressure of parties, he imagined a superior legislative authority that embodied the legitimacy of the Constitution without being affected by opinion. But can any constitution simply rule by itself, and if so, by what means? During the remaining 36 years of his long life, Sieyès no doubt had plenty of time – as an imperial dignitary in Paris, in comfortable exile in Brussels during the Restoration, then back in Paris after the Revolution of 1830 – to reflect on this puzzling question.

7

The Indispensable Counsel: Jean-Jacques-Régis Cambacérès (1753–1824)

The long list of positions occupied by Jean-Jacques-Régis Cambacérès during his career – from counsel at the Court of Aids (*Cour des aides*) of Montpellier in 1774 to Archchancellor of the Empire thirty years later – does not include that of Director. At the time of the election of the first Directory in October 1795, Cambacérès, who had closely followed the shaping of the new government, had been confident that he would be part of it. But a timely scandal – the discovery of a document that suggested his implication in a royalist conspiracy – intervened to sink his candidature. His hopes were revived when Emmanuel Sieyès refused the position, but once again the Councils chose Lazare Carnot as a replacement, instead of Cambacérès.

Not only was there no conspiracy, but the accusations of royalist complicity, eagerly exploited by Cambacérès' political enemies, were unfounded. Although he had been opposed to the king's trial and execution, attachment to the fallen monarchy had nothing to do with Cambacérès' stance. In common with other jurists, including Sieyès, he had doubts about the legitimacy of the Convention acting as a penal court, and believed that Louis XVI should be judged by a special board of magistrates. It is true, on the other hand, that Cambacérès was generally reluctant to adopt the radical, bellicose rhetoric of other revolutionary deputies, thus acquiring a reputation for moderation that made many suspect him of disloyalty, if not treason. His attitude was partly dictated by prudence (or even cowardice), but it also reflected the natural inclination of someone who recalled with nostalgia the tranquillity of the old regime and, as a magistrate, shied away as much as possible from the full severity of the law.[1]

The incident of the royalist plot left Cambacérès temporarily stranded as simple deputy of the Five Hundred, at the margins of the new executive that he joined only belatedly, in 1799, as minister of justice.[2] All things considered, the years of the Directory represented a setback in the steady progress of his political career, allowing him to focus instead on his flourishing practice as a legal consultant. Yet it is impossible to capture in full the nature of the Directory without coming to terms with the ever-present, indispensable, unavoidable lawyer from Montpellier. Few political figures embody as fully as he does the effort to pilot 'the vessel of the Revolution' out of the storms towards the safe shores of a pacified, stable regime.[3] Few made such a massive and lasting (if largely forgotten) contribution to the shaping of modern French institutions, among them the Council of State (1800), the new Civil Code (1804) and the Court of Audits (*Cour des comptes*; 1807).[4] When the Directory was hastily discarded in 1799 as an unhappy constitutional experiment, it was Cambacérès, as he rose to the top of the consular and imperial governments, who rescued and consolidated its achievements.

The prudent deputy

Born in Montpellier, the elder son of a family of the *noblesse de robe*, as a teenager Cambacérès had imagined for himself a brilliant future in the royal administration. Louis XV's conflict with the parliament of Paris in 1771 unsettled the whole edifice of legal institutions, however, making the traditional career prospects for the new generation of magistrates highly uncertain. Although Cambacérès' family was originally fairly wealthy, the misguided ambitions of his authoritarian, quarrelsome father resulted in costly litigation and heavy indebtedness, finally

Henri Frédéric Schopin, *Jean-Jacques Régis de Cambacérès*, 1824–42, oil on canvas.

leaving his elder son to pick up the bill.[5] In the end the young lawyer had to resign himself to taking up his father's not-so-exciting position of counsel in Montpellier's Court of Aids, a post that he was to occupy for fifteen years. Although the job was in itself uninspiring, his experience in the court proved instructive. The Court of Aids had just merged with the Court of Audits and with the Royal Estates (*Domaines*), and all these institutions dealt with fiscal matters, but from different perspectives, which included scrutinizing the fiscal position of the nobility and the expenses of the king's household. As a private lawyer, having realized early on that he had no great talent or taste for pleading, Cambacérès specialized in advising on international and commercial law. It was a sought-after expertise in Montpellier, since several prominent local families were involved in the maritime trade and profited from the economic fallout of the American war.

Serious, discreet and hard-working, the young Cambacérès was soon appreciated for his solid juridical competence and his capacity to master the most complex dossiers. It was a reputation that would accompany him for the rest of his life. Despite his professional success, the summoning of the Estates General came as a desirable opportunity for new prospects. In Montpellier, dressed in the old-fashioned black coat and wig of the magistracy, the shy, very short-sighted lawyer kept to his quiet provincial routine, yet an early visit to Paris in the company of his friend Jean-Antoine Chaptal (a distinguished chemist and future minister of the interior for the Empire) had given him a taste for a more hedonistic, pleasurable lifestyle.[6] While moving his legal practice to Paris was too hazardous, since it would involve facing harsh competition, joining the delegates of the Estates in Versailles seemed a promising start.

Cambacérès contributed to the drafting of the *cahiers des doléances*, and was duly elected as one of the two deputies of the nobility for Montpellier; unfortunately, the doubling of the number of representatives requested by the town was not endorsed by the king, and Cambacérès' election was invalidated. Instead of going to Versailles, he was first chosen as Procureur-Syndic of Montpellier, an essentially administrative post; then, in September 1791, he was elected president of the new Criminal Tribunal for the *département* of the Hérault, with a large majority. Although criminal law was not his favourite domain, he soon became an expert, especially when it came to adjusting the old legislation to the flood of new measures produced since 1789, an exercise that most of his colleagues were unable to master. His good service was rewarded in September 1792, when he was elected to the Convention. Finally, at the age of 39, he was able to begin a new life in Paris.

Cautious as ever, in the Convention Cambacérès avoided siding openly with the Girondins or the Montagnards, sitting instead with the moderate deputies of the *plaine*. Similarly, he politely declined the approaches of the Duke of Orléans, who, to Cambacérès' considerable astonishment, turned up early one morning at his modest lodgings with the explicit purpose of recruiting him to his cause – namely the plan to take the place of his cousin Louis XVI – as the duke had done with other promising deputies.[7] However, despite his effort to keep away from factional involvement, there was one question on which Cambacérès could not avoid taking sides, namely the king's trial in December 1792. He was among those who thought the monarch should be judged by some special court, not by a legislative assembly like the Convention. Defeated on this point of procedure, he led a small delegation of four lawyers who visited Louis XVI, then imprisoned at the Temple, to consult him on his choice of defence counsels.[8]

When it came to the vote in the Convention, Cambacérès, who had unsuccessfully opposed the open vote by nominal appeal, was part of the large majority who declared the king guilty, but sided with the minority who voted in favour of suspending his execution. He was not on principle an abolitionist – at least, he never expressed any legal opinion to that effect – but as a magistrate he always tried to avoid pronouncing death sentences. Moreover, in Louis XVI's case there were political considerations that pleaded for the option of keeping him alive, from the possible impact of his death on domestic and international opinion, to the value he might have as a hostage in negotiating with the coalition of European powers at war with France. In 1804, as Second Consul, Cambacérès in vain used the same arguments to persuade Napoleon to spare the life of the Duke of Enghien – a member of the Bourbon family executed for bearing arms against France – one of the rare occasions on which they disagreed.[9] Unsurprisingly, Cambacérès' ambivalent attitude at the king's trial left a negative impression on both sides. His fellow revolutionaries mistrusted him because he had opposed the death, as their readiness to believe the false accusations of conspiracy in 1795 showed. The royalists, for their part, regarded him as a regicide on the strength of his first vote on the king's culpability; it was only in 1818 that, faced with the prospect of permanent exile, he managed to clarify his position, persuading Louis XVIII of the sincere efforts he had made to save his brother's life.[10]

Master of committees

The focus of Cambacérès' activity in the Convention was his participation in different committees, an exercise of which he soon became master. During the Revolution the number of committees emanating from the assembly had grown from 3 under the Constituent Assembly to 23 under the Convention, and in 1793 a dozen had been created to replace the ministers and their departments, so that all executive tasks might be controlled by the legislative.[11] Some of these committees had a nominal membership of up to fifty deputies, but in practice few of those attended the meetings regularly or made any contribution to the drafting of reports and documents, leaving diligent professionals, such as Cambacérès, to carry out most of the work. In time, on their behalf, Cambacérès produced more than 1,000 legal opinions on different subjects. His most important commitment was to the rewriting of the Civil Code, a task first undertaken by the Committee of Legislation in May 1793. The titanic enterprise of integrating into

French legislation some 15,000 decrees voted since 1789 would be achieved only eleven years later, under the Consulate. The difficulty – in Cambacérès' metaphor – was keeping hold of the thread through the intricate labyrinth of the law. He was especially interested in questions of succession and family law, and militated for legalizing the position of 'natural' (illegitimate) children, lowering the age of majority from 25 to 21, and reducing the scope of parental authority. His proposals for the overall structure of the new code, however, were judged (not for the last time) as too elaborate and technical, and were rejected by the Convention.[12]

In the spring of 1793, before engaging in this eminently juridical undertaking, Cambacérès had contributed to the creation of two crucial revolutionary institutions: the Committee of Public Safety and the Revolutionary Tribunal. He had also contributed to drafting the famous Law of Suspects, the special measures designed for the arrest and prosecution of enemies of the Republic. It is paradoxical that the reputation of this moderate lawyer should be associated with the most distinctive symbols of revolutionary dictatorship. While his interventions in the assembly on the necessity of what became the Committee of Public Safety have attracted little attention, his contribution to the Tribunal and its special legislation represents a permanent stain on his reputation, and in later years, unsurprisingly, he attempted to deny any involvement.[13]

In both cases, Cambacérès had no intention of introducing instruments of dictatorship and persecution; he was merely trying to impose legal order on the abusive arrests and executions that were spiralling rapidly out of control. Regarding the Tribunal and the special anti-suspects legislation, the aim was to discipline the flood of arrests and sentencing of supposed public enemies carried out since the beginning of the war by all manner of central and local authority. This attempt to bring the whole machinery of repression under the control of the magistracy, introducing some legal guarantees to protect the accused, was not appreciated by the revolutionary government, which soon set it aside so as to act more speedily and without constraint. As for the formation of the Committee of Public Safety – replacing the extraordinary and improvised Committee of General Defence – the idea was to re-establish some coherent central authority to direct the Convention's actions, unravelling the confusion created by the overlapping competences of the various commissions. In practice, it meant re-creating an executive council with extensive prerogatives, although formally the Committee was merely another subcommission of the assembly.

Cambacérès told the Convention in March 1793: 'You need more than ever a firm and strong government. The existing one is weak and incoherent, organized as if there were two powers, when in practice there is only one.'[14] Later he explained:

> This was the origin of the institution that later became so dreadful. It was born of the impotence of the Convention to govern by decrees that subordinate agents were responsible for executing. The existence of an assembly uniting all powers will always require resorting to extraordinary resolutions.[15]

In other words, the Committee had been designed with the intention of preventing dictatorship, rather than making it possible. Significantly, after advocating its creation, Cambacérès declined the offer to sit on it (he would join it only after Thermidor). While his involvement in the activity of the various commissions gave him the opportunity to exercise his legal expertise, it also offered him a refuge from the escalation of factional conflict within the Convention. His strategy of survival during the Terror, as he described it in retrospect, consisted in '*passer au milieu*', burying himself in the humdrum routine of meetings and reports, while carefully avoiding the front of the political stage.

Predictably, given his cautious attitude, Cambacérès did not take an active part in the Thermidor conspiracy and later – unlike many in the same position – claimed no undeserved credit from it. According to his *Memoirs*, on the eve of the coup he received two unexpected visits.[16] The first was from Maximilien Robespierre. The two men had never been close; Cambacérès explained that he disliked the Jacobin leader's 'lawyer's arrogance', contrasting it with his own innate magistrate's 'reserve'. While there had never been any personal animosity between them, Cambacérès confessed to having been very frightened when the Incorruptible turned up unannounced. The latter questioned him in seemingly friendly terms on the rumours about ongoing intrigues ('What is Fouché up to?'); obviously Cambacérès denied having any knowledge of the matter and insisted on his own determination not to be part of any plot. Robespierre replied that this was the right thing to do ('keep your quiet attitude') and left with the reassurance that the agitation would soon blow over.[17]

The second visit was from the deputy for Montpellier Joseph Cambon, a wealthy local businessman whom Cambacérès knew well. A few days earlier, as chairman of the Committee of Finances, Cambon had openly defied Robespierre in the Convention, defending the action of his committee against the Jacobin leader's attacks and even suggesting that the latter was not competent to discuss financial matters.[18] He now came, accompanied by two other plotters, Jean-Lambert Tallien and François Paul Legendre, to ask Cambacérès whether he was ready to side with them: 'To vote, yes,' was his reply; 'to fight, no, as I have no idea of how to load a gun.'[19] The next day he did vote with the 'rebel' majority of the Convention. The coup opened significant opportunities for him, in any case, since, unlike other Thermidorians, he had no Terrorist past to answer for and could be safely promoted to the top of the new government.

Some of the self-proclaimed heroes of Thermidor, pursued by accusations of mass executions and corruption, were soon replaced in positions of power by men who, like Cambacérès, had survived the Terror labouring away behind the scenes. Before the end of 1794 the prudent lawyer had become chairman of the Committee of Legislation, president of the Convention, and finally president of the Committee of Public Safety. If he had not been ready to fight openly against Robespierre, Cambacérès was perfectly in tune with the new Thermidorian ethos. In his speeches he repeatedly denounced Terrorism and factionalism, urging his compatriots to flee from those 'who talk incessantly of blood and scaffolds' while digging the grave of France's liberty. On 11 October, as newly elected president of the Convention, Cambacérès celebrated the solemn reburial of Jean-Jacques Rousseau's remains in the Panthéon. On that occasion he provided the Genevan philosopher with surprisingly moderate (not to say Thermidorian) credentials, stressing in his speech Rousseau's feelings of compassion. Goodness, the speaker claimed, had been the basis of Rousseau's legislation; his politics had been 'sublime' yet always 'wise and benevolent'.[20]

Public and private affairs

Promotion to the top of these political institutions did not slow Cambacérès' relentless activity; if anything, they intensified it and widened its scope, stretching it from legislative to executive objects.[21] As chairman of the Committee of Legislation he resumed, with Merlin, the project of the new Civil Code; he also addressed a tricky reform of civil administration, since, in a scenario that was destined to recur in French history, the number of civil servants was thought to be unnecessarily large, and their performance unsatisfactory. Turning his attention to foreign affairs, he commissioned a detailed study of all political and commercial agreements subscribed to by France from the Treaty of Westphalia (1648) to the present. He reorganized the diplomatic bureau, which now included future Directors Merlin, Sieyès and Jean-François Reubell, and in 1795 the bureau negotiated the Treaty of Basel. As president of the Committee of Public Safety, fortified by the *pot-au-feu* he had made every morning to sustain himself and his colleagues in their efforts, Cambacérès examined every scrap of correspondence and supervised every detail in his effort to restore order to the administration.[22]

However, one of the main difficulties the new regime had to face was represented by the very institution he had originally advocated for, and over which he now presided. One priority of the Thermidorians became limiting the powers of the Committee of Public Safety to prevent the resurgence of some form of dictatorial rule by a faction or individual leader. Accordingly, membership was increased from twelve to sixteen, and a quick turnover of tenure was established; between November 1794 and October 1795 Cambacérès was appointed three times, with an interval of one month between mandates. Yet the problem the Committee had originally been created to address – how to establish a functioning executive, extricating the practice of government from the maze of parliamentary commissions – remained unsolved.

In principle, the answer should have come from the return to normal constitutional rule, which had been suspended when France was facing the threat of foreign invasion. Yet the type of executive designed in the Constitution of 1793 (never applied but still theoretically in force) did not look promising. The Constitution introduced an 'executive council' of 24 members; these were chosen by the legislative body from lists voted for by the electoral assemblies of the *départements*, and half of them would be replaced at each annual election (Articles 62–77). This executive council would be de facto totally dependent on the legislative, since all initiatives, including the choice of the 'agents' of the administration (as ministers were called), had to be approved by the assembly. The council did not even have a physical seat of its own, but must meet on the premises of the Convention.

It is difficult to imagine how the system might have worked if it had been put into application. In the event, the combination of semi-direct popular election and lack of autonomy embodied the revolutionary doctrine of the executive as a mere emanation of the legislative that the Thermidorians were struggling to overcome. Like other aspects of the 1793 text, it was the expression of a radical phase of the Revolution that the Convention now wished to bring to an end. When, on 21 March 1795, a crowd of sans-culottes broke into the assembly to reclaim the Constitution of 1793, it was Cambacérès who suggested the creation of the Commission of the Eleven, allegedly to examine the application of the old Constitution, but in fact to draft a new one. Having proposed the Commission, though, Cambacérès – like Sieyès – chose not to join it, instead holding on to his position at the Committee of Public Safety, confident that he would be part of the new executive whatever form it might take.

The Directory established by the Constitution of 1795 seemed, at least on paper, a reasonable compromise between a too-powerful government and a weak one: a collegial body selected by the two legislative Councils, but with sufficiently wide prerogatives. Cambacérès' name circulated in the press as one of those likely to be elected to it, but his ubiquitous presence and relentless interventions on all fronts were not universally appreciated by his colleagues. The useful jurist now looked far too much like a man with a firm grip on power. Shortly before the election of the Directory, Cambacérès' enemies were offered the perfect opportunity to block his appointment. Following the arrest of a royalist agent, Pierre-Jacques Le Maître, the police found at his Parisian lodgings a letter in which Cambacérès' name was mentioned among those of other supposed royalist sympathizers who might favour the king's return.

The letter had been written to Le Maître by another known exponent of the somewhat shambolic network of royalist agents, the Count d'Antraigues.[23] The count was, like Cambacérès, from Montpellier, and the two men had moved in the same circles in their youth before d'Antraigues left France to pursue an adventurous career in such exotic places as Turkey and Egypt.[24] Cambacérès could assert truthfully in his own defence that he had not been in touch with d'Antraigues for more than a decade, and that the inclusion of his name in the letter as a royalist supporter was pure speculation on the writer's part (other prominent personalities, such as the president of the Eleven, François-Antoine de Boissy d'Anglas, were also mentioned). Yet, while he assured the Convention of his innocence in the affair, he must have known that the problem was a political one. In the eyes of his fellow deputies, he was not quite 'sound'. In the words of the former Montagnard Antoine-Claire Thibaudeau, he was undoubtedly committed to the Revolution, but was he also devoted to the Republic? Later, however, Thibaudeau admitted that had Cambacérès been elected to the Directory, he would have performed far better than any of the chosen five.[25]

This reluctance to be associated with any party, which had protected Cambacérès during the Terror, now became a handicap. Unlike Sieyès, who was similarly averse to parties, he had no past revolutionary credentials to fall back on. Moreover, the press brought up the fact that Cambacérès was a member of the Five Hundred, not of the Elders as became a senior politician, because he was neither married nor a widower (a snide reference to his not-so-secret homosexuality).[26] While obviously disappointed, Cambacérès reacted to these personal attacks, and to his exclusion from the Directory, with his usual avoidance of conflict. As a member of the Five Hundred he continued to serve on various committees, collaborating, for example, with Reubell and his minister Dominique-Vincent Ramel-Nogaret in the Commission of Finances on the project of forced borrowing and discovering some errors in their calculations. In June 1796 he published his *Projet de Code Civil*, a voluminous compilation of more than 1,000 articles that received more attention from jurists all over Europe than in France.[27] At the elections for the Five Hundred in 1797 he withdrew in the face of repeated personal attacks, refusing various alternative positions as consolation prizes; at 44, he felt almost ready to leave politics for good.

Rather than accepting some sinecure with a stable income, Cambacérès decided to go back to work privately as legal advisor. Although he had lost touch to some extent with Montpellier society, partly because of his difficult relationship with his quarrelsome father, he had maintained his networks of professional (and Masonic) contacts. Under the old regime, the scope of legal counsel had focused mainly on questions of inheritance and feudal regulations, although Cambacérès had found a more promising area of expertise in commercial law. The Revolution had brought about massive transfers of property through the confiscation of Church and émigrés' lands, and had facilitated the emergence of fortunes built on army contracting and financial speculation. The protracted war had created both complications and opportunities for international commerce. Those participating in these new and expanding activities needed guidance through the maze of still-uncharted post-1789 legislation.

With an established reputation as an expert in maritime trade, Cambacérès became advisor to the French East India Company (Compagnie des Indes Orientales et de la Chine). Another important client was the Anzin Mining Company, which exploited the coal mines in northern France, mining being a relatively novel sector and one that was still unregulated. Through the Genevan businessman Jean-Pierre Vieusseux, Cambacérès found himself close to the influential circle of bankers and army contractors – including Gabriel-Julien Ouvrard, Casimir-Pierre Périer, François-Louis Michel and Jacques-Rose Récamier – who were to provide crucial financial backing for the coup of Brumaire.[28] As a private lawyer Cambacérès had been able to make a living and acquire some national properties, and in 1793 he had opposed in vain the obligation for deputies to disclose their financial situation to the Convention. However, politics was not especially lucrative for those who, like him, relied on their official income without resorting to corrupt practices. Now, backed by an efficient staff of young lawyers, he began making serious money and could profit from the best possible opportunities to invest it. Finally, he was able to indulge in the love of luxury and extravagant consumption that he had repressed in his youth, and which would become his political enemies' favourite object of mockery.

The second man in France

As he was busy building his private fortune, Cambacérès had kept in touch with the men in power, in particular Merlin and Sieyès. It was Sieyès, once re-elected to the Directory, who in July 1799 proposed him for the ministry of justice, on the strength of his impeccable professional credentials. This time Cambacérès, who had previously turned down various offices in the magistracy, accepted the position. In common with most in governmental circles, he must have been aware that some major political change was about to occur, but there is no evidence as to his expectations. The role he played a few months later in the coup of Brumaire is bound to remain to some extent a matter of speculation. His own version of events is very similar to the one he offered for Thermidor: that he knew there were plans to overturn the Directory but had no part in them, confining himself to safeguarding the department for which he was responsible. He even described his own situation as the coup unfolded as 'painful' and 'dangerous'.[29] Indeed, when the Provisional Consulate took over from the Directory, he insisted on resigning his position of minister of justice (to the annoyance of Napoleon, who thought the gesture a futile formality), only to be immediately reconfirmed in his portfolio.[30]

Yet, while Cambacérès' claim to have been merely a cautious bystander (although one who profited from the change of regime) is plausible for Thermidor, it is difficult to accept it for Brumaire. He emerged from the latter coup in the role of Second Consul, a position that was not – like that of Third Consul or the presidency of the Senate offered to Sieyès – merely honorary, but that turned him effectively into Napoleon's deputy and, eventually, into the second man in France. His appointment came as an unwelcome surprise to Sieyès, who until then had regarded himself as the *deus ex machina* of the conspiracy, treating Cambacérès as a marginal actor.

The key to the whole affair must be in the personal connection Cambacérès had built with Napoleon. The two had met a few years before, in the autumn of 1794, in rather curious circumstances. Once again Cambacérès had been surprised by an early morning visit, his visitor an unknown, shabbily dressed, furious young man who, without any preliminaries, accused him of having unjustly dismissed him from the army. As a member of the War Committee, Cambacérès had indeed signed the document that suspended the 25-year-old artillery officer for insubordination. Briefly arrested after Thermidor on account of his friendship with Robespierre's brother Augustin, Napoleon had then been assigned to an infantry regiment bound for the Vendée, but, since neither the infantry nor the repression of guerrillas suited him, he had refused to take up the post. Cambacérès, who knew nothing whatsoever of the case, had simply countersigned the decision made by the chairman of the War Committee, Captain François Xavier Aubry. However, always inclined to conciliation, he was ready to listen to the young officer's grievances and to admit that Napoleon might indeed have been the victim of an injustice. The following year he endorsed Napoleon's promotion to divisional general.[31]

Nothing noticeable transpires about the two men's relationship during the Italian and Egyptian campaigns until Napoleon's return to France in October 1799, but then no correspondence between the two for that period (assuming there was any) has survived.[32] Cambacérès was not part of the small crowd of dignitaries who gathered at the general's house or solicited meetings with him. Instead, it was Napoleon who came to see Cambacérès the day after his return, apparently (to his 'extreme surprise') to discuss a matter of no pressing relevance, namely the émigrés' legal status. Then, the evening before the coup, the general dined at his house. As member of the government, Sieyès complained to Cambacérès of this preference: 'He has treated you better than me, [for] I have seen him only in the cabinet.'[33]

One plausible explanation of the connection between Napoleon and Cambacérès, set forth by some historians, is that the latter served as a contact between the general and the financiers who backed the coup. Unsurprisingly, nothing to this effect is mentioned in

Cambacérès' own memoirs. There he writes that he was initially surprised by Napoleon's choice of Sieyès as his main political supporter, since Paul Barras would have been much easier to deal with. But then, he admits, Barras was discredited, and there were rumours of ongoing negotiations between him and the emissaries of Louis XVIII. As to Sieyès, so full of 'speculative knowledge', he took offence at any contradiction, an attitude that 'led to no results'. Cambacérès concludes that the developments of Brumaire showed how relations between Napoleon and Sieyès rested on a degree of mutual misunderstanding as to their respective intentions.[34] Whatever his actual role in the coup, Cambacérès kept his usual cautious attitude, claiming that he had no expectations and expressing surprise at Napoleon's choice of himself as Second Consul. Apparently, as they were debating the choice of the Third Consul (Charles-François Lebrun), Napoleon declared that public opinion had already indicated the minister of justice for the second place.[35] The ballots filled by the members of the special Legislative Commission with their choice of consul were discreetly tossed unopened into the fireplace.[36]

Whatever the case, the Consular Constitution of 13 December 1799 (Year VIII) corresponded largely to Cambacérès' own views as they had emerged from the revolutionary experience. The Proclamation of the Provisional Consuls of 15 December declared that the Revolution, now 'fixed upon the principles that had started it', was over; in other words, the ship of state had finally reached the safe shore advocated by Cambacérès in 1794.[37] The new text created a strong executive with both elected and nominated councils as organs of discussion and consultation, rather than decision. Unlike Sieyès, Cambacérès was more concerned with questions of governance than with the mechanisms of popular representation, such as electoral assemblies and voting procedures. Moreover, his attitude reflected the classical position of the magistracy, which focused essentially on the structure of the law. For him, liberty and equality were empty words unless they were firmly inscribed in the civil and penal codes, the object of his lasting concern.

In this respect Cambacérès' first reaction to the constitutional text of 1799 is revealing. He noticed the absence from it of any preliminary statement on rights and freedom of expression, but he concluded that the omission, if deliberate, was reasonable, since in such matters much depended on circumstance, and legislation should not be 'bound by maxims'.[38] It was a view that several jurists had expressed at the time of the drafting of the Declaration of Rights in 1789.

The new Constitution introduced the Council of State, an institution that was destined to play a pivotal role in the vast plan of reform undertaken by the Consulate. Often described inaccurately as being modelled on the old king's council, and therefore as anticipating the monarchical character of the new regime, it was created to address an essentially modern problem that had been brought out by the revolutionary experience: the coordination of the legislative's activity with that of the executive, of the production of laws with their effective application. Its purpose was to avoid that the legislative should issue any more of the decrees that had been piling up since 1789, and that the executive had been unable to apply. The Council had to some extent been a joint invention of Sieyès and Cambacérès', but after the former's retirement from active politics the latter – who presided over it from 1799 to 1814 – was left to turn it into a functioning institution, overseeing the necessary adjustments alone.[39]

Given his general disposition, in 1804 Cambacérès had no reason to object to the transformation of the Consulate into a hereditary regime. Predictably enough, the speech he gave in front of the Senate at the opening session on 16 May (26 Floréal Year XII) contained the expected laudatory comments about the 'hero who had saved [France] on the brink of the abyss'. It did, however, include an unintentionally revealing remark: 'As you know, the art of the legislator consists in regenerating states on the existing basis, and his task is to face circumstances with the materials on hand.'[40]

In this case the 'materials on hand' consisted of the emperor-to-be – but in selecting Cambacérès as his deputy, Napoleon had also made very good use of the materials on hand. Indeed, he had made the perfect choice: someone he knew to be both competent and loyal, a reliable 'collaborator' with no ambitions of power on his own account. He might have joked about Cambacérès' habit of using special diplomatic couriers to deliver his personal supply of *pâté de foie gras*, or mocked his time-consuming meetings with mysterious 'demoiselles' whom he knew to be men, but the lawyer was the only one in Napoleon's close entourage whom he trusted to run civil government when he was away on military campaigns. At the same time, in adopting Cambacérès the First Consul inherited the many unfinished projects of reform that the Consulate was finally able to accomplish – the least visible but bulkiest and most durable legacy of the Directory. Most important of these was the new Civil Code, now rescued from the vagaries of the legislative assemblies and entrusted to an administrative commission over which Cambacérès presided. The new Code finally saw the light of day in 1804, ready to be exported across the new Empire.[41]

According to a contemporary witness,

> The choice of a well-known and respected man surprised those who supposed that Bonaparte would surround himself with nonentities . . . [Cambacérès] never abandons his solemn calm. He bends in front of what he cannot oppose and, once the storm has passed, he works to repair the damage, showing a tenacity unusual in the French character.[42]

Cambacérès dealt with the First Consul and later emperor as he used to deal with his important clients: patiently and respectfully, advising, suggesting and smoothing away any potential conflict. His friend Chaptal claimed that Cambacérès and the emperor's wife, Joséphine, were the only people who could subdue Napoleon's occasional explosions of rage. The two men's successful partnership did not simply grant Cambacérès several honours (he became Duke of Parma, among other things) and, of course, considerable wealth, but gave him an effective role in government. After the collapse of the Empire his habitually calm, reassuring attitude allowed him to obtain Louis XVIII's pardon, and in 1818 he was able to return from exile in Brussels to enjoy his famously beautiful *hôtel particulier*, the Hôtel d'Elbeuf, his membership of the Académie and his quiet life in Paris.

The reverse of the medal

The sumptuous premises of the ministry of justice at the Hôtel de Bourvallais in Place Vendôme display an imposing piece of furniture known as the *bureau de Cambacérès*. It is not, as the name suggests, a working desk, but rather a long table with gilded columns and exotic divinities in the neoclassical-cum-Egyptian style of the First Empire. Famous historical documents are said, perhaps inaccurately, to have been signed on it. It seems that the table was indeed commissioned by Cambacérès, although not at the time of his brief mandate as minister of justice in 1799, nor on the occasion of his even shorter tenure of the same post in 1815 during the Hundred Days, but around 1810. In the safer years of the Empire the Archchancellor was probably more at leisure to address the choice of luxury furniture. Whatever the case, it is fitting that his name should still be associated with the writing of laws, the cause to which most of his life was dedicated.[43]

Reflecting in retrospect on his life, Cambacérès admitted that he had chosen to follow the Revolution out of reason and not from personal taste. He had not been motivated by resentment or ambition, he wrote, and in a different age occupying a simple place of 'notable' would have satisfied his aspirations fully. However, given the circumstances in which his generation had been placed, forced to follow the 'general movement' of the times, his desire had been to lead, as far as possible, an 'honourable life'.[44] This admission – made public only with the belated appearance of his *Memoirs* at the end of the twentieth century – seems to confirm the suspicions of his fellow revolutionaries, who felt he was not really 'one of them': not fully committed to the brave new world they had struggled to create, but rather resigned to the inevitable changes it had generated.

In some ways Cambacérès' profile can be added to the long line that runs from the 'bourgeois' ministers of Louis XIV to the graduates of the Grandes Écoles who sit today in French government, often having dispensed with the traditional validation of party militance.[45] Historians have found it only too easy to write him off as the embodiment of that 'technocratic' side of the Revolution that asserted itself with the Directory, of the exercise of government as a simple professional performance. As the inscription on a commemorative medal issued around 1804 asserted, he was 'a skilful jurist and prudent legislator who kept away from the factions'.

Yet this image is only one side of the medal. The label 'technocrat' suggests the blind application of rules and procedures, but after 1789 rules and procedures no longer existed; they had to be reinvented, and the invention required considerable imagination and creativity, as well as great determination. As for Cambacérès' professed attachment to the values of the past, this was to some extent a provocative pose, a sign of nonconformity against conventional revolutionary morality, just like his taste for showy clothing, perfumes, attractive grenadiers and sophisticated food. On some subjects (such as individual and family rights), his views were in fact more advanced than those of most of his contemporaries. Besides, one did not need to be nostalgic for the old regime to be horrified by the display of popular violence, and there was nothing unmodern about the desire for stability or the wish to protect property.

More importantly, Cambacérès was, just like his more radical and outspoken fellow revolutionaries, in thrall to a powerful utopia. His somewhat pompous declaration to the Duke of Orléans of having as his cause 'the reign of the law' was sincere. Establishing the rule of law was an older ideal than the sovereignty of the nation, the triumph of the Third Estate or the creation of the Republic. Cherished by the French magistrates through the centuries, it became an essential component of the project of 1789, as one might expect of a revolution essentially fashioned (if not made) by lawyers. It was to this old yet honourable cause, far more than to the powers in place, that the lawyer from Montpellier dedicated his lifelong service.

Conclusion: Changing Palaces

If you can look into the seeds of time,
And say which grain will grow and which will not,
Speak then to me.
WILLIAM SHAKESPEARE,
Macbeth (1.3)

Once the uncertain events of 18 and 19 Brumaire were over, as they travelled back to Paris from Saint-Cloud in the middle of the night, Napoleon told his secretary Louis-Antoine Fauvelet de Bourrienne: 'Tomorrow night we shall sleep at the Luxembourg.' What he meant was that the coup had succeeded and that the Consulate would replace the Directory as the new government. As to sleeping at the Luxembourg, the phrase was not to be taken literally.[1]

Napoleon made his own low-key entrance into the palace the next day for the investiture of the Provisional Consulate, the government that was briefly installed, pending the adoption of the new Constitution, to replace the Directory. The general wore plain civilian clothing – a dark green redingote – for the occasion, rather than his army uniform. In line with the strategy he had adopted since his return to France, he wished to present himself as a magistrate rather than a military commander.[2] Brumaire had been no military coup. Although Napoleon owed his reputation to his campaigns in Italy and Egypt, the conspiracy had been planned among the civil government's entourage, and the troops deployed in support of their action had not been called on to intervene other than by providing an intimidating presence. In any case, with or without uniform, the newly appointed First Consul had no intention of taking up residence in the somewhat overcrowded Petit Luxembourg. Of the five Directors, only Paul Barras had left for good after signing his resignation; Louis-Jérôme Gohier and Jean-François Moulin, who had initially refused to do the same, were kept in their apartments under temporary house arrest next door to Emmanuel Sieyès and Roger Ducos, who had been party to the coup and were promoted to the ephemeral role of Provisional Consuls.[3]

This strange cohabitation was soon over. On 24 December, shortly after the adoption of the Constitution of 1799 (Year VIII) on 13 December, a decree indicated the palace of the Tuileries as the official residence of the consuls Napoleon, Jean-Jacques-Régis Cambacérès and Charles-François Lebrun. Second Consul Cambacérès declined the honour, choosing instead for himself the elegant Hôtel d'Elbeuf near the Carousel, while at the Tuileries Napoleon undertook the first of a series of enthusiastic restorations of former royal palaces.[4] Emptied of both the losers and the winners at Brumaire, the Petit Luxembourg was hastily refurbished by the ever-present Jean-François Chalgrin on the First Consul's instructions. Refashioned in neoclassical, neo-Egyptian style, it became the seat of one of the new legislative councils, the Senate, until 1814, when the restoration of the larger palace was finally completed.[5] The new furnishings included a set of eighty chairs (for the eighty senators), each inlaid with the image of a snake looking into a mirror to watch its back: a symbol of political prudence but also, for some of the occupants, a belated warning.

The inevitable outcome?

Bonapartist propaganda lost no time in presenting the coup of Brumaire as inevitable, the necessary consequence of the inadequacy of the Directory. Historians have stressed the feeble reaction of the political class and of the public at large to yet another change in government. There was no unrest in Paris, no clamour in the press, and only a few *départements* refused at first to endorse the new Constitution. The army manifested no enthusiasm but also no significant opposition, and the arrest and deportation (on Sieyès' initiative, against Napoleon's advice) of a group of Jacobin militants constituted the only instance of active repression. Contemporary accounts suggest that the strongest motive for the general acceptance of the new status quo was simply the shared fear of Jacobinism. Nobody was prepared to relive the experience of the Terror, so any moderate alternative seemed a reasonable compromise.

It is important to bear in mind that even the most critical liberal observers, as well as those who mistrusted Napoleon, did not imagine in 1799 that what had occurred was a radical change of regime. Considering the recurrent difficulties the Directors experienced over the Constitution of 1795, the idea of introducing changes to it without waiting for the passing of the nine years indicated in Article 338 under Heading XIII as the term for revision seemed acceptable. After all, the Consulate was, just like the Directory, a republican government; the adjustments made to the organization of powers in the Constitution of 1799, hastily put together in the aftermath of the coup (see Chapter Six), conformed to the criticism that had been addressed from all sides to the text of 1795. First among them was the necessity to strengthen the executive, abandoning the collegial formula that nobody had ever seriously believed in, and introducing instead the figure of the First Consul as head of government.

Besides the reinforced executive, the Consular Constitution maintained a plural legislative now divided into three councils:

Legislative Body, Tribunate and Senate. It retained the practice of partial annual elections, while with the introduction of universal male suffrage without property conditions, citizens' voting rights were more extensive than they had been under the 1795 text. The mechanisms introduced to control the outcome of elections – such as the creation of an intricate hierarchy of lists of 'eligible' candidates – seemed at first to be merely technical adjustments, and the limits they

Auguste Couder, *Establishment of the Conseil d'Etat, 25 December 1799*, 1856, oil on canvas.

would impose on the electors' choices were not immediately apparent.[6] Basic individual rights were reasserted; in the very succinct text Title VII – on guarantees against arbitrary arrest – was one of the few sections to be formulated in detail.

Annotating the projected constitutional text for the First Consul, Cambacérès noticed that the freedom of the press had somehow disappeared from the draft, but he assumed that the omission, if deliberate, was probably justified. He wrote in the margin: 'As the spirit of the project is to confer great strength to the government, whatever will be done to this purpose will never be unconstitutional.'[7] In taking power in December 1799, the consuls could boast of adopting a constitution 'founded upon the true principles of representative government and the sacred rights of property, equality and liberty'. Because these were the principles the Revolution had originally proposed to establish in 1789, the Revolution itself – they famously concluded – had now come to an end.[8]

Despite the omissions and ambiguities in the Constitution of 1799, no one at this stage (not even Napoleon himself) anticipated the process that would lead in a few years to the replacement of the Republic with a new hereditary regime.[9] Only some over-optimistic royalists hoped that the consuls might be open to negotiating the return of the Bourbons. While the Consulate lasted, Napoleon took great care to maintain the forms of republican rule. Even the label 'empire' (rather than 'monarchy') was chosen in 1804 because it belonged to the republican tradition, in an attempt to preserve symbolic continuity with the revolutionary heritage.[10] Difficult to predict in 1799, the transition from republic to monarchy was neither necessary nor inevitable; it was mainly the product of circumstantial factors that were connected only indirectly to the experience of the Directory.

Napoleon's ambition, audacity and unsuspected political talent played a major role, of course. Paradoxically, the great care the revolutionaries had taken to quash the emergence of any individual leadership, be it civil or military, had left a void that favoured the rise of personal rule. The several attempts made on the First Consul's life in the following years increased the anxiety to preserve a strong individual presence by making it permanent, and finally even hereditary.[11] Similarly, the constant concern with protecting France's frontiers and securing peace had created the conditions for the military undertakings and conquests of the Empire. All things considered, the authoritarian evolution of the Consulate, far from being a necessary outcome, marked a discontinuity from the experience of the Directory. The fall of the Directorial Republic had been caused precisely by the Directors' reluctance to pursue consistently illiberal, anti-democratic measures to ensure their political survival. Although they were occasionally tempted to overstep the limits of their prerogatives, they were unable to see themselves as a novel Committee of Public Safety, holding power by intimidation and determined to destroy their political opponents; the new generation that took over with Napoleon did not have such scruples.

In the mirror of the future

The modern Republic established in France in the 1790s had the uncertain consistency of a ghost. It was a vision from the future, and – like the apparitions in prophecies, like Macbeth's glimpse of Scotland's future kings in the witches' mirror – it was evanescent and difficult to interpret. The elements identified by the theorists of modern republicanism were all there: the dedicated commitment to the rule of law; the ambition to promote prosperity in a free commercial economy; and above all the determination, born out of the experience of the Terror, to protect citizens not just from the ordinary abuse of power, but from the murderous tendencies of some regimes. With the Directory the ghost had taken material form in a hostile environment, marked by the instability and partisan divisions of the Revolution, where it had been impossible for it to survive. Yet it proved very resilient, for a phantom. Repeatedly crushed by its more aggressive, more ambitious competitors, it was destined to resurface tenaciously in different institutional shapes whenever favourable circumstances presented themselves. Writing in the early 1990s, in the aftermath of the bicentenary of the Revolution of 1789 but also of the collapse of the Soviet bloc, the political theorist John Dunn commented: 'At present the modern constitutional republic stands virtually unchallenged as the sole surviving candidate for a model of legitimate political authority in the modern world.'[12]

In Dunn's analysis, if this two-centuries-old model had finally emerged as the political victor against the competition of totalitarian systems, it was because of the unique combination of two factors: the democratic legitimation of governmental power; and a realistic understanding of how this power could be made to work in practice. Predictably, as Dunn fully realized at the time, this could hardly be the end of the story. Since the collapse of twentieth-century socialist regimes, the model of the constitutional republic has been faced with new challenges ranging from international terrorism to the return of war in Europe and the emergence of conservative authoritarian movements within democratic states. Interestingly, the most embattled opponents of the modern republic today are no longer those who denounce its vices – the angry crowds and militant groups protesting against economic inequality, blindness to climate change or insufficient democracy – but rather those rulers who condemn its virtues: individual freedom, religious toleration and the rejection of violence by the State against its citizens. It is to all these advantages that they oppose the merits of their own autocratic powers.

The Directors' ambitions did not stretch so far into the future. In their most optimistic and prophetic moments, they hoped that the system of government they had built, following the aspirations of the Revolution, was going to last. This hope was at least partly realized, since for two centuries France – as empire, monarchy or republic – has been sustained by the formidable legal and administrative architecture they created. Over the course of just a few years the desk revolutionaries succeeded in turning the principles of 1789 into viable legislation and governmental practices; they drafted new penal and civil codes, reorganized ministries and tribunals, and devised procedures to educate and recruit civil servants; they stabilized the economy and created a fiscal system that remained in place until the First World War; and they designed institutions – such as the Council of State and the new Court of Audits – that are still working in the twenty-first century.

Although the large majority of French citizens are unaware of it, contemporary France is still functioning on the solid institutional mechanisms and offices these men created. If the Directors failed to secure a durable peace, they at least settled questions and concluded agreements that opened the way for that possibility, as shown by the treatises made with the European powers under the Consulate. Possibly the ideals of the rule of law and the creation of a smooth governmental machine that they had pursued since the old regime were not fully realized, but they went a long way towards these objectives.

Where they did fail was in finding effective solutions to the puzzling relationship between government and democracy. All along they believed sincerely in the sovereignty of the people, an ideal that was an essential part of their original engagement in the Estates General, as was the establishment of a national system of representation. Even the experience of violent confrontations in the streets of Paris, the clubs and the assembly did not change their attitude on the matter. However, once they were in government, the gap between the theory and practice of representation proved impossible to bridge. No constitutional rules, no institutional machinery could guarantee popular consensus on the government's activity. The will of the people turned out to be inscrutable, unpredictable, full of unexpected twists and turns, impervious to the rational arguments of men who were not themselves persuasive demagogues. In common with many politicians since then, they felt impotent when faced with popular discontent and the volatility of electoral choices.[13]

It was a frustrating setback, since for their generation, and for them personally, modern constitutional government represented a conquest and a point of arrival, not an object of contempt or an enemy to fight against. It was, in a recurrent metaphor, the safe harbour where the vessel of the state, and those at its helm, had found shelter after a season of terrible storms. Benjamin Constant wrote in 1796: 'The choice [was] between finding rest in the Republic, or walking backwards towards tyranny along the terrible road France had followed through floods of blood spilled in the name of liberty.'[14]

While those Directors who were excluded from power in 1799 must have felt some bitterness, it is possible to detect in their attitude, together with resignation and fatigue, a sense of relief. Their long struggle had come to an end and the Republic they had fought so hard to maintain from the embattled trench of their desks was now someone else's responsibility. If not all of them were seduced by Napoleon's personality, they were at least able to recognize the energy, imagination and ruthlessness of a new generation for whom the old regime, as well as the experience of Terror, was no longer a tenacious memory, but a remote legend. As this narrative has shown, some left politics altogether for a comfortable retirement; others stayed on, resuming the congenial role of expert that had served them so well in the past and collecting the substantial benefits that accompanied the garish decorations and fanciful titles of the new regimes. Walking today around the gardens of the Luxembourg, where the two palaces now stand under the guard of patrols holding machine guns, ready to defend the Senate's premises and its occupants from a new breed of unknown assailants, one can easily understand their feelings.

TIMELINE, 1789–99

1789

5 May	Meeting of the Estates General at Versailles
20 June	Oath of the Tennis Court
9 July	Beginning of the Constituent Assembly
14 July	Storming of the Bastille
4 August	The Constituent Assembly abolishes feudal privileges
26 August	Adoption of the Declaration of the Rights of Man and Citizen
5–6 October	March of the women on Versailles; the king and the royal family forced to return to Paris
2 November	The Constituent Assembly votes for the confiscation of the lands of the Church

1791

21 June	King Louis XVI and his family arrested at Varennes as they try to flee France
3 September	Adoption of Constitution of 1791
1 October	Beginning of the Legislative Assembly after the dissolution of the Constituent Assembly

1792	
20 April	France declares war on Austria; Prussia, Britain and Russia join Austria in the anti-French coalition
10 August	Palace of the Tuileries stormed by a crowd; massacre of the Swiss Guard; the king and his family imprisoned at the Temple
20 September	Battle of Valmy: the French army defeats the Prussians led by the Duke of Brunswick
20–21 September	Legislative Assembly replaced by the Convention
22 September	Proclamation of the Republic
3 December	King Louis XVI put on trial by the Convention
1793	
21 January	Execution of Louis XVI
31 May/2 June	Girondin deputies put on trial and sentenced to death after an attempted insurrection defeated by the Montagnards
24 June	Adoption of Constitution of 1793 (Year I)
September	Beginning of Terror
16 October	Execution of Queen Marie-Antoinette
1794	
5 April	Execution of Georges Danton
27–28 July	Coup of Thermidor: arrest and execution of Maximilien Robespierre and his group
1795	
22 July	Treaty of Basel; peace agreements signed with Prussia and Spain
22 August	Adoption of Constitution of 1795 (Year III)
5 October	Failed royalist insurrection of Vendémiaire
26 October	Beginning of government of the Directory

1796

May	Failed insurrection of the Equals

1797

May	Babeuf arrested and executed
4 September	Failed royalist coup of Fructidor; Lazare Carnot and Balthazar François de Barthélemy evicted from the Directory
30 September	Bankruptcy of the Two-Thirds: Directory cancels two-thirds of national debt
17 October	General Napoleon Bonaparte signs Treaty of Campo-Formio after his victories against Austria during the Italian campaigns

1798

March	French army occupies Switzerland
1 July	Beginning of Napoleon's campaign in Egypt

1799

18 June	Coup of Prairial; Jacobins win a majority in Councils
8 October	Napoleon returns from Egypt
9–10 November	Coup of Brumaire; resignation of Directors
13 December	Adoption of Constitution of 1799 (Year VIII); beginning of Consulate

FRENCH REPUBLICAN CALENDAR

The French Republican (Revolutionary) Calendar was adopted by the Convention on 23 October 1793; it remained in place until 31 December 1805 (but it was briefly revived during the insurrection of the Paris Commune in 1871). The new calendar removed all references to traditional names and religious festivities and was associated with the introduction of the decimal system. Years were counted from the foundation of the Republic on 22 September 1792; the calendar established twelve months of thirty days, each divided into three decades (five extra days had to be added during the year to fit the solar year of 365 days). The new names of the months were inspired by the natural cycle of seasons; they were created by the poet Philippe Fabre d'Eglantine, who was executed in 1794 with Danton's faction. Under the Empire it was decided to abandon the new calendar, since the discrepancies with the solar year were a source of endless complications, as were the differences from other countries' calendars; it was suppressed on 9 September 1805.

REFERENCES

Introduction: At the Luxembourg

1 He left on the same day, 21 June, on which his brother Louis XVI and his family made their unsuccessful attempt to escape; while they were famously stopped at Varennes, Provence managed to reach Coblenz without difficulty. Timothy Tackett, *When the King Took Flight* (Cambridge, MA, 2003); Mona Ozouf, *Varennes: La Mort de la royauté* (Paris, 2005).

2 About 1,000 prisoners had been kept there, including one of the future Directors, Nicolas François de Neufchâteau (see Chapter Five).

3 'Hôtel du Luxembourg' was the name of the original *hôtel particulier* bought with its grounds by Marie de Medici in order to build the larger palace. In the seventeenth and eighteenth centuries the two buildings were passed down to various members of the Bourbon-Condé and Orléans families; from 1750 onwards the larger one was used as a public art gallery. Finally, in 1778 Louis XVI gave the whole property to the Count of Provence, who wanted an appropriate Parisian residence to rival the Palais Royal of the Orléans, in settlement of their joint family inheritance. Today the Petit Luxembourg is the official residence of the president of the Senate; the Senate itself occupies the Luxembourg Palace, which has been rebuilt and extended in stages since the creation of the institution by Napoleon in 1800. Sara Galetti, *Le Palais du Luxembourg de Marie de Medici* (Paris, 2012); Claude d'Anthenaise, Michel Richard and Philippe Martial, eds, *Palais du Luxembourg* (Paris, 1992); Jean Mounicq, *Le Sénat: Palais et jardins du Luxembourg* (Paris, 1994); Charles-Eloi Vial, *Les Lieux de Napoléon* (Paris, 2025), pp. 147–52; Thierry Sarmant, *Histoire des palais: Le Pouvoir et sa mise en scène en France du V au XXIème siècle* (Paris, 2025), pp. 231–47.

4 The number of these subcommittees increased from 3 under the Constituent to 23 under the Convention. On the role of the executive, see Biancamaria Fontana, 'The Absent Power: The Restoration of the Executive from Necker to Constant', in *Les Usages de la séparation des pouvoirs*, ed. Biancamaria Fontana and Sandrine Baume (Paris, 2008), pp. 98–113.

5 A handsome, elegant man, Barras firmly refused to appear in public in this official disguise. Dominique Waquet, 'Costumes et vêtements sous le Directoire: Signes politiques ou effets de mode?', *Cahiers d'histoire*, CXXIX (2015), pp. 19–54.

6 Articles 165 and 168 of the Constitution of 1795; for the constitutional texts cited here, see Jacques Godechot, ed., *Les Constitutions de la France depuis 1789* (Paris, 1970). The most important study of the Constitution of 1795 is Michel Troper, *Terminer la Révolution: La Constitution de 1795* (Paris, 2006).

7 There were complaints from the Councils about the secrecy of the procedure, but the Constitution gave no specific indications on the matter. The Director who left was also tacitly entitled to financial compensation settled by unofficial agreement. Antoine-Claire Thibaudeau, *Mémoires sur la Convention et le Directoire*, ed. François Pascal (Paris, 2007), pp. 380–81.

8 The same age limit applied to the Elders, with the additional restriction that only married men (or widowers) were eligible on grounds of the sense of responsibility conferred by a household. On the general profile of the first generation of revolutionaries, see Timothy Tackett, *Becoming a Revolutionary: The Deputies of the French National Assembly and the Emergence of a Revolutionary Culture (1789–1790)* (Princeton, NJ, 1996).

9 To give a measure of this age limit, supposing Danton and Robespierre had escaped execution in 1794, they would have been ineligible in 1795; the fact that Napoleon was only thirty in 1799 prevented his election to the Directory, forcing him and his supporters to plan a different route to power.

10 The only exception was Barras, who belonged to the old nobility, had left home in his teens to join a colonial regiment, and possessed no professional skills (see Chapter One). On the sociological background of the revolutionary political class, see Haim Burstin, *Révolutionnaires: Pour une anthropologie politique de la Révolution française* (Paris, 2013); Daniel de Montplaisir, *Ces nobles qui ont fait la Révolution: Précurseurs, agitateurs, fondateurs* (Paris, 2024).

11 Alsace had been annexed by France in 1648, Lorraine in 1766; however, by the end of the eighteenth century both regions were still poorly integrated and retained distinctive cultural and administrative features. On the changes brought by the Revolution to international order, see Jacques Godechot, *La Grande Nation: L'Expansion révolutionnaire de la France, 1789–1799* [1957] (Paris, 2004); Stuart Woolf, *Napoleon's Integration of Europe* [1992] (London, 2015); Paul W. Schroeder, *The Transformation of European Politics, 1763–1848* (Oxford, 1994); Jeremy Black, *European International Relations, 1648–1815* (New York, 2002); and Jean-Pierre Bois, *De la paix des rois à l'ordre des empereurs, 1714–1815* (Paris, 2003).

12 See Chapters Three and Six for details of Carnot's and Sieyès' careers.

13 The proposal was rejected, since it was feared that the popular vote might save Louis XVI's life. See Albert Soboul, ed., *Le Procès de Louis XVI*

(Paris, 1966); Michael Walzer, *Regicide and Revolution: Speeches at the Trial of Louis XVI* (New York, 1992); and David Peter Jordan, *The King's Trial: Louis XVI vs the French Revolution* (Berkeley, CA, 2004).

14 Some of them exaggerated in retrospect their contribution to the fall of Robespierre, while others chose to be discreet about their role. On the Thermidor conspiracy, see Gérard Walter, *La Conjuration du 9 thermidor* (Paris, 1974), and Colin Jones, *The Fall of Robespierre* (Oxford, 2021).

15 David Hume, 'Of Parties in General' and 'Of the Parties of Great Britain', in *Essays, Moral, Political and Literary* [1777], ed. E. F. Miller (Indianapolis, IN, 1985), pp. 54–72; Alexander Hamilton, James Madison and John Jay, *The Federalist Papers* [1787], ed. Ian Shapiro (New Haven, CT, 2009).

16 Germaine de Stäel, *Considerations on the Principal Events of the French Revolution* [1818–20], ed. Aurelian Craiutu (Indianapolis, IN, 2008), part III, ch. 21, p. 384.

17 A significant indication of the level of inflation was that the remuneration of Directors was established in Article 173 of the Constitution in a given quantity of grain, rather than a sum of money: 50,000 *myriagrams* (more than 10,000 quintals) of wheat.

18 The most famous attempt against Napoleon, known as the Plot of the Infernal Machine, was organized by royalist agents on Christmas night 1800. A barrel of gunpowder exploded in a narrow, busy street in the heart of Paris, missing the First Consul but killing more than twenty passers-by. See Carlos de la Huerta, *The Great Conspiracy: Britain's Secret War against Revolutionary France, 1794–1805* (Stroud, 2016), and Jonathan North, *Killing Napoleon: The Plot to Blow Up Bonaparte* (Stroud, 2019). On conspiracy theories and the Revolution, see Edmond Dziembowski, *La Main cachée: Une autre histoire de la Révolution française* (Paris, 2023).

19 R. D. d'Angers, ed., *Mémoires de La Révellière-Lépeaux* (Paris, 1895), vol. I, p. 363.

20 Georges Lefebvre, *La France sous le Directoire*, ed. Albert Soboul and Jean-René Suratteau (Paris, 1984); Martyn Lyons, *France under the Directory* (Cambridge, 1975); Christine Le Bozec, *La Première République* (Paris, 2014); see also the more recent Loris Chavanette, ed., *Le Directoire: Forger la République* (Paris, 2020).

21 Under the ambiguous phrase *la pensée du gouvernement*; see Troper, *Terminer la Révolution*. See also Nicolas Rousselier, *La Force de gouverner: Le Pouvoir exécutif en France, XIX–XXI siècles* (Paris, 2013).

22 In 1790 there were 83 *départements*; today, following the growth of the population, there are 96, plus 4 *outre mer* (overseas) *départements*.

23 Patrice Gueniffey, *Le Nombre et la raison: La Révolution française et les élections* (Paris, 1993); Malcolm Crook, *Elections in the French Revolution: An Apprenticeship in Democracy (1789–1799)* (Cambridge, 1996).

24 Napoleon intervened financially to rescue Carnot, who had invested his family inheritance unwisely, and Reubell's family, who were left in difficult circumstances despite the former Director having been accused of accumulating a large fortune by nefarious means.

25 For details on Barras' experience as 'missionary' of the Republic, and the Committee of Public Safety's lack of reaction, see Chapter One.

26 When the Constitution of 1795 was exported to Switzerland in 1798, the Constitution of the Helvetic Republic did not reproduce this particular clause in defining the powers of the Directory; clearly the Swiss had more experience of the functioning of republican executives. See n. 34 below.

27 On the atmosphere of Thermidorian society, see Biancamaria Fontana, 'The Thermidorian Republic and Its Principles', in *The Invention of the Modern Republic*, ed. Biancamaria Fontana (Cambridge, 1994), pp. 118–38.

28 Michelet (himself born in 1798) claimed to have heard the story from an 'old man' who had been ten years old at the time; see Jules Michelet, *Histoire de la Révolution française*, ed. Paule Petitier and Michel Biard (Paris, 2019), vol. II, p. 1096. See also Albert Mathiez, *La Réaction thermidorienne* [1928] (Paris, 2010); François Furet, 'La République thermidorienne, 1795–1799', in *La Révolution française* (Paris, 2007), pp. 381–441; and Denis Woronoff, *La République bourgeoise de thermidor à brumaire, 1794–1799* (Paris, 1972).

29 The confiscation of Church lands was justified using the argument that they belonged not to individual owners, but to confraternities or associations that the State had the power to dissolve; as for the émigrés, their properties were forfeited by virtue of the traditional accusation of treason. Rafe Blaufarb, *The Great Demarcation: The French Revolution and the Invention of Modern Property* (Oxford, 2016).

30 The circumstances of the exit from the *assignats* are discussed in Chapter Two.

31 For an account of this episode, see Chapter Five.

32 Edmund Burke, *Reflections on the Revolution in France* [1790], ed. Conor Cruise O'Brien (Harmondsworth, 1969), p. 130. See Thierry Sarmant and Mathieu Stoll, *Régner et gouverner: Louis XIV et ses ministres* (Paris, 2010); Isser Woloch, *Napoleon and His Collaborators* (New York, 2001); and Thierry Lentz, *Les Ministres de Napoléon* (Paris, 2016).

33 R. R. Palmer, *The Improvement of Humanity: Education and the French Revolution* (Princeton, NJ, 1985); Charles Coutel, *Instituer le citoyen* (Paris, 1999); R. D. Anderson, 'France from the Enlightenment to the Napoleonic University', in *European Universities from the Enlightenment to 1914* (Oxford, 2004), pp. 39–50.

34 'Constitution de la République helvétique du 12 avril 1798', in *Quellenbuch zur neueren schweizerischen Verfassungsgeschichte*, ed. Alfred Kölz (Bern, 1992), pp. 126–52; see also Alfred Kölz, *Histoire constitutionnelle de la Suisse moderne* (Bern, 2006).

35 Biancamaria Fontana, *La République helvétique: Laboratoire de la Suisse moderne* (Lausanne, 2020).

36 Pierre Serna, *L'Extrême Centre, ou le poison français, 1789–2019* (Ceyzérieu, 2019), pp. 103–52. See also Marc Belissa and Yannick Bosc, *Le Directoire: La République sans la démocratie* (Paris, 2018). The movement En Marche was created to support Emmanuel Macron's presidential campaign of 2017; the party has now been rechristened 'Renaissance'.

37 In Benjamin Constant, *The Political Writings of Benjamin Constant*, ed. Biancamaria Fontana (Cambridge, 1988), pp. 307–28; in time the definition of the modern republic was stretched to involve some forms of constitutional monarchy.
38 Fontana, *The Invention of the Modern Republic*. The only constitutional text to adopt the term was the Constitution of the Helvetic Republic of 1798; the French Constitution of 1795 speaks of a 'united republic' in which 'the universality of citizens is the sovereign', avoiding the term 'democracy' altogether, since at the time it was still suggestive of 'anarchy'.
39 Pasquale Pasquino, *Sieyès et l'invention de la constitution en France* (Paris, 1998); Bernard Manin, *Principes du gouvernement représentatif* (Paris, 1995).
40 Pasquino, *Sieyès et l'invention de la constitution*, pp. 73–97.
41 The term 'bourgeois liberal republic' was used by the Chinese leader Deng Xiaoping in 1989 to describe the aspiration of the protesters in Tiananmen Square. See John Dunn, 'The Identity of the Bourgeois Liberal Republic', in Fontana, *The Invention of the Modern Republic*, pp. 206–25 (p. 210).
42 For an overview, see Jacques Godechot, *Les Institutions de la France sous la Révolution et l'Empire* [1951] (Paris, 1998), and Isser Woloch, *The New Regime: The Transformation of the French Civic Order, 1789–1820s* (New York, 1994). See also, for a recent survey, Alexandre Guermanzi, Jeanne-Laure Le Quang and Virginie Martin, eds, *Exécuter la loi (1789–1804)* (Paris, 2018), and Benjamin Morel, *Le Parlement: Temple de la République de 1789 à nos jours* (Paris, 2024).
43 Troper, *Terminer la Révolution*, pp. 163–80. See also John Dunn, *The Cunning of Unreason: Making Sense of Politics* (London, 2000).
44 R. R. Palmer, *Twelve Who Ruled* [1941] (Princeton, NJ, 1989). For a recent overview of the endless debate over the interpretation of the Revolution, see Antonino De Francesco, *La Guerre des deux cents ans* (Paris, 2018).

1 The Viscount on Horseback: Paul Barras (1755–1829)

1 Germaine de Staël, *Considerations on the Principal Events of the French Revolution* [1818–20], ed. Aurelian Craiutu (Indianapolis, IN, 2008), part IV, ch. 2, p. 429. For Barras' unflattering account of his exchanges with de Staël, see the (abridged) current edition of his memoirs: Paul Barras, *Mémoires de Barras*, ed. Jean-Pierre Thomas (Paris, 2010), pp. 212–23.
2 At the time of his election, it was rumoured that he had falsified his certificate of baptism (the only official record of births at the time), since he may have been a few months short of forty.
3 For the full edition of the memoirs, see Georges Duruy, ed., *Mémoires de Barras, membre du Directoire*, 4 vols (Paris, 1895–6). On Barras' life, see Jacques Vivent, *Barras le 'roi' de la République* (Paris, 1938); Jean-Paul Garnier, *Barras roi du Directoire* (Paris, 1970); Eric Le Nabour, *Barras* (Paris, 1982); Christine Le Bozec, *Barras* (Paris, 2016); and Pierre Temin, *Barras* (Geneva, 1992).
4 Thomas Carlyle, *The Affair of the Diamond Necklace* [1837] (Cambridge, MA, 1913); Evelyne Lever, *L'Affaire du collier* (Paris, 2013).

5 In October 1791, following the assassination of Nicolas Lescuyer, secretary of the commune of Avignon, some sixty 'papist' prisoners were summarily executed and their bodies thrown into a pit in a tower of the papal palace that served as a place for cool storage (*glacière*). See René Moulinas, *Le Massacre de la glacière: Enquête sur un crime impuni* (Aix-en-Provence, 2004), and Jean-Clément Martin, *Violence et révolution* (Paris, 2006).

6 Barras' biographers have given great emphasis to his relations with two influential society hostesses, Thérèse Cabarrus and Joséphine de Beauharnais, the future wives of Tallien and Napoleon respectively. Barras remained on friendly terms with Thérèse, who had remarried, during the years of his retirement, but his supposed affair with the future empress seems merely a legend.

7 Pierre Cornut-Gentille, *Madame Roland: Une femme en révolution* (Paris, 2004).

8 On the role of deputies in military missions, see Michel Biard, *Missionnaires de la République: Les Représentants du peuple en mission (1793–1795)* (Paris, 2002).

9 Fréron was named Stanislas after his godfather, the king of Poland; under the Consulate, following his injudicious affair with Napoleon's sister Pauline, he was sent on a hazy diplomatic mission to Saint Domingue, where he died of fever in 1802.

10 Louis-Marie Stanislas Fréron, *Mémoire historique sur la réaction royale du midi* (Paris, 1824).

11 Bernard Ireland, *The Fall of Toulon* (London, 2005). In later years Barras, driven by his resentment against Napoleon, claimed that the young artillery officer owed his appointment at Toulon to him; this was not quite true, since Napoleon's main sponsor at the time was his compatriot the Corsican deputy Antoine-Christophe Saliceti. Barras also insisted that the author of the French victory at the siege of Toulon was not Napoleon, but General Jacques François Dugommier, ignoring the contradiction implicit in such a claim (if Napoleon had not distinguished himself, why boast of being his patron?).

12 For a recent comprehensive study, see Colin Jones, *The Fall of Robespierre* (Oxford, 2021); see also Henry Monteagle, 'Barras au neuf thermidor', *Annales historiques de la Révolution française*, XLIX/229 (1977), pp. 377–84.

13 The nine-year-old dauphin was already suffering from the form of bone tuberculosis that had killed his elder brother in 1789; Barras found him in appalling conditions of neglect and entrusted him to the care of a doctor with instructions to improve his situation, although not much could be done to save his life. During the Restoration, several impostors claimed to be the dead dauphin; at the end of the twentieth century DNA tests on the heart of the dead boy (preserved by the surgeon after the autopsy) have confirmed his identity. His fifteen-year-old sister, Marie-Thérèse, was physically as well as could be expected in the circumstances; in 1795, after her brother's death, the Directory exchanged her with some French hostages, sending her to her relatives in Vienna. Deborah Cadbury, *The Lost King of France* (London, 2002).

14 Benjamin Constant, *Portraits, mémoires, souvenirs*, ed. E. Harpaz (Paris, 1992).
15 On Thermidorian society, see Bronislaw Baczko, *Politiques de la Révolution française* (Paris, 2006), pp. 341–491.
16 The rise in prices followed the abandonment by the government of the *maximum*, the law that limited the price of bread.
17 The four were sentenced to deportation to French Guiana, which at the time was not yet organized as a penal colony; Barère and Vadier managed to escape before they were transported. See Loris Chavanette, *Quatre-vingt-quinze: La Terreur en procès* (Paris, 2017).
18 A tenacious legend represents Napoleon attacking the insurgents with heavy artillery; in fact he ordered his soldiers to load their rifles with real bullets rather than the blanks that had been suggested by the Councils. Two volleys were sufficient to disperse the crowd. The marks on the front of the church of St Roch were made by rifles, not cannon. See Patrice Gueniffey, *Bonaparte (1769–1802)* (Paris, 2013), pp. 159–60.
19 Antoine-Claire Thibaudeau, *Mémoires sur la Convention et le Directoire*, ed. François Pascal (Paris, 2007), p. 283.
20 Emmanuel de Las Cases, *Le Mémorial de Sainte-Hélène*, ed. Jean Prévost (Paris, 1948), vol. II, pp. 749–50.
21 The paintings were moved to the Louvre in 1816.
22 Las Cases, *Le Mémorial*, vol. II, pp. 749–50; Pierre François Pinaud, 'Entre rumeur et réalité: La Fortune de Paul Barras', *Napoleonica: La Revue*, XXVIII (2017), pp. 4–18.
23 Albert Meynier, *Les Coups d'état du Directoire* (Paris, 1928).
24 The Count of Provence had assumed the title of king of France after his nephew's death.
25 Garnier, *Barras roi du Directoire*, pp. 302–3. On Barras' real or imagined exchanges with royalist agents, see Le Nabour, *Barras*, pp. 274–8. On royalist conspiracies, see also Jacques Godechot, *La Contre-Révolution, 1789–1804: Doctrine et action* (Paris, 1984), and Jean Tulard, ed., *La Contre-Révolution: Origine, histoire, postérité* (Paris, 1990).
26 *Il n'était pas fort en politique*; Joseph Fouché, *Mémoires* [1824], ed. Louis Madelin [1945] (Paris, 2015), p. 69.
27 On the coup of Brumaire, see Thierry Lentz, *Le 18 Brumaire* (Paris, 1997), and Patrice Gueniffey, *Le Dix-Huit Brumaire* (Paris, 2008).
28 Le Bozec, *Barras*, Annexe [Appendix] 4, in Alexandre Dumas, *Mes mémoires* [1852–6] (Paris, 1989), 2 vols, vol. I, pp. 377–9.

2 The Difficult Lawyer from Alsace: Jean-François Reubell (1747–1807)

1 David's unfinished sketch 'Le Serment du jeu de paume', a 'wash drawing' in pencil, ink and oil, is displayed at Versailles; the oil painting at the Musée Carnevalet in Paris is a copy, probably made by a different artist. See Marie-Catherine Sahut and Régis Michel, *David: L'Art et la politique* (Paris, 1988), pp. 58–61.

2 Raymond Guyot, 'Documents biographiques sur Jean-François Reubell (1747–1807)' [1911], complementary thesis (Clichy, 2011); Gerlof D. Homan, *Jean-François Reubell: French Revolutionary, Patriot and Director (1747–1807)* (The Hague, 1971); Jean-René Suratteau and Alain Bischoff, *Jean-François Reubell: L'Alsacien de la Révolution française* (Colmar, 1995).

3 Emmanuel de Las Cases, *Le Mémorial de Sainte-Hélène*, ed. Jean Prévost (Paris, 1948), vol. II, pp. 751–2.

4 Henry Swinburne, *The Courts of Europe at the Close of the Last Century* (London, 1895), vol. II, p. 136; Homan, *Jean-François Reubell*, p. 105. On Reubell's abilities, see also Antoine-Claire Thibaudeau, *Mémoires sur la Convention et le Directoire* [1828], ed. François Pascal (Paris, 2007), p. 282.

5 Under the old regime, France's main towns had an institution called a *parlement*. These were not, however, elected legislative assemblies as the name suggests, but large tribunals in charge of civil and penal justice. Their members were magistrates who bought or inherited their positions.

6 Henri Strohl, *Le Protestantisme en Alsace* (Strasbourg, 2000).

7 Roland Oberlé, *La Révolution en Alsace* (Roanne, 1989); Jean-Luc Eichenlaub, *L'Alsace et la Révolution* (Strasbourg, 1989).

8 Traditionally each of the three estates had a single vote, which meant the Third was always outvoted by the clergy and nobility. Necker persuaded the king to adopt a system by which each individual delegate had a vote, while the number of delegates from the Third was doubled; as a result, it was now the Third that had a guaranteed majority.

9 On the debate over the status of Jews, see Homan, *Jean-François Reubell*, pp. 6–8, and Suratteau and Bischoff, *Jean-François Reubell*, pp. 42ff.

10 *Les Révolutions de France et de Brabant*, 29 December 1789, n.5, p. 204; quoted in Homan, *Jean-François Reubell*, pp. 45–6.

11 Zosa Szajkowski, *The Economic Status of Jews in Alsace, Metz and Lorraine, 1648–1789* (New York, 1954).

12 Joseph Smets, 'Le Rhin, frontière naturelle de la France: Genèse d'une idée à l'époque révolutionnaire, 1789–1799', *Annales historiques de la Révolution française*, IV (1998), pp. 675–98.

13 Homan, *Jean-François Reubell*, p. 57.

14 Patrice Gueniffey, 'Les Généraux et la Révolution: Entre incompréhension et trahison', in *Traîtres*, ed. F. Favier and V. Haegele (Paris, 2023), pp. 103–14.

15 Homan, *Jean-François Reubell*, p. 60.

16 Michel Biard, *Missionnaires de la République: Les Représentants du peuple en mission (1793–1795)* (Paris, 2002).

17 Bernard Nabonne, *La Diplomatie du Directoire et Bonaparte, d'après les papiers inédits de Reubell* (Paris, 1951).

18 Quoted in Homan, *Jean-François Reubell*, p. 96.

19 See his own retrospective assessment of France's financial situation in Dominique-Vincent Ramel-Nogaret, *Des finances de la République française en l'an IX* (Paris, 1801).

20 On the general financial situation, see René Sturm, *Les Finances de l'Ancien Régime et de la Révolution*, 2 vols (Paris, 1885); Florin Aftalion, *L'Économie de la Révolution française* (Paris, 2007). On the issue of monetary circulation, see Rebecca Spang, *Stuff and Money in the Time of the French Revolution* (Cambridge, MA, 2015).
21 As suggested in the Introduction, this conflict was at the origin of the repeated accusations of corruption directed against the executive.
22 On the problem of deforestation, see Chapter Five.
23 Michael Sonenscher, *Before the Deluge: Public Debt, Inequality and the Intellectual Origins of the French Revolution* (Princeton, NJ, 2006); Pierre de Saint-Phalle, *Normes et valeurs de la dette (1787–1791)* (Paris, 2022); Jerome Greenfield, *The Making of a Fiscal-Military State in Post-Revolutionary France* (Cambridge, 2022), pp. 30–38.
24 Claude Mazauric, *Babeuf et la conspiration pour l'égalité* (Paris, 1962); R. B. Rose, *Gracchus Babeuf: The First Revolutionary Communist* (Stanford, CA, 1978); Ian Birchall, *The Spectre of Babeuf* (Chicago, IL, 2016); Laura Mason, *The Last Revolutionaries* (New Haven, CT, 2022); Jean-Marc Schiappa, *Gracchus Babeuf* (Paris, 2023).
25 Clément Weiss, 'Principes, méthode et efficacité de la chasse au "vampires" du Palais Royal', in *Exécuter la loi (1789–1804)*, ed. Alexandre Guermanzi, Jeanne-Laure Le Quang and Virginie Martin (Paris, 2018), pp. 189–203.
26 Michel Bruguière, *Gestionnaires et profiteurs de la Révolution: L'Administration des finances françaises de Louis XVI à Bonaparte* (Paris, 1986).
27 In his capacity as Louis XVI's director of finances, the Swiss banker Jacques Necker had decided in 1781 to publish a (partial) account of the budget of the monarchy; the initiative had cost him his position while enhancing his reputation as an economist and statesman. Jacques Necker, *Compte rendu au roi* [1781], ed. Léonard Burnand (Geneva, 2005).
28 Georges Dejoint, *La Politique économique du Directoire* (Paris, 1951); Arnaud Decroix, *Question fiscale et réforme financière en France (1749–1789)* (Aix-en-Provence, 2006).
29 Joris Oddens, Mart Rutjes and Erik Jacobs, eds, *The Political Culture of the Sister Republics* (Amsterdam, 2015).
30 Biancamaria Fontana, *La République helvétique: Laboratoire de la Suisse moderne* (Lausanne, 2020).
31 Las Cases, *Le Mémorial*.
32 Jacques Godechot, *Les Commissaires aux armées sous le Directoire*, 2 vols (Paris, 1937).
33 Reubell published a meticulous and detailed refutation of all charges against him: *Mémoire justificatif* (Paris, 1799).
34 François-Auguste Mignet, *Histoire de la Révolution française depuis 1789 jusqu'à 1814* [1824] (Paris, 2012).
35 Suratteau and Bischoff, *Jean-François Reubell*.
36 Joseph Fouché, *Mémoires* [1824], ed. Louis Madelin [1945] (Paris, 2015), p. 78.

3 Master of the Maps: Lazare Carnot (1753–1823)

1 Jules Michelet, *Histoire de la Révolution française*, ed. Paule Petitier and Michel Biard (Paris, 2019), vol. II, p. 676.

2 Charles de Gaulle, *La France et son armée* [1938], ed. Hervé Gaymard (Paris, 2016).

3 Carnot died in exile in Magdeburg (then Prussia) in 1823. His body was reburied in the Panthéon in 1889, as part of the celebrations for the centenary of the Revolution. The major biographical works on him remain those by Marcel Reinhard, *Le Grand Carnot* [1950–52], 2 vols (Paris, 1994), and Jean Dhombres and Nicole Dhombres, *Lazare Carnot* (Paris, 1997).

4 Emmanuel de Las Cases, *Le Mémorial de Sainte-Hélène*, ed. Jean Prévost (Paris, 1948), vol. II, p. 752.

5 Lazare Carnot, *Éloge du Marechal de Vauban: Discours qui a remporté le prix de l'Académie de Dijon en 1784* (Paris, 2016).

6 Lazare Carnot, *De la défense des places fortes: Ouvrage composé par ordre de Sa Majesté Impériale et Royale pour l'instruction des élèves du Corps du Génie* [1810] (London, 2018). On the debate over fortresses, see Hervé Drévillon, *Penser et écrire la guerre: Contre Clausewitz, 1780–1837* (Paris, 2021), pp. 183–213.

7 Shocked by the king's execution and by the Terrorist turn of the government, in April 1793 General Dumouriez, one of the victors in the Battle of Valmy in September 1792, had attempted to defect to Austria with the troops under his command; however, his officers had refused to follow him and he had been forced to escape. Marc Belissa, ed., *Le Moment thermidorien de Charles-François Dumouriez* (Paris, 2019).

8 *Corréspondance générale de Carnot* (Paris, 1892–7). On Carnot and the Committee of Public Safety, see Emmanuel Grison, 'Lazare Carnot et le grand Comité de Salut Public', *Bulletin de la Sabix*, XXIII (2000): *Huit portraits de fondateurs de l'École Polythecnique.*

9 'Idée d'un classement méthodique des sciences et des arts, ou aperçu systématique des conaîssances humaines'; the table is reproduced in Dhombres, *Lazare Carnot*, pp. 94–5.

10 On the Committee, see Bronislaw Baczko, ed., *Une éducation pour la démocratie: Textes et projets de l'époque révolutionnaire* (Geneva, 2000).

11 Quoted in Hippolyte Carnot, *Mémoires sur Carnot par son fils* (Paris, 1863), vol. II, p. 129.

12 On Carnot's scientific profile, see Jean-Paul Charnay, ed., *Lazare Carnot ou le Savant Citoyen* (Paris, 1990).

13 *Le Moniteur universel*, CCXCVIII (28 Messidor Year V/16 July 1797), pp. 1189–90.

14 'Rosati' is an anagram of the name of the patron of the circle, the Count of Artois, the king's youngest brother and the future Charles X.

15 Dhombres, *Lazare Carnot*, pp. 379–83.

16 On the transformation of the agents of the executive during the Revolution, see Michel Biard, *Les Lilliputiens de la centralisation* (Seyssel, 2007).

17 On the issue of executive power, see Paolo Colombo, 'La Question du pouvoir exécutif dans l'évolution institutionnelle et le débat politique révolutionnaire', *Annales de l'histoire de la Révolution française*, CCCXIX (January–March 2000), pp. 1–26.
18 Dhombres, *Lazare Carnot*, pp. 417–20.
19 Collot d'Herbois and Billaud-Varenne were sent to French Guiana, while Barère and Vadier avoided deportation by going into hiding. In 1799 all were granted amnesty by the First Consul; by then Collot d'Herbois was dead, while Billaud-Varenne chose to remain in the colony. See Loris Chavanette, *Quatre-vingt-quinze: La Terreur en procès* (Paris, 2017).
20 To preserve continuity in office of the Thermidorian political class, at the elections held in October 1795 some 500 out of the 750 seats in the new Councils (the Five Hundred and the Elders) were reserved for former deputies of the Convention.
21 The accusations were unfounded (see Chapter Seven), although Cambacérès did represent a more moderate political line than Carnot.
22 Claude Mazauric, 'Carnot et les babeuvistes', in Charnay, *Lazare Carnot ou le Savant Citoyen*, pp. 99–115. On the Babeuf conspiracy, see Chapter Two, including the references at n. 24.
23 Carnot to Wilhelm Körte, 2 February 1821, quoted in Dhombres, *Lazare Carnot*, p. 421.
24 Ibid., p. 322. On the different positions towards the war within the revolutionary political class, see Jacques Godechot, *La Grande Nation* (Paris, 2004), pp. 67ff.
25 For a recent overview of the evolution of international perspectives, see Marc Belissa, 'De l'ordre d'Ancien Régime à l'ordre international: Approches de l'histoire des relations internationales', in *La Révolution à l'œuvre*, ed. Jean-Clément Martin (Rennes, 2015), pp. 217–27.
26 Pierre Ambroise Choderlos de Laclos, 'De la guerre et de la paix', in *Œuvres complètes*, ed. L. Versini (Paris, 1979), p. 708.
27 Constitution of 1791, Heading VI; 'Des rapports de la nation française avec les nations étrangères', in *Les Constitutions de la France depuis 1789*, ed. Jacques Godechot (Paris, 1970), p. 65.
28 Carnot, *Mémoires*, pp. 29–30.
29 Biancamaria Fontana, *La République helvétique: Laboratoire de la Suisse moderne* (Lausanne, 2020).
30 For the official report on the conspiracy, see Charles Bailleul, *Le Coup d'état du 18 fructidor an V* (Paris, 1798); and for Carnot's self-defence, see *Réponse de L.N.M. Carnot, citoyen français . . . au rapport fait sur la conjuration du 18 fructidor . . .* (London, 1799). See also Albert Mathiez, 'Le Coup d'état du 18 fructidor, an V', *Annales historiques de la Révolution française*, XXXVI (November–December 1929), pp. 521–50, and Loris Chavanette, 'La Chûte de Carnot, ou l'échec d'une république', in *Le Directoire: Forger la République*, ed. Loris Chavanette (Paris, 2020), pp. 249–72.
31 In *La Proclamation du premier Empire*, ed. Thierry Lentz (Paris, 2001), pp. 59–62. Carnot's speech can also be found on the website of the French National Assembly, www.assemblee-nationale.fr.

32 On the figure of the saviour in French history, see Patrice Gueniffey, *Napoléon et De Gaulle: Deux héros français* (Paris, 2017).

4 The Emperor's Beacon: Philippe-Antoine Merlin de Douai (1754–1838)

1 Emmanuel de Las Cases, *Le Mémorial de Sainte-Hélène*, ed. Jean Prévost (Paris, 1948), vol. II, p. 333.

2 Unlike other Directors, Merlin left no memoirs and there are very few biographical studies on him. On his life, see Louis Gruffy, *La Vie et l'œuvre juridique de Merlin de Douai* (Paris, 1934), and Hervé Leuwers, *Un juriste en politique: Merlin de Douai (1754–1838)* (Arras, 1994). See also the commemorative speeches cited below.

3 Jean-Louis Halperin, *Le Tribunal de cassation et les pouvoirs sous la République (1790–1799)* (Paris, 1987).

4 André Cocatre-Zilgien, 'Merlin de Douai et le droit public de la monarchie française', *Revue historique de droit français et étranger*, XXXVII (1960), pp. 603–25.

5 For a list of Merlin's publications, see Leuwers, *Un juriste*, pp. 344–6.

6 An early example of this ideal model can be found in Jean Bodin's *Methodus ad facilem historiarum cognitionem* of 1566. Published in French as Pierre Mesnard, ed., *La Méthode de l'histoire* (Paris, 1941).

7 Jean-Pierre Hirsch, *La Nuit du 4 août* [1978] (Paris, 2013).

8 'Rapport de M. Merlin (de Douai) sur la suppression et le rachat des droits féodaux, lors de la séance du 8 février 1790', *Archives parlementaires de la Révolution française* (1880), vol. XI, pp. 498–501.

9 Paul Janet, 'La Propriété pendant la Révolution française', *Revue des deux mondes*, Third Series, XXIII/2 (1877), pp. 320–54; Rafe Blaufarb, *The Great Demarcation: The French Revolution and the Invention of Modern Property* (Oxford, 2016).

10 'Rapport de M. Merlin.'

11 Marie-Clémence Perrot, 'La Politique linguistique de la Révolution française', *Mots*, LII (1997), pp. 158–67; Philippe Blanchet, 'Langues et pouvoirs en France de 1780 à 1850: Un problème de définition', in *Pouvoir local et révolution*, ed. Roger Dupuy (Rennes, 1999), pp. 537–55. The ruined castle of Villers-Cotterêts is now being restored to host the Cité Internationale de la Langue Française.

12 Jacques Godechot, *La Grande Nation* (Paris, 2004), pp. 67ff.

13 Eric Hartmann, *La Révolution française en Alsace et Lorraine* (Paris, 1990).

14 The phrases were used by Hippolyte Taine in his work *Les Origines de la France contemporaine* [1875–93] (Paris, 2011).

15 Leuwers, *Un juriste*, pp. 78–9.

16 Ibid.

17 It is important to recall that, while prisoners may occasionally have been threatened and brutalized, torture was not employed to extract confessions, since its use was associated with the abuses characteristic of the old regime. The practice of systematic legal torture had been introduced in

France during the religious wars and had been abolished by the monarchy only in 1787. Similarly, there is no evidence of a systematic practice of rape.

18 Bronislaw Baczko, *Comment sortir de la Terreur: Thermidor et la République* (Paris, 1989); Loris Chavanette, 'Le Procès de Fouquier-Tinville, ou l'accusation de terreur en l'an III', *Histoire de la justice*, XXXII/2 (2021), pp. 47–59.

19 Georges Bernier, *Marie-Jean Hérault de Séchelles: Biographie* (Paris, 1995). Hérault was executed in 1794 with Danton's faction.

20 Its rapporteur, the young magistrate Michel-Louis Le Peletier de Saint-Fargeau, was assassinated in 1793 in retaliation for having voted for the king's death. The debates at the Constituent on the reform of the penal code and the abolition of the death penalty can be found on the website of the French National Assembly, www.assemblee-nationale.fr.

21 Isser Woloch, *The New Regime: The Transformation of the French Civic Order, 1789–1820s* (New York, 1994), pp. 297–379.

22 Annie Jourdan, 'La Convention ou l'empire des lois: Le Comité de législation et la commission de classification des lois', *Cahiers de l'Institut d'Histoire de la Révolution Française*, III (2012), pp. 1–29.

23 Jean-Claude Farcy, *Histoire de la justice en France de 1789 à nos jours* (Paris, 2015); Bernard Durand et al., *Histoire de la justice en France du XVIII siècle à nos jours* (Paris, 2016).

24 Jacques Godechot, *Les Institutions de la France sous la Révolution et l'Empire* [1951] (Paris, 1998); Woloch, *The New Regime*, pp. 297–379.

25 Quoted in Leuwers, *Un juriste*, p. 118.

26 Hervé Robert, 'Le Retour des juristes sous le Consulat', in *Napoléon et le droit*, ed. Thierry Lentz (Paris, 2017), pp. 29–72.

27 'Mémoire sur la nécessité d'un code universel et uniforme pour toute la République', in Leuwers, *Un juriste*, pp. 295–310.

28 'La Constitution de l'an VIII', in Jacques Godechot, ed., *Les Constitutions de la France depuis 1789* (Paris, 1970), p. 157.

29 Ainé Dupin, *La Profession d'avocat* [1832] (Paris, 2013).

30 See the two celebratory speeches for the Ordre des Avocats and the Institute: Auguste Mathieu, *Éloge historique de Merlin, prononcé le 23 novembre 1839* (Paris, 1839); Auguste Mignet, 'Notice historique sur la vie et les travaux de M. le comte Merlin (15 mai 1841)', *Mémoires de l'Institut*, IV (1844), pp. xli–lxxvi.

5 Voltaire's Eclectic Heir: Nicolas François de Neufchâteau (1750–1828)

1 The title *bailli* was used in the north of France (and also in parts of Switzerland) to describe a kind of governor of a particular region, with both executive and judicial powers; after the Revolution the *baillis* were replaced by the *préfets*, who essentially had executive functions.

2 'Il faut bien qu'on me succède/ Et j'aime en vous mon héritier' (Voltaire to Neufchâteau). A natural father more attractive than the legal one may have been a trait that Neufchâteau shared with Voltaire; on the latter's supposed illegitimacy, see Pierre Milza, *Voltaire* (Paris, 2007), pp. 9–12.

3 The only modern biography of Neufchâteau is the one by Dominique Margairaz, *François de Neufchâteau: Biographie intellectuelle* (Paris, 2005).

4 The national assembly known as the Legislative Assembly replaced the Constituent on 1 October 1791; it was replaced in turn by the Convention on 20–21 September 1792, at the time of the proclamation of the Republic.

5 François de Neufchâteau, *Paméla, ou la vertu récompensée*, ed. Martial Poirson (Oxford, 2007).

6 For a full list of his publications, see Margairaz, *François de Neufchâteau*, pp. 518–23.

7 *Les Lectures du citoyen, adressées à MM. les administrateurs des départements* (Toul, 1790).

8 *Abus de pouvoir, ou Vexations exercés contre M. François de Neufchâteau, et autres électeurs* (Paris, 1789).

9 *L'Origine ancienne des principes modernes, ou les décrets constitutionnels conférés avec les maximes des sages de l'antiquité* (Paris, 1791).

10 James Livesey, 'A Revolutionary Career? François de Neufchâteau Does Well by Doing Good, 1774–1794', *French History*, XVIII/2 (2004), pp. 1–23.

11 *L'Origine ancienne*, pp. 10–12.

12 *Notice historique et littéraire sur la vie et les écrits du Comte François de Neufchâteau* (Paris, 1843).

13 Charles Conus, *François de Neufchâteau ministre de l'intérieur (17 juin 1798–22 juin 1799)* (Épinal, 1874); Dominique Margairaz, 'La Figure de l'exécutif pendant les deux ministères de Neufchâteau', *Annales historiques de la Révolution française*, CCCXXXII/2 (April–June 2003), pp. 81–99.

14 Catherine Kawa, 'Les Employés du ministère de l'intérieur pendant la première république (1792–1800)', *Annales historiques de la Révolution française*, CCXCV (1994), pp. 110–20.

15 Just like civil servants, they were not elected, although their tenure might depend on the permanence in government of the Director who had appointed them.

16 Eric Szulman, 'Administrer la navigation intérieure sous la République', *Annales historiques de la Révolution française*, CCCLXXXIX (March 2017), pp. 57–76.

17 Yveline Cantarel-Besson, ed., *Musée du Louvre (janvier 1797–juin 1798): Procès verbaux du Conseil d'administration du 'Musée Central des Arts'* (Paris, 1992).

18 On the reform of schools, see Isser Woloch, *The New Regime: The Transformation of the French Civic Order, 1789–1820s* (New York, 1994), pp. 173–236.

19 Jean Tulard, 'François de Neufchâteau et la politique économique du Directoire', *Journal des savants*, IV (1966), pp. 234–42.

20 Octave Fasty, 'Les Essais de statistique économique pendant le Directoire et le Consulat', *Annales historiques de la Révolution française*, XXV/131 (April–June 1953), pp. 161–76; Bertrand Gille, *Les Sources statistiques de l'histoire de France: Des enquêtes du XVIIème à 1870* (Paris, 1964).

21 See also his report of 8 January 1799 (19 nivôse Year VII).
22 The architect who had worked for the Count of Provence and would be employed by Napoleon to restore the Luxembourg and build the Arc de Triomphe.
23 Charles Simian, *François de Neufchâteau et les expositions* (Paris, 1889); Arthur Chandler, 'L'Exposition publique des produits de l'industrie française, Paris, 1798', *World's Fair*, X/1 (1990), pp. 2–22; Christiane Demeulenaere-Douyère, 'Pour le progrès des "arts" en France: Les Expositions nationales des produits de l'industrie (1798–1849)', *Artefact*, X (2019), pp. 53–73.
24 *Le Moniteur*, Year VI (1798), pp. 402–3.
25 Georges Lefebvre, *La France sous le Directoire, 1795–1799* (Paris, 1984), pp. 653–706.
26 Adélaïde de Place, *Etienne Nicolas Méhul* (Paris, 2005). Mozart's *Clemenza di Tito* had been first performed in Prague in 1791.
27 Germaine de Staël, *Considerations on the Principal Events of the French Revolution*, ed. Aurelian Craiutu (Indianapolis, IN, 2008), part III, ch. 26, pp. 411–13. Admittedly, sitting at a dinner party between Napoleon and Sieyès (as de Staël did) must have been a somewhat stressful experience.
28 The position of consul had been turned into a life appointment (instead of the ten-year one established by the Constitution of the Year VIII in 1799) by the Constitution of the Year X (4 August 1802). Neufchâteau's speech is reprinted in *La Proclamation du premier Empire*, ed. Thierry Lentz (Paris, 2001), pp. 282–91.
29 Ibid.
30 The term 'oxymoron' applied to the Empire was used by President Emmanuel Macron when he celebrated the bicentenary of Napoleon's death at the Institut de France on 5 May 2021.
31 Simian, *François de Neufchâteau et les expositions*, p. 84.
32 Margairaz, *François de Neufchâteau*, pp. 36, 380.

6 Unsuited to the Post: Emmanuel Sieyès (1748–1836)

1 The president in charge, La Révellière-Lépeaux, was himself elected to the Directory on the same day; he was replaced by Pierre-Charles-Louis Baudin des Ardennes.
2 Heading XIII, Article 338.
3 On Sieyès' life and political thought, see Paul Bastid, *Sieyès et sa pensée* [1939] (Geneva, 1978); Murray Forsyth, *Reason and Revolution: The Political Thought of the Abbé Sieyes* (Leicester, 1987); Jean-Denis Bredin, *Sieyès: La Clé de la Révolution française* (Paris, 1988); and Erwan Sommerer, *Sieyès: Le Révolutionnaire et le conservateur* (Paris, 2011).
4 *Notice sur la vie de Sieyès* (Paris, 1795). The official author of the *Notice* (which appeared anonymously in various editions in French, English and German) was Sieyès' German friend Konrad Oelsner; however, Sieyès himself seems to have inspired or even drafted most of it. Erwan Sommerer, 'La *Notice sur la vie de Sieyès d'Œlsner*: Autopromotion inavouée et évolution post-thermidorienne', in *Biographie et politique:*

Vie publique et vie privée de l'Ancien Régime à la Restauration, ed. Olivier Ferret and Anne-Marie Mercier-Faivre (Lyon, 2014), pp. 169–81.

5 Bishop of Tréguiez and then of Chartres, he was elected to the Estates and joined the Constituent, but emigrated after the adoption of the Civil Constitution of the clergy.

6 Olivier Christin, *Vox populi: Une histoire du vote avant le suffrage universel* (Paris, 2014).

7 The *vingtième* was a kind of generalized income tax introduced in 1749, from which privileged orders were largely exempt.

8 See Emmanuel-Joseph Sieyès, *Écrits politiques*, ed. Roberto Zapperi (Brussels, 1994), and Emmanuel-Joseph Sieyès, *Essai sur les privileges et autres textes*, ed. Pierre-Yves Quiviger (Paris, 2007). Both pamphlets are published in English in Emmanuel-Joseph Sieyès, *Political Writings*, ed. Michael Sonenscher (Indianapolis, IN, 2003).

9 Jules Michelet, *Histoire de la Révolution française*, ed. Paule Petitier and Michel Biard (Paris, 2019), vol. I, p. 103.

10 Emmanuel de Waresquiel, *Sept jours: 17–23 juin 1789, la France entre en Révolution* (Paris, 2020); Loris Chavanette, *Le 14 Juillet de Mirabeau* (Paris, 2023).

11 On Sieyès' constitutionalism, see Pasquale Pasquino, *Sieyès et l'invention de la constitution en France* (Paris, 1998).

12 Alphonse Armant Bigeon, *Sieyès: L'Homme, le constituant* (Paris, 1893).

13 On the debate over the confiscation of Church lands, see Germain Sicard, 'L'Église et l'état dans les débats de l'Assemblée Nationale Constituante (1789–1790)', in *Mélanges Germain Sicard* (Toulouse, 2000), vol. I, pp. 517–41, and Bernard Bodinier, 'La Révolution française et la question agraire', *Histoire et sociétés rurales*, XXX/1 (January 2010), pp. 7–47.

14 Sieyès' approach was finally adopted by the Directory in 1796. See Laurent Martin, *Histoire de la censure en France* (Paris, 2022).

15 Germaine de Staël, *Considerations on the Principal Events of the French Revolution*, ed. Aurelian Craiutu (Indianapolis, IN, 2008), part II, ch. 6; de Staël used the term *parti populaire* as a synonym for the English phrase 'country party', which is the current expression used in English political debates since the seventeenth century to describe the party of the people, as opposed to the party of the king.

16 Benjamin Constant, 'Fragments de mémoires de Madame Récamier', in *Oeuvres*, ed. A. Roulin (Paris, 1957), pp. 965–6.

17 Timothy Tackett, *Becoming a Revolutionary: The Deputies of the French National Assembly and the Emergence of a Revolutionary Culture (1789–1790)* (Princeton, NJ, 1996).

18 For a full list, see Bredin, *Sieyès*, p. 130: *Préliminaire à la constitution*; *Reconnaissance . . . des droit de l'homme*; *Observations . . . sur les biens ecclésiastiques*; *Observations . . . sur la nouvelle organisation de la France*.

19 For de Staël's portrait of Sieyès, see de Staël, *Considerations*, part II, ch. 7, pp. 203–4.

20 In Pasquino, *Sieyès et l'invention de la constitution*, pp. 193–6.

21 *Notice.*
22 Bredin, *Sieyès*, p. 329.
23 Merlin de Douai and Jean-Jacques-Régis Cambacérès were the main authors; see Chapters Four and Seven.
24 Antoine-Claire Thibaudeau, *Mémoires sur la Convention et le Directoire*, ed. François Pascal (Paris, 2007), p. 206.
25 Bredin, *Sieyès*, pp. 336–7. See also Chapter Three.
26 On the Batavian Republic and France, see Annie Jourdan, 'The National Dimension of the Batavian Revolution', in *The Political Culture of the Sister Republics*, ed. Joris Oddens, Mart Rutjes and Erik Jacobs (Amsterdam, 2015), pp. 187–99.
27 Sentenced to death with the Girondins, Condorcet died in 1794 while in custody, in obscure circumstances, possibly committing suicide by poison. See Elisabeth Badinter and Robert Badinter, *Condorcet, 1743–1794: Un intellectuel en politique* (Paris, 1989).
28 Laurence Chatel de Brancion, ed., *Mémoires inédits de Cambacérès* (Paris, 1999), vol. I, pp. 58–9.
29 Michel Troper, *Terminer la Révolution: La Constitution de 1795* (Paris, 2006), pp. 31–72; Marc Latimer, 'Sieyès lors des débats constituant en l'an III: Autopsie d'un échec', in *Figures de Sieyès*, ed. Pierre-Yves Quiviger and Vincent Denis (Paris, 2008), pp. 43–82.
30 Angus Harwood Brown, 'Republican Nostalgia, the Division of Labour and the Origins of Inequality in the Thought of the Abbé Sieyès', *Intellectual History Review*, XXXIV/2 (2024), pp. 1–38.
31 Pasquino, *Sieyès et l'invention de la constitution*, pp. 73–97.
32 Ibid., pp. 193–6.
33 Thibaudeau, *Mémoires*, pp. 206–33.
34 Bredin, *Sieyès*, pp. 388–9.
35 Such as *Le Mercure*, *Le Spectateur du nord* and *Le Magazin encyclopédique*. Sieyès himself had no German.
36 *Réponse du Professeur Kant de Königsberg à l'abbé Sieyès de Paris* (Paris, 1796). Ferenc Fehér, 'Practical Reason in the Revolution: Kant's Dialogue with the French Revolution', *Social Research*, LVI/1 (1989), pp. 161–85; Reidar Maliks, 'Revolutionary Epigones: Kant and His Radical Followers', *History of Political Thought*, XXXIII/4 (Autumn 2012), pp. 647–71.
37 For Benjamin Constant's views on the abuse of constitutional violations, see the section on 'Coups d'état' in the unpublished *Principes de politique*: Benjamin Constant, *Les 'Principes de politique' de Benjamin Constant*, ed. Etienne Hofmann (Geneva, 1980), vol. II, pp. 105–23.
38 In 1804 Pichegru took part in the royalist conspiracy organized by Georges Cadoudal against Napoleon; he was arrested and died while in custody. See Jonathan North, *Killing Napoleon: The Plot to Blow Up Bonaparte* (Stroud, 2019), and Jacques-Olivier Boudon, *Ils voulaient tuer Napoléon: Attentats, conspirations et complots* (Paris, 2022), pp. 103–15.
39 On Sieyès' attitude and the unfolding of Brumaire, see Thierry Lentz, *Le 18 Brumaire* (Paris, 1997), and Patrice Gueniffey, *Le Dix-Huit Brumaire* (Paris, 2008).

40 Edmund Burke, *Letter to a Noble Lord* [1796], ed. Albert H. Smyth (London, 2019).
41 'I shall not become a fattening pig' was allegedly Napoleon's comment on the prospect of becoming the Great Elector; quoted in Gueniffey, *Le Dix-Huit Brumaire*, p. 338.
42 The Senate was housed in the Petit Luxembourg, hastily and lavishly done up in the fashionable neo-Egyptian style. The refurbishing of the larger palace (the seat of today's Senate) took more than a decade and was finally completed under Louis XVIII.
43 For Napoleon's views on Sieyès, see Emmanuel de Las Cases, *Le Mémorial de Sainte-Hélène*, ed. Jean Prévost (Paris, 1948), vol. I, pp. 868ff.

7 The Indispensable Counsel: Jean-Jacques-Régis Cambacérès (1753–1824)

1 On Cambacérès' life, see Pierre-François Pinaud, *Cambacérès* (Paris, 1996); Laurence Chatel de Brancion, *Cambacérès: Maître d'œuvre de Napoléon* (Paris, 2001); and Louis Faivre d'Arcier, *Cambacérès: L'Art de servir tous les régimes* (Paris, 2015). The publication of his own memoirs, suspected by different French governments to contain explosive revelations, was possible only at the end of the twentieth century: Laurence Chatel de Brancion, ed., *Mémoires inédits de Cambacérès*, 2 vols (Paris, 1999). Other supposedly autobiographical narratives are collected in *Les Après-Diners de Cambacérès*, ed. Étienne-Léon de Lamothe-Langon [1837], 4 vols (Paris, 1946).
2 He chose not to stand for re-election in 1797.
3 The naval metaphor was used by Cambacérès himself in a speech to the Convention in October 1794.
4 Isser Woloch, *The New Regime: The Transformation of the French Civic Order, 1789–1820s* (New York, 1994), pp. 297–320.
5 Jean-Jacques-Régis and a younger brother (who became a priest) were the only survivors in a family of twelve children: an unusually high mortality rate even for the times.
6 On Chaptal, see Patrice Gueniffey, 'Chaptal, un libéral autoritaire', in *Histoires de la Révolution et de l'Empire* (Paris, 2013), pp. 473–519.
7 According to Cambacérès, he explained to the prince that his only concern was to establish 'the reign of the law', a statement to which Orléans agreed readily. Quoted in Pinaud, *Cambacérès*, pp. 51–3; the source of this, as well as of the other anecdotes about meeting Robespierre and Napoleon (not reported in the *Mémoires inédits*), is *Les Après-Diners de Cambacérès*. For Cambacérès' judgement on Orléans, see Chatel de Brancion, *Mémoires inédits*, vol. I, pp. 142–3.
8 In later years one of the king's chosen defence lawyers, François-Denis Tronchet, worked with Cambacérès on the team that prepared the new Civil Code.
9 In 1804 Louis-Antoine-Henri de Bourbon-Condé, Duke of Enghien, was accused of being involved in a plot organized by royalist agents to assassinate the First Consul; he was sentenced to death and shot. See Jean-Paul Bertaud, *Le Duc d'Enghien* (Paris, 2001).

10 For his own account of the king's trial, see Chatel de Brancion, *Mémoires inédits*, vol. I, pp. 95–119.
11 Virginie Martin, 'Pour une histoire du "gouvernement d'Assemblée": Les comités à la charnière du Législatif et de l'exécutif', *La Révolution française*, XVII (2020), pp. 1–23.
12 On the protracted development of the new Civil Code, see Bernard Schwartz, ed., *The Code Napoleon and the Common-Law World* (New York, 1954); Jean-Louis Halpérin, *L'Impossible Code Civil* (Paris, 1992); and Saman Safatian, 'La Rédaction du Code Civil', *Napoleonica: La Revue*, XVI (January 2013), pp. 49–63. On Cambacérès' contribution, see Jean Hilaire, 'Cambacérès et le Code Civil', *Bulletin mensuel de l'Académie des Sciences et des Lettres de Montpellier*, New Series, XXXVIII (2008), pp. 61–8.
13 He found himself in a position similar to that of Merlin de Douai; see Chapter Four. On the Terror and Terrorist legislation, see Patrice Gueniffey, *La Politique de la Terreur* (Paris, 2003); Marisa Linton, *Choosing Terror* (Oxford, 2013); and Timothy Tackett, *The Coming of Terror in the French Revolution* (Cambridge, MA, 2015).
14 Chatel de Brancion, *Mémoires inédits*, vol. I, p. 152.
15 Ibid., pp. 145–60.
16 We have only Cambacérès' (unconfirmed) version of these episodes as reported in *Les Après-Diners de Cambacérès*. As for the practice of paying early morning visits, given the working schedule of assemblies and councils, it must have been the only time when one could be confident of catching a deputy at home.
17 Quoted in Pinaud, *Cambacérès*, p. 94.
18 Antoine-Claire Thibaudeau, *Mémoires sur la Convention et le Directoire*, ed. François Pascal (Paris, 2007), pp. 108–10.
19 Pinaud, *Cambacérès*, p. 95.
20 'Discours du président pour la translation des restes de Rousseau Panthéon, lors de la séance du 20 vendémiaire an III (11 octobre 1794)', *Archives parlementaires*, First Series (1787–99), vol. XCIX (Paris, 1795), p. 97.
21 Jean d'Andlau, 'Le Comité de législation: D'un organe législatif à un "comité de gouvernement"?', *Cahiers de l'Institut d'Histoire de la Révolution Française*, XVII (2020), pp. 1–16.
22 The future Director La Révellière-Lépeaux recalled: 'My principle – Cambacérès used to tell us – is that men who must take on both the workload of the Assembly and that of the Committee need good restaurants, or else they might succumb to the weight of their labours.' Quoted in Pinaud, *Cambacérès*, p. 111.
23 At the time there were at least three clandestine royalist 'agencies': one organized around Louis XVIII; another run by his younger brother, the Count d'Artois; and a third operating on behalf of the English government. Inevitably their plans of *coups d'état* and assassinations overlapped and often interfered with one another. See Jacques Godechot, *La Contre-Révolution, 1789–1804: Doctrine et action* (Paris, 1984);

Carlos de la Huerta, *The Great Conspiracy: Britain's Secret War against Revolutionary France, 1794–1805* (Stroud, 2016); and Jonathan North, *Killing Napoleon: The Plot to Blow Up Bonaparte* (Stroud, 2019).

24 In 1809 d'Antraigues and his wife were murdered at their house in London, apparently by a disgruntled servant, although there were suspicions of a political assassination. See Jacques Godechot, *Le Comte d'Antraigues: Un espion dans l'Europe des émigrés* (Paris, 1986).

25 Thibaudeau, *Mémoires*, p. 271.

26 Sieyès, who found himself in the same position, did not attract similar insinuations, possibly because his celibacy was attributed to his clerical past.

27 For the text of his presentation of his project to the Convention, see Chatel de Brancion, *Mémoires inédits*, vol. I, pp. 176–82.

28 The backing was necessary not to finance the coup as such, but to guarantee the absence of financial backlash afterwards. On these financial circles, see Michel Bruguière, *Gestionnaires et profiteurs de la Révolution: L'Administration des finances françaises de Louis XVI à Bonaparte* (Paris, 1986).

29 Chatel de Brancion, *Mémoires inédits*, vol. I, p. 440.

30 Joseph Fouché was also reconfirmed as minister of police, while Charles-Maurice de Talleyrand was recalled to the ministry of foreign affairs. Ibid., p. 442.

31 Pinaud, *Cambacérès*, pp. 106–7.

32 In 1815 all the correspondence between Cambacérès and Napoleon disappeared. A large stock of more than 1,000 letters resurfaced in a private collection in the 1960s and was duly deposited in the State archives and published, but they date from 1802 to 1814. See Jean Tulard, ed., *Jean-Régis Cambacérès: Lettres inédites à Napoléon, 1802–1814* (Paris, 1973).

33 Chatel de Brancion, *Mémoires inédits*, vol. I, pp. 431–3.

34 Ibid.

35 Chatel de Brancion, *Cambacérès*, p. 248.

36 Patrice Gueniffey, *Le Dix-Huit Brumaire* (Paris, 2008), p. 344.

37 'Proclamation des consuls de la République du 24 frimaire an VIII (15 décembre 1799)', in *Les Constitutions de la France depuis 1789*, ed. Jacques Godechot (Paris, 1970), p. 162.

38 Chatel de Brancion, *Mémoires inédits*, vol. I, pp. 455–6; however, Cambacérès claimed that his comments had no impact whatsoever on the finished document.

39 See Constitution of the Year VIII, Heading IV, Article 52, for a description of the function of the institution. Godechot, *Les Constitutions*, p. 157. On the Council of State, see Jean-Louis Mestre, 'Le Conseil d'État de France du Consulat au début de la IIIème République (1799–1872)', *La Revue administrative*, LII/8 (1999), pp. 17–32. See also Hervé Robert, 'Le Retour des juristes sous le Consulat', in *Napoléon et le droit*, ed. Thierry Lentz (Paris, 2017), pp. 29–72.

40 In *La Proclamation du premier Empire*, ed. Thierry Lentz (Paris, 2001), pp. 227–8. See also Annie Jourdan, 'Le Premier Empire: Un nouveau pacte social', *Cités*, XX (2004), pp. 51–64.

41 To reach a conclusion, Cambacérès had to give up some of his most advanced views on divorce and family law.
42 Mme Reinhart, wife of the diplomat Charles-Frédéric Reinhart, quoted in Chatel de Brancion, *Cambacérès*, p. 250.
43 D'Arcier, *Cambacérès*, p. 98.
44 Chatel de Brancion, *Mémoires inédits*, vol. I, pp. 47–8.
45 Thierry Sarmant and Mathieu Stoll, *Régner et gouverner: Louis XIV et ses ministres* (Paris, 2010); see also Isser Woloch, *Napoleon and His Collaborators* (New York, 2001), and Thierry Lentz, *Les Ministres de Napoléon* (Paris, 2016).

Conclusion: Changing Palaces

1 On the unfolding of the Brumaire coup, see Thierry Lentz, *Le 18 Brumaire* (Paris, 1997), and Patrice Gueniffey, *Le Dix-Huit Brumaire* (Paris, 2008). See also Patrick Lagoueyte, *Les Coups d'états: Une histoire française* (Paris, 2021).
2 In June 1800, after his victory at Marengo, Napoleon stopped at Lyon, where he was presented with a 'First Consul dress coat', a magnificent suit of coral-red silk velvet. It was immortalized in the official portrait by Antoine-Jean Gros, but he never wore it in real life.
3 They were soon released. Gohier accepted a diplomatic position in Amsterdam, and Moulin retired from public life but later re-entered the army and ended his career as Count of the Empire.
4 On Cambacérès and the Hôtel d'Elbeuf, see Jean Tulard, *L'Empire de l'argent: S'enrichir sous Napoléon* (Paris, 2023), pp. 154–5. On Napoleon and the Tuileries, see Gueniffey, *Le Dix-Huit Brumaire*, pp. 368–9. Returning to the Tuileries in 1816, Louis XVIII, impressed by the improvements Napoleon had made, wrote to the Count of Artois: 'My brother, we've had a very good concierge!'
5 Chalgrin had been employed to work on the palace by the Count of Provence in the late 1770s. See Thierry Sarmant, *Histoire des palais: Le Pouvoir et sa mise en scène en France du V au XXIème siècle* (Paris, 2025), pp. 231–47, and Charles-Eloi Vial, *Les Lieux de Napoléon* (Paris, 2025), pp. 147–52.
6 However, elections under the Consulate were more than mere formalities; see Josiane Bourguet-Rouveyre, 'La Survivance d'un système électoral sous le Consulat et l'Empire', *Annales historiques de la Révolution française*, CCCXLVI (October–December 2006), pp. 17–29.
7 See Chapter Seven and Laurence Chatel de Brancion, ed., *Mémoires inédits de Cambacérès* (Paris, 1999), vol. I, p. 417.
8 'Proclamation des consuls de la République du 24 frimaire an VIII (15 décembre 1799)', in *Les Constitutions de la France*, ed. Jacques Godechot (Paris, 1970), p. 162.
9 See the documents collected in *La Proclamation du premier Empire*, ed. Thierry Lentz (Paris, 2002).
10 The term 'empire' had been used since 1792 to describe France's relationship with its territorial possessions abroad. See Thierry Lentz,

Le Grand Consulat, 1799–1804 (Paris, 2014), pp. 815–56, and Jean Tulard, *Le Grand Empire, 1804–1815* [1982] (Paris, 2009), pp. 15–35.

11 On the monarchical heritage in today's 5th Republic, see James B. Collins, *La Monarchie républicaine: État et société dans la France moderne* (Paris, 2016), and Jean-Dominique Merchet, *Macron Bonaparte* (Paris, 2017).

12 John Dunn, 'The Identity of the Bourgeois Liberal Republic', in *The Invention of the Modern Republic*, ed. Biancamaria Fontana (Cambridge, 1994), p. 206.

13 On the controversial revolutionary heritage in today's France, see François Cherix, *Le Crépuscule du récit révolutionnaire* (Geneva, 2021); Loris Chavanette, *La Tentation du désespoir* (Paris, 2024); David A. Bell, *Shadows of Revolution: Reflections on France Past and Present* (Oxford, 2016); and Loris Chavanette, ed., *Le Directoire: Forger la République* (Paris, 2020).

14 Philippe Raynaud, ed., *De la force du gouvernement actuel de la France et de la nécessité de s'y rallier* [1796] (Paris, 2013), p. 88.

BIBLIOGRAPHY

Aftalion, Florin, *L'Économie de la Révolution française* (Paris, 2007)

Anderson, R. D., 'France from the Enlightenment to the Napoleonic University', in *European Universities from the Enlightenment to 1914* (Oxford, 2004), pp. 39–50

Baczko, Bronislaw, *Comment sortir de la Terreur: Thermidor et la République* (Paris, 1989)

——, *Politiques de la Révolution française* (Paris, 2006)

Badinter, Elisabeth, and Robert Badinter, *Condorcet, 1743–1794: Un intellectuel en politique* (Paris, 1989)

Barras, Paul, *Mémoires de Barras, membre du Directoire*, ed. Georges Duruy, 4 vols (Paris, 1895–6)

——, *Mémoires de Barras*, ed. Jean-Pierre Thomas (Paris, 2010)

Barstin, Haim, *Révolutionnaires: Pour une anthropologie politique de la Révolution française* (Paris, 2013)

Bastid, Paul, *Sieyès et sa pensée* [1939] (Geneva, 1978)

Belissa, Marc, and Yannick Bosc, *Le Directoire: La République sans la démocratie* (Paris, 2018)

Bell, David A., *Shadows of Revolution: Reflections on France Past and Present* (Oxford, 2016)

Bernier, Georges, *Marie-Jean Hérault de Séchelles: Biographie* (Paris, 1995)

Bertaud, Jean-Paul, *Le Duc d'Enghien* (Paris, 2001)

Biard, Michel, *Missionnaires de la République: Les Représentants du peuple en mission (1793–1795)* (Paris, 2002)

——, *Les Lilliputiens de la centralisation* (Seyssel, 2007)

Bigeon, Alphonse Armant, *Sieyès: L'Homme, le constituant* (Paris, 1893)

Birchall, Ian, *The Spectre of Babeuf* (Chicago, IL, 2016)

Black, Jeremy, *European International Relations 1648–1815* (New York, 2002)

Blanchet, Philippe, 'Langues et pouvoirs en France de 1780 à 1850: Un problème de définition', in *Pouvoir local et révolution*, ed. Roger Dupuy (Rennes, 1999), pp. 537–55

Blaufarb, Rafe, *The Great Demarcation: The French Revolution and the Invention of Modern Property* (Oxford, 2016)

Bodin, Jean, *Methodus ad facilem historiarum cognitionem* [1566], published in French as Pierre Mesnard, ed., *La Méthode de l'histoire* (Paris, 1941)
Bodinier, Bernard, 'La Révolution française et la question agraire', *Histoire et sociétés rurales*, XXX/1 (January 2010), pp. 7–47
Bois, Jean-Pierre, *De la paix des rois à l'ordre des empereurs, 1714–1815* (Paris, 2003)
Boudon, Jacques-Olivier, *Ils voulaient tuer Napoléon: Attentats, conspirations et complots* (Paris, 2022)
Bourguet-Rouveyre, Josiane, 'La Survivance d'un système électoral sous le Consulat et l'Empire', *Annales historiques de la Révolution française*, CCCXLVI (October–December 2006), pp. 17–29
Bredin, Jean-Denis, *Sieyès: La Clé de la Révolution française* (Paris, 1988)
Brown, Angus Harwood, 'Republican Nostalgia, the Division of Labour and the Origins of Inequality in the Thought of the Abbé Sieyès', *Intellectual History Review*, XXXIV/2 (2024), pp. 433–56
Bruguière, Michel, *Gestionnaires et profiteurs de la Révolution: L'Administration des finances françaises de Louis XVI à Bonaparte* (Paris, 1986)
Burke, Edmund, *Reflections on the Revolution in France* [1790], ed. Conor Cruise O'Brien (Harmondsworth, 1969)
——, *Letter to a Noble Lord* [1796], ed. Albert H. Smyth (London, 2019)
Cadbury, Deborah, *The Lost King of France* (London, 2002)
Carlyle, Thomas, *The Affair of the Diamond Necklace* [1837] (Cambridge, MA, 1913)
Carnot, Lazare, *Éloge du Marechal de Vauban: Discours qui a remporté le prix de l'Académie de Dijon en 1784* (Paris, 2016)
——, *De la défense des places fortes: Ouvrage composé par ordre de Sa Majesté Impériale et Royale pour l'instruction des élèves du Corps du Génie* [1810] (London, 2018)
Chandler, Arthur, 'L'Exposition publique des produits de l'industrie française, Paris, 1798', *World's Fair*, X/1 (1990), pp. 2–22
Chatel de Brancion, Laurence, ed., *Mémoires inédits de Cambacérès*, 2 vols (Paris, 1999)
——, *Cambacérès: Maître d'œuvre de Napoléon* (Paris, 2001)
Chavanette, Loris, *Quatre-vingt-quinze: La Terreur en procès* (Paris, 2017)
——, ed., *Le Directoire: Forger la République* (Paris, 2020)
——, 'Le Procès de Fouquier-Tinville, ou l'accusation de terreur en l'an III', *Histoire de la justice*, XXXII/2 (2021), pp. 47–59
——, *Le 14 Juillet de Mirabeau* (Paris, 2023)
——, *La Tentation du désespoir* (Paris, 2024)
Cherix, François, *Le Crépuscule du récit révolutionnaire* (Geneva, 2021)
Christin, Olivier, *Vox populi: Une histoire du vote avant le suffrage universel* (Paris, 2014)
Cicatre-Zilgien, André, 'Merlin de Douai et le droit public de la monarchie française', *Revue historique de droit français et étranger*, XXXVII (1960), pp. 603–25
Collins, James B., *La Monarchie républicaine: État et société dans la France moderne* (Paris, 2016)

Constant, Benjamin, 'Fragments de mémoires de Madame Récamier', in *Oeuvres*, ed. A. Roulin (Paris, 1957), pp. 965–6

——, *Les 'Principes de politique' de Benjamin Constant*, ed. Etienne Hofmann, 2 vols (Geneva, 1980)

——, *The Political Writings of Benjamin Constant*, ed. Biancamaria Fontana (Cambridge, 1988)

——, *Portraits, mémoires, souvenirs*, ed. E. Harpaz (Paris, 1992)

——, *De la force du gouvernement actuel de la France et de la nécessité de s'y rallier* [1796], ed. Philippe Raynaud (Paris, 2013)

Conus, Charles, *François de Neufchâteau ministre de l'intérieur (17 juin 1798–22 juin 1799)* (Épinal, 1874)

Cornut-Gentille, Pierre, *Madame Roland: Une femme en Révolution* (Paris, 2004)

Coutel, Charles, *Instituer le citoyen* (Paris, 1999)

Crook, Malcolm, *Elections in the French Revolution: An Apprenticeship in Democracy (1789–1799)* (Cambridge, 1996)

d'Anthenaise, Claude, Michel Richard and Philippe Martial, eds, *Palais du Luxembourg* (Paris, 1992)

d'Arcier, Louis Faivre, *Cambacérès: L'Art de servir tous les régimes* (Paris, 2015)

De Francesco, Antonino, *La Guerre des deux cents ans* (Paris, 2018)

de Gaulle, Charles, *La France et son armée* [1938], ed. Hervé Gaymard (Paris, 2016)

de Staël, Germaine, *Considerations on the Principal Events of the French Revolution* [1818–20], ed. Aurelian Craiutu (Indianapolis, IN, 2008)

Decroix, Arnaud, *Question fiscale et réforme financière en France (1749–1789)* (Aix-en-Provence, 2006)

Dejoint, Georges, *La Politique économique du Directoire* (Paris, 1951)

Demeulenaere-Douyère, Christiane, 'Pour le progrès des "arts" en France: Les Expositions nationales des produits de l'industrie (1798–1849)', *Artefact*, x (2019), pp. 53–73

Dhombres, Jean, and Nicole Dhombres, *Lazare Carnot* (Paris, 1997)

Drévillon, Hervé, *Penser et écrire la guerre: Contre Clausewitz, 1780–1837* (Paris, 2021)

Dunn, John, ed., *Democracy: The Unfinished Journey, 508 BC to AD 1993* (Oxford, 1992)

——, *The Cunning of Unreason: Making Sense of Politics* (London, 2000)

Dupin, Ainé, *La Profession d'avocat* [1832] (Paris, 2013)

Durand, Bernard, et al., *Histoire de la justice en France du XVIII siècle à nos jours* (Paris, 2016)

Eichenlaub, Jean-Luc, *L'Alsace et la Révolution* (Strasbourg, 1989)

Farcy, Jean-Claude, *Histoire de la justice en France de 1789 à nos jours* (Paris, 2015)

Fasty, Octave, 'Les Essais de statistique économique pendant le Directoire et le Consulat', *Annales historiques de la Révolution française*, XXV/131 (April–June 1953), pp. 161–76

Fontana, Biancamaria, ed., *The Invention of the Modern Republic* (Cambridge, 1994)

——, *Germaine de Staël: A Political Portrait* (Princeton, NJ, 2016)

——, *La République helvétique: Laboratoire de la Suisse moderne* (Lausanne, 2020)
——, and Sandrine Baume, eds, *Les Usages de la séparation des pouvoirs* (Paris, 2008)
Forsyth, Murray, *Reason and Revolution: The Political Thought of the Abbé Sieyès* (Leicester, 1987)
Fouché, Joseph, *Mémoires* [1824], ed. Louis Madelin [1945] (Paris, 2015)
Fréron, Louis-Marie Stanislas, *Mémoire historique sur la réaction royale du midi* (Paris, 1824)
Furet, François, *Penser la Révolution française* (Paris, 1978)
——, 'La République thermidorienne, 1795–1799', in *La Révolution française* (Paris, 2007), pp. 381–441
Galetti, Sara, *Le Palais du Luxembourg de Marie de Medici* (Paris, 2012)
Garnier, Jean-Paul, *Barras roi du Directoire* (Paris, 1970)
Gille, Bertrand, *Les Sources statistiques de l'histoire de France: Des enquêtes du XVIIème à 1870* (Paris, 1964)
Godechot, Jacques, *Les Commissaires aux armées sous le Directoire*, 2 vols (Paris, 1937)
——, ed., *Les Constitutions de la France depuis 1789* (Paris, 1970)
——, *La Contre-Révolution, 1789–1804: Doctrine et action* (Paris, 1984)
——, *Le Comte d'Antraigues: Un espion dans l'Europe des émigrés* (Paris, 1986)
——, *Les Institutions de la France sous la Révolution et l'Empire* [1951] (Paris, 1998)
——, *La Grande Nation: L'Expansion révolutionnaire de la France, 1789–1799* [1957] (Paris, 2004)
Greenfield, Jerome, *The Making of a Fiscal-Military State in Post-Revolutionary France* (Cambridge, 2022)
Gruffy, Louis, *La Vie et l'œuvre juridique de Merlin de Douai* (Paris, 1934)
Gueniffey, Patrice, *Le Nombre et la raison: La Révolution française et les élections* (Paris, 1993)
——, *La Politique de la Terreur* (Paris, 2003)
——, *Le Dix-Huit Brumaire* (Paris, 2008)
——, *Bonaparte (1769–1804)* (Paris, 2013)
——, 'Chaptal, un libéral autoritaire', in *Histoires de la Révolution et de l'Empire* (Paris, 2013), pp. 473–519
——, 'Les Généraux et la Révolution: Entre incompréhension et trahison', in *Traîtres*, ed. F. Favier and V. Haegele (Paris, 2023), pp. 103–14
Guermanzi, Alexandre, Jeanne-Laure Le Quang and Virginie Martin, eds, *Exécuter la loi (1789–1804)* (Paris, 2018)
Guyot, Raymond, 'Documents biographiques sur Jean-François Reubell (1747–1807)' [1911], complementary thesis (Clichy, 2011)
Halperin, Jean-Louis, *Le Tribunal de cassation et les pouvoirs sous la République (1790–1799)* (Paris, 1987)
——, *L'Impossible Code Civil* (Paris, 1992)
Hartmann, Eric, *La Révolution française en Alsace et Lorraine* (Paris, 1990)
Hilaire, Jean, 'Cambacérès et le Code Civil', *Bulletin mensuel de l'Académie des Sciences et des Lettres de Montpellier*, New Series, XXXVIII (2008), pp. 61–8
Hirsch, Jean-Pierre, *La Nuit du 4 août* [1978] (Paris, 2013)

Homan, Gerlof D., *Jean-François Reubell: French Revolutionary, Patriot and Director (1747–1807)* (The Hague, 1971)
Huerta, Carlos de la, *The Great Conspiracy: Britain's Secret War against Revolutionary France, 1794–1805* (Stroud, 2016)
Ireland, Bernard, *The Fall of Toulon* (London, 2005)
Janet, Paul, 'La Propriété pendant la Révolution française', *Revue des deux mondes*, Third Series, XXIII/2 (1877), pp. 320–54
Jones, Colin, *The Fall of Robespierre* (Oxford, 2021)
Jordan, David Peter, *The King's Trial: Louis XVI vs the French Revolution* (Berkeley, CA, 2004)
Jourdan, Annie, 'Le Premier Empire: Un nouveau pacte social', *Cités*, XX (2004), pp. 51–64
——, 'La Convention ou l'empire des lois: Le Comité de législation et la commission de classification des lois', *Cahiers de l'Institut d'Histoire de la Révolution Française*, III (2012), pp. 1–29
Kawa, Catherine, 'Les Employés du ministère de l'intérieur pendant la première république (1792–1800)', *Annales historiques de la Révolution française*, CCXCV (1994), pp. 110–20
Kolz, A., ed., 'Constitution de la République helvétique du 12 avril 1798', in *Quellenbuch zur neueren schweizerischen Verfassungsgeschichte* (Bern, 1992), pp. 126–52
——, *Histoire constitutionnelle de la Suisse moderne* (Bern, 2006)
Laclos, Pierre Ambroise Choderlos de, *Œuvres complètes*, ed. L. Versini (Paris, 1979)
Lagoueyte, Patrick, *Les Coups d'états: Une histoire française* (Paris, 2021)
Lamothe-Langon, Étienne-Léon de, ed., *Les Après-Diners de Cambacérès*, 4 vols [1837] (Paris, 1946)
Las Cases, Emmanuel de, *Le Mémorial de Sainte-Hélène*, ed. Jean Prévost, 2 vols (Paris, 1948)
Latimer, Marc, 'Sieyès lors des débats constituant en l'an III: Autopsie d'un échec', in *Figures de Sieyès*, ed. Pierre-Yves Quiviger and Vincent Denis (Paris, 2008), pp. 43–82
Le Bozec, Christine, *Barras* (Paris, 2016)
Le Nabour, Eric, *Barras* (Paris, 1982)
Lefebvre, Georges, *La France sous le Directoire, 1795–1799* (Paris, 1984)
Lentz, Thierry, *Le 18 Brumaire* (Paris, 1997)
——, ed., *La Proclamation du premier Empire* (Paris, 2001)
——, *Le Grand Consulat, 1799–1804* (Paris, 2014)
——, *Les Ministres de Napoléon* (Paris, 2016)
——, ed., *Napoléon et le droit* (Paris, 2017)
Leuwers, Hervé, *Un juriste en politique: Merlin de Douai (1754–1838)* (Arras, 1994)
Lever, Evelyne, *L'Affaire du collier* (Paris, 2013)
Linton, Marisa, *Choosing Terror* (Oxford, 2013)
Livesey, James, 'A Revolutionary Career? François de Neufchâteau Does Well by Doing Good, 1774–1794', *French History*, XVIII/2 (2004), pp. 1–23
Maliks, Reidar, 'Revolutionary Epigones: Kant and His Radical Followers', *History of Political Thought*, XXXIII/4 (Autumn 2012), pp. 647–71

Manin, Bernard, *Principes du gouvernement représentatif* (Paris, 1995)
——, *Un voile sur la liberté* (Paris, 2025)
Margairaz, Dominique, 'La Figure de l'exécutif pendant les deux ministères de Neufchâteau', *Annales historiques de la Révolution française*, CCCXXXII/2 (April–June 2003), pp. 81–99
——, *François de Neufchâteau: Biographie intellectuelle* (Paris, 2005)
Martin, Jean-Clément, *Violence et révolution* (Paris, 2006)
Martin, Laurent, *Histoire de la censure en France* (Paris, 2022)
Martin, Virginie, 'Pour une histoire du "gouvernement d'Assemblée": Les Comités à la charnière du Législatif et de l'exécutif', *La Révolution française*, XVII (2020), pp. 1–23
Mason, Laura, *The Last Revolutionaries* (New Haven, CT, 2022)
Mathiez, Albert, *La Réaction thermidorienne* [1928] (Paris, 2010)
Mazauric, Claude, *Babeuf et la conspiration pour l'égalité* (Paris, 1962)
Merchet, Jean-Dominique, *Macron Bonaparte* (Paris, 2017)
Mestre, Jean-Louis, 'Le Conseil d'État de France du Consulat au début de la IIIème République (1799–1872)', *La Revue administrative*, LII/8 (1999), pp. 17–32
Meynier, Albert, *Les Coups d'état du Directoire* (Paris, 1928)
Michelet, Jules, *Histoire de la Révolution française*, ed. Paule Petitier and Michel Biard, 2 vols (Paris, 2019)
Mignet, François-Auguste, *Histoire de la Révolution française depuis 1789 jusqu'à 1814* [1824] (Paris, 2012)
Milza, Pierre, *Voltaire* (Paris, 2007)
Monteagle, Henry, 'Barras au neuf thermidor', *Annales historiques de la Révolution française*, XLIX/229 (1977), pp. 377–84
Montplaisir, Daniel de, *Ces nobles qui ont fait la Révolution: Précurseurs, agitateurs, fondateurs* (Paris, 2024)
Morel, Benjamin, *Le Parlement: Temple de la République de 1789 à nos jours* (Paris, 2024)
Mottironi, Henri-Pierre, *Commerce et république en France au XVIIIème siècle* (Bordeaux, 2023)
Moulinas, René, *Le Massacre de la glacière: Enquête sur un crime impuni* (Aix-en-Provence, 2004)
Nabonne, Bernard, *La Diplomatie du Directoire et Bonaparte, d'après les papiers inédits de Reubell* (Paris, 1951)
Necker, Jacques, *Du pouvoir exécutif dans les grands états*, 2 vols (Paris, 1792), published in English as *On Executive Power in Large States*, 2 vols (London, 1792)
——, *Compte rendu au roi* [1781], ed. Léonard Burnand (Geneva, 2005)
Neufchâteau, François de, *L'Origine ancienne des principes modernes, ou les décrets constitutionnels conférés avec les maximes des sages de l'antiquité* (Paris, 1791)
——, *Paméla, ou la vertu récompensée*, ed. Martial Poirson (Oxford, 2007)
North, Jonathan, *Killing Napoleon: The Plot to Blow Up Bonaparte* (Stroud, 2019)
Oberlé, Roland, *La Révolution en Alsace* (Roanne, 1989)

Oddens, Joris, Mart Rutjes and Erik Jacobs, eds, *The Political Culture of the Sister Republics* (Amsterdam, 2015)
Ozouf, Mona, *Varennes: La Mort de la royauté* (Paris, 2005)
Palmer, R. R., *The Improvement of Humanity: Education and the French Revolution* (Princeton, NJ, 1985)
——, *Twelve Who Ruled* [1941] (Princeton, NJ, 1989)
Pasquino, Pasquale, *Sieyès et l'invention de la constitution en France* (Paris, 1998)
Perrot, Marie-Clémence, 'La Politique linguistique de la Révolution française', *Mots*, LII (1997), pp. 158–67
Pinaud, Pierre-François, *Cambacérès* (Paris, 1996)
——, 'Entre rumeur et réalité: La Fortune de Paul Barras', *Napoleonica: La Revue*, XXVIII (2017), pp. 4–18
Place, Adélaïde de, *Etienne Nicolas Méhul* (Paris, 2005)
Ray, Jean-Philippe, *Les Hommes de Bonaparte: La Conquête du pouvoir 1793–1800* (Paris, 2012)
Reinhard, Marcel, *Le Grand Carnot* [1950–52], 2 vols (Paris, 1994)
Robert, Hervé, 'Le Retour des juristes sous le Consulat', in *Napoléon et le droit*, ed. Thierry Lentz (Paris, 2017), pp. 29–72
Rose, R. B., *Gracchus Babeuf: The First Revolutionary Communist* (Stanford, CA, 1978)
Safatian, Saman, 'La Rédaction du Code Civil', *Napoleonica: La Revue*, XVI (2013), pp. 49–63
Sahut, Marie-Catherine, and Régis Michel, *David: L'Art et la politique* (Paris, 1988)
Saint-Phalle, Pierre de, *Normes et valeurs de la dette (1787–1791)* (Paris, 2022)
Sarmant, Thierry, *Histoire des palais: Le Pouvoir et sa mise en scène en France du V au XXIème siècle* (Paris, 2025)
——, and Mathieu Stoll, *Régner et gouverner: Louis XIV et ses ministres* (Paris, 2010)
Schiappa, Jean-Marc, *Gracchus Babeuf* (Paris, 2023)
Schroeder, Paul W., *The Transformation of European Politics, 1763–1848* (Oxford, 1994)
Schwartz, Bernard, ed., *The Code Napoleon and the Common-Law World* (New York, 1954)
Serna, Pierre, *L'Extrême Centre, ou le poison français, 1789–2019* (Ceyzérieu, 2019)
Sièyes, Emmanuel-Joseph, *Écrits politiques*, ed. Roberto Zapperi (Brussels, 1994)
——, *Political Writings*, ed. Michael Sonenscher (Indianapolis, IN, 2003)
——, *Essai sur les privileges et autres textes*, ed. Pierre-Yves Quiviger (Paris, 2007)
Simian, Charles, *François de Neufchâteau et les expositions* (Paris, 1889)
Sobul, Albert, ed., *Le Procès de Louis XVI* (Paris, 1966)
Sommerer, Erwan, *Sieyès: Le Révolutionnaire et le conservateur* (Paris, 2011)
Sonenscher, Michael, *Before the Deluge: Public Debt, Inequality and the Intellectual Origins of the French Revolution* (Princeton, NJ, 2006)

Spang, Rebecca, *Stuff and Money in the Time of the French Revolution* (Cambridge, MA, 2015)
Strohl, Henri, *Le Protestantisme en Alsace* (Strasbourg, 2000)
Sturm, René, *Les Finances de l'Ancien Régime et de la Révolution*, 2 vols (Paris, 1885)
Suratteau, Jean-René, and Alain Bischoff, *Jean-François Reubell: L'Alsacien de la Révolution française* (Colmar, 1995)
Swinburne, Henry, *The Courts of Europe at the Close of the Last Century*, 2 vols (London, 1895)
Szaikowski, Zosa, *The Economic Status of Jews in Alsace, Metz and Lorraine, 1648–1789* (New York, 1954)
Szulman, Eric, 'Administrer la navigation intérieure sous la République', *Annales historiques de la Révolution française*, CCCLXXXIX (March 2017), pp. 57–76
Tackett, Timothy, *Becoming a Revolutionary: The Deputies of the French National Assembly and the Emergence of a Revolutionary Culture (1789–1790)* (Princeton, NJ, 1996)
——, *When the King Took Flight* (Cambridge, MA, 2003)
——, *The Coming of Terror in the French Revolution* (Cambridge, MA, 2015)
Taine, Hippolyte, *Les Origines de la France contemporaine* [1875–93] (Paris, 2011)
Temin, Pierre, *Barras* (Geneva, 1992)
Thibaudeau, Antoine-Claire, *Mémoires sur la Convention et le Directoire*, ed. François Pascal (Paris, 2007)
Troper, Michel, *Terminer la Révolution: La Constitution de 1795* (Paris, 2006)
Tulard, Jean, 'François de Neufchâteau et la politique économique du Directoire', *Journal des savants*, IV (1966), pp. 234–42
——, ed., *Jean-Régis Cambacérès: Lettres inédites à Napoléon, 1802–1814* (Paris, 1973)
——, ed., *La Contre-Révolution: Origine, histoire, postérité* (Paris, 1990)
——, *Le Grand Empire, 1804–1815* [1982] (Paris, 2009)
Vial, Charles-Eloi, *Les Lieux de Napoléon* (Paris, 2025)
Vivent, Jacques, *Barras le 'roi' de la République* (Paris, 1938)
Walter, Gérard, *La Conjuration du 9 thermidor* (Paris, 1974)
Walzer, Michael, *Regicide and Revolution: Speeches at the Trial of Louis XVI* (New York, 1992)
Waquet, Dominique, 'Costumes et vêtements sous le Directoire: Signes politiques ou effets de mode?', *Cahiers d'histoire*, CXXIX (2015), pp. 19–54
Waresquiel, Emmanuel de, *Sept jours: 17–23 juin 1789, la France entre en Révolution* (Paris, 2020)
Woloch, Isser, *The New Regime: The Transformation of the French Civic Order, 1789–1820s* (New York, 1994)
——, *Napoleon and His Collaborators* (New York, 2001)
Woolf, Stuart, *Napoleon's Integration of Europe* [1992] (London, 2015)
Woronoff, Denis, *La République bourgeoise de thermidor à brumaire, 1794–1799* (Paris, 1972)

ACKNOWLEDGEMENTS

This book could not have been written without the support and encouragement of both John Dunn and the late Bernard Manin. I am grateful to my friends in Cambridge, Milan and Lausanne, in particular the colleagues of the Centre Walras Pareto at the University of Lausanne, for bearing with me while I pursued my odd obsession with the French Directory. I wish to thank Michael Leaman for adopting Desk Revolutionaries for Reaktion Books, and Amy Salter and Alex Ciobanu for their help with the text and illustrations.

PHOTO ACKNOWLEDGEMENTS

The author and publishers wish to express their thanks to the sources listed below for illustrative material and/or permission to reproduce it. Some locations of artworks are also given below, in the interest of brevity:

Château de Versailles: pp. 139, 185, 208; Harvard Art Museums/Fogg Museum, Cambridge, MA, photo © President and Fellows of Harvard College: p. 161; Musée Carnavalet, Histoire de Paris: pp. 6, 19; Musée Unterlinden, Colmar/ Christian Kempf: p. 67; private collection: pp. 42, 88, 112.

INDEX

Page numbers in *italics* indicate illustrations